LearnTCI Access Code

8513-0001-AD7N-RSKJ-7YWD-4XG5

Social Studies Alive!®
Regions of Our Country

Chief Executive Officer: Bert Bower

Chief Operating Officer: Amy Larson

Director of Product Development: Liz Russell

Managing Editor: Laura Alavosus

Editorial Project Manager: Lara Fox

Project Editors: Wendy Frey and Nancy O'Leary

Editorial Associates: Anna Embree and Sarah Sudano

Production Manager: Lynn Sanchez

Design Manager: Jeff Kelly

Graphic Designer: Victoria Philp

Photo Edit Manager: Margee Robinson

Photo Editor: Diane Austin

Art Editors: Eric Houts and Sarah Wildfang

Audio Manager: Katy Haun

TCi™   Teachers' Curriculum Institute
PO Box 50996
Palo Alto, CA 94303

Customer Service: 800-497-6138
www.teachtci.com

ISBN 978-1-58371-851-3

1 2 3 4 5 6 7 8 9 10 QW 15 14 13 12 11 10 09

Program Director
Bert Bower

Program Consultant
Vicki LaBoskey, Ph.D., Professor
of Education, Mills College,
Oakland, California

Student Edition Writers
Susan Buckley
Diane Hanover
Diane Hart
Peter Lacey

Curriculum Developers
Joyce Bartky
Anne Maloney
Elizabeth Sarica
Steve Seely
Kelly Shafksy

Reading Specialist
Barbara Schubert, Ph.D., Reading Specialist,
Saint Mary's College, Moraga, California

Teacher and Content Consultants
Lynn Casey, Teacher, Husmann Elementary
School, Crystal Lake, Illinois

Jane Crowe, Teacher, Brookwood Elementary
School, Tuscaloosa County, Alabama

Khieta Davis, Teacher, Flower City
School #54, Rochester, New York

Ann Dawson, Educational Consultant,
Intermediate Curriculum Specialist,
Gahanna, Ohio

Shirley Jacobs, Library Media Specialist,
Irving Elementary School, Bloomington,
Illinois

Elizabeth McKenna, Teacher, St. Thomas
Aquinas Catholic School, Diocese of Orlando,
Florida

Mitch Pascal, Social Studies Specialist,
Arlington County Schools, Arlington, Virginia

Becky Suthers, Retired Teacher, Stephen F.
Austin Elementary, Weatherford, Texas

Tiffany Wilson, Teacher, Corbell Elementary,
Frisco, Texas

Literature Consultant
Regina M. Rees, Ph.D., Assistant Professor,
Beeghly College of Education, Youngstown
State University, Youngstown, Ohio

Music Specialist
Beth Yankee, Teacher, The Woodward School
for Technology and Research, Kalamazoo,
Michigan

Maps
Mapping Specialists, Ltd., Madison, Wisconsin

Contents

Maps

Discovering the Social Sciences

What do social scientists do?

1.1 Introduction

Why are some people rich and others poor? How can studying the past help us live better today? These are the kinds of questions that **social scientists** ask.

Social scientists study the ways people live in groups. Their field is called **social science**. Some social scientists study small groups, such as families. Others study large groups, such as nations. They learn about the economy, geography, politics, and history of the groups they study.

Social scientists want to understand why people behave as they do. To find out, they watch people. They ask questions. They study written records, such as letters and news stories.

They also study other artifacts. Artifacts are things people have made. Your clothes are a kind of artifact. So are all the things you carry in your backpack. What would a social scientist learn about you by studying these artifacts? You might be surprised by the answer!

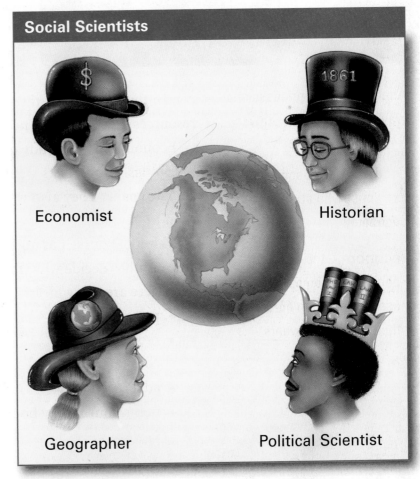

Social Scientists

Economist

Historian

Geographer

Political Scientist

1.2 The Social Science of Economics

You find a dollar in your pocket. Should you spend it on a snack? Save it for a new comic book? You might think that no one cares about how you choose to spend your money. Not true! Some social scientists are **economists**. They are very interested in the choices people make about money every day.

Economists study the **economy** of a city, state, or country. An economy is the way people in a community use resources to meet their needs and wants. We all need food, clothing, and shelter. And we all want things that we don't really need. You may want a new game. Your parents may want a new car. In the economy of the United States, a variety of resources meets people's needs and wants.

Economics is the study of how people make, buy, and sell things. Economists want to know how people decide what to make. They also want to know how people decide what to buy.

Think of yourself as an economist. You are studying how families decide what to buy. What artifacts might help you? Here are a few ideas:

- price tags
- receipts
- coupons
- advertisements
- items your family bought recently

Analyzing rising prices is one way to study an economy.

economist a social scientist who studies the economy

economy the way people in a community use resources to meet their needs and wants

1.3 The Social Science of Geography

You are on a trip somewhere new. Nothing looks familiar. You begin to feel a little lost. Finally, you ask yourself, "Where am I?"

You could use some help from another social scientist— a **geographer**. Geographers like to know where places are on a map. They study Earth's surface to find out what physical features lie around them. They also study climate and plant and animal life.

Geographers use maps and globes to show the features of our planet's surface. Land, water, plants, and animals are part of nature. They are called natural features. People build towns, roads, bridges, and dams. These things are called human features.

The United States has a great range of natural and human features. It has mountains, deserts, rivers, and lakes. It has large cities filled with people and buildings. It has tiny towns. It also has vast empty spaces.

Think of yourself as a geographer. You are studying the natural and human features of your community. These artifacts and natural objects might help you:

- maps
- weather records
- newspaper articles
- wildflowers
- birds' nests

geographer a social scientist who studies the natural and human features of Earth's surface, and its climate and life-forms

Learning to use maps is an important part of thinking like a geographer.

1.4 The Social Science of Political Science

You are riding your bike down the street when—*bam!*—your front wheel hits a pothole. You fall to the ground. As you pick yourself up, you grumble, "This is dangerous! Who's in charge of fixing the streets, anyway?"

This is just the type of question a **political scientist** might ask. Political scientists are interested in who is in charge. They want to know how people get the power to run a city, state, or nation. They also look at how the people in charge use their power.

political scientist
a social scientist who studies governments

Political science is the study of governments. All groups—even families—have some sort of government. A government is a system for deciding what is best for the group. Its main job is to make and carry out rules and laws.

These rules help people live together in peace. Governments also supply things that people need. Your local government provides things that you need, such as schools and safe streets.

Suppose a political scientist is visiting your home. What artifacts might interest him or her? Here are a few ideas:

- election advertisements
- stories about government
- information about how and where to vote
- newspaper articles about laws

Protest signs such as these are one way that people tell the government what they want and need.

1.5 The Social Science of History

Your class takes a field trip to the cemetery. Your assignment is to make a rubbing of a tombstone and report on it to the class. When you read the tombstone, you think, "I wonder how many people buried here were related to this person." Now you are thinking like a **historian**.

History is the study of the past. Human beings have been around a very long time. As a result, we have a lot of past to study. Historians, however, are most interested in the last few thousand years. This is when people began leaving written records.

The first question historians ask is *What happened in the past?* To find out, they study all kinds of artifacts, including records made by people in the past. Once historians know what happened, they ask other questions to help them interpret or understand the past, such as *Who took part in these events? How did these things happen?* and *Why did they happen this way?*

Suppose you have been asked to write a history of your family. What artifacts would help you? Here are some suggestions:

- birth certificates
- baby books
- family photos
- letters
- diaries
- family treasures

This old school photograph is an artifact that might interest a historian.

1.6 Thinking Like a Social Scientist

Now that you know more about social scientists, can you start thinking like one?

Try this experiment. Choose one object from your desk or backpack to study. Ask yourself, *What kind of social scientist would be most interested in this artifact? An economist? A geographer? A political scientist? A historian? What would that person want to know about this artifact—who made it, how much it cost, where it came from, or something else?*

One group of fourth graders tried this experiment with a pair of shoes. To their surprise, the shoes turned out to be a rather interesting artifact. Here are the group's results.

An economist might ask these questions:

1. How much did the shoes cost to make?
2. How much did you pay for them?
3. Why did you choose to buy these shoes instead of another pair of shoes?

A geographer might ask these questions:

1. Where were these shoes made?
2. What route did the shoes travel from the factory to your shoe store?

A political scientist might ask these questions:

1. Are there any laws about making these shoes, and did the maker follow them?
2. Who was in charge of buying this pair of shoes?

A historian might ask these questions:

1. How have shoes changed over time?
2. What is the history of these shoes? When were they made? Who made them? Why did they make them? What has happened to these shoes since they were made?

Summary

As you have learned, the social sciences are the study of how people live in groups. Some social scientists study small groups like families. Others study large groups like nations.

Social scientists want to understand why people behave as they do. To find out, they watch people. They ask questions. They look at written records and other artifacts.

Economists are interested in the choices people make about money. They look at what people make, buy, and sell.

Geographers want to know what lies around them. They examine mountains and lakes, roads and towns.

Political scientists study governments. They look at how people get power. They look at what people do with power.

Historians study the past. They look at items like old letters and photographs to learn what happened in the past. Historians are most interested in the last few thousand years, when people began leaving written records.

But human beings have been around for a very long time—since long before people started writing. How do social scientists study the past when there are no written clues to follow?

Clues from Cahokia

In southern Illinois, a large mound rises from the ground. But it is not a natural hill. People built it long ago. Who? Why? How? These are questions social scientists ask. How do social scientists help us learn about life long ago?

"What a strange looking hill!" you might think as you walk toward the mound. "It's squared off instead of round. Look, the top is flat. And it has different levels. Is it really a hill?"

These questions and observations show that you're thinking like an **archaeologist**. Archaeologists are a special kind of social scientist. Like historians, they study the past. But they don't study people's written records. To find clues about the past, they hunt for and examine objects that people have left behind.

This huge mound, called Monks Mound, is one *giant* artifact! It is about as tall as a ten-story building. It is the largest of several mounds in the area. Archaeologists have learned that the mounds were part of a 1300-year-old American Indian city called Cahokia.

How did archaeologists begin their explorations at Cahokia? What did they find?

archaeologist a social scientist who studies the past by looking at artifacts people have left behind

Monks Mound at Cahokia

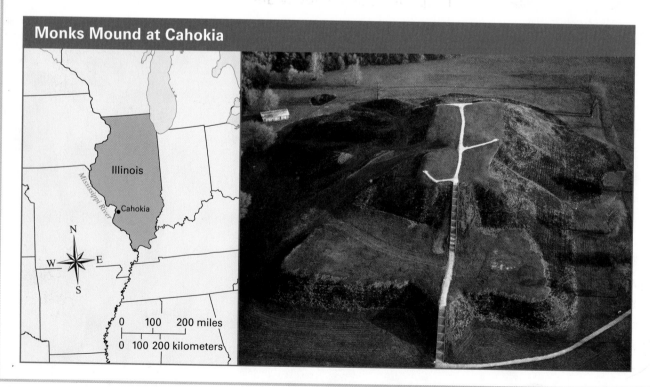

Illinois

Mississippi River

Cahokia

N
W   E
S

0   100   200 miles
0 100 200 kilometers

Help from Geography

The people who built Monks Mound left the area more than 600 years ago. Why did they build these mounds? The people left no written language. So how can we know?

Luckily, there are archaeologists eager to search for clues. Modern-day archaeologists use high-tech tools to look in the ground and underneath the soil that has collected on top of these very old structures over time. They also dig into the soil for clues—slowly and very carefully.

Before they start investigating, archaeologists need to figure out where to focus their attention. So they turn to geography for help. They look at the land. They think about where people might have lived. Are there places where it is easy to get water? Are there fertile places to grow food? They also study areas that appear to have been changed by the people who lived there. This helps archaeologists choose the likeliest places to search for more clues.

Archaeologists have made many discoveries at Cahokia since the 1920s. One of the most exciting was at the top of Monks Mound. They discovered the remains of a large wooden building. It stood on top of the hill about 850 years ago. It was probably the biggest building in the city. Here was a wonderful clue about life long ago.

An archaeologist carefully sifts the soil in search of clues about the past.

An artist created this view of Cahokia based on what archaeologists learned about the city.

Help from Political Science

Archaeologists now knew that a building once stood at the top of the great mound. But what was it for?

Nothing they found on the mound explained it. So they turned to political science for help. Political scientists study how people organize into governments. To make such a large mound, thousands of people would have had to work together. These people must have had leaders. Could this explain the building atop the mound?

Picture the scene a thousand years ago. Everywhere you look, people are at work. Some are in the vast fields beyond the city, raising corn for food. Others dig soil from pits and place it in baskets. People carry the heavy baskets to the foot of the mound. Up and up they climb. At last, exhausted, they drop their loads. Slowly, very slowly, the mound grows taller. Who is in charge of all this work?

Convincing thousands of people to move 22 million cubic feet of soil takes powerful leadership! Political scientists say that a group of high-ranking nobles must have ruled Cahokia. They may have lived on top of this mound, while the people lived in the city below.

Help from Economics

Archaeologists now knew that nobles ruled the large, rich city. But how had the city grown so large and become so wealthy? Archaeologists turned to economics for help. Economists ask questions about resources. What resources did Cahokia have?

Rich soil for farming was one. The rich soil along the Mississippi River allowed people to grow as much food as they needed. That meant more people could live in one place. It also meant that not everyone had to work in the fields or hunt for food. Some people could work on building a great city.

Rivers were another resource. They served as water highways for trade. Traders brought salt to Cahokia in canoes. They also carried shells from the Gulf of Mexico and copper from the Great Lakes. People used these things to make objects of great beauty. Archaeologists have found carved-shell jewelry, copper ornaments, and stone figures.

So why did people leave? Nobody knows exactly. Part of the answer may be that people *used up* the resources. They cut down trees and farmed the same fields until the land could no longer support so many people. Today, the mounds at Cahokia are an important monument. Thanks to the work of social scientists, we now know that, long ago, a large, lively city existed in this place.

People at Cahokia made the wooden bowl shown to the left and the carving shown above.

Midwest

Northeast

West

Southwest

Southeast

Exploring Regions of the United States

How do geographers study the regions of the United States?

2

2.1 Introduction

Because Earth is so large, geographers divide it into regions to study. A region is an area with common features that set it apart from other areas. In this book, we have divided the United States into five regions to study.

In this chapter, you will learn how geographers study regions. One way is by using maps. Geographers use maps to help them think about five topics, or themes, of geography. These are the five themes of geography:

Location: Where is this place located? What is it near?

Place: What is this place like?

Human-environmental interaction: How does this place affect the people living here? How do the people who live here affect this place?

Movement: How do people, goods, and ideas move to and away from this place?

Regions: What features about this place set it apart from other places?

Try answering the questions above about a place you know well—your school. Now you are thinking like a geographer. Keep thinking that way as you read more about the regions of the United States.

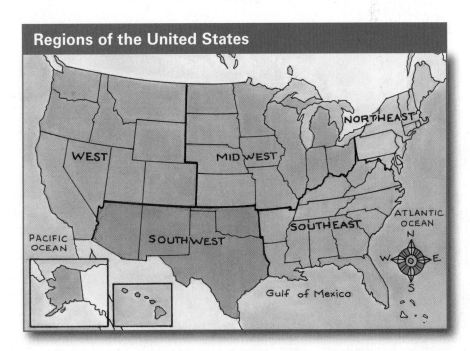

Regions of the United States

2.2 Location and Direction

Every place has its own location. A location is the site where something can be found. People describe locations in many ways. You might describe the location of your home by talking about what it is near. This is the relative location of your home. Or you might use your street address. This is the exact location of your home.

Geographers use globes and maps to show the locations of places on Earth. Globes are round like Earth. They are useful when you want to know where places are on the planet. When you need to see where many places are all at once, maps can be more useful. Maps show all or part of Earth on a flat surface.

To use a map, you need to know the four cardinal directions. North is the direction toward the North Pole. When you face north, your back is facing south. East is to your right. West is to your left. On a map, the letters N, S, E, and W stand for the cardinal directions.

The intermediate directions are halfway between the cardinal directions. Northeast, for example, lies halfway between north and east. The other intermediate directions are southeast, southwest, and northwest. On a map, the letters NE, SE, SW, and NW stand for the intermediate directions.

Most maps use a compass rose to show directions. It sits on each map with N pointing toward the North Pole. This tells you which way is north.

North Pole

South Pole

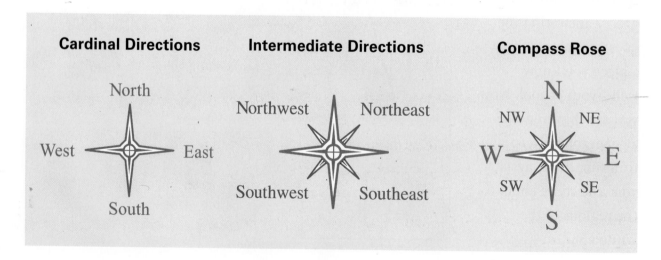

| Cardinal Directions | Intermediate Directions | Compass Rose |

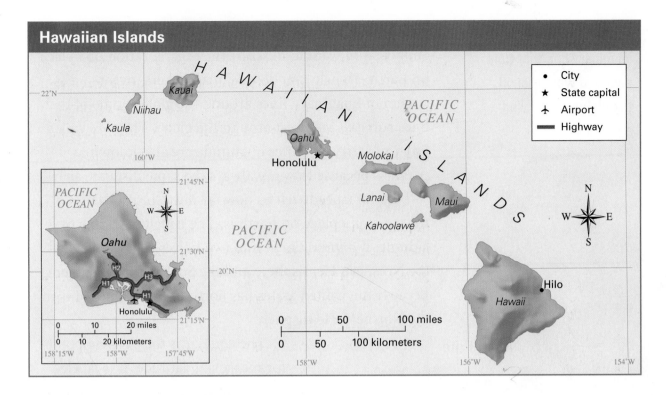

Hawaiian Islands

2.3 Scales and Symbols

Maps never show sizes and distances as they really are. They are always much smaller than the part of Earth they represent. A short distance on a map stands for a much greater distance on Earth.

The **scale** of a map shows the relationship between map distances and real distances. A map's scale can be shown in many ways. The most common is a line scale. The maps on this page have two line scales. One is for miles, and the other is for kilometers.

Maps use symbols to show other kinds of information. A symbol is anything that stands for something else. Sometimes symbols look like what they stand for. For example, mapmakers often use tiny airplane symbols to stand for airports.

Color is another important map symbol. The color blue usually stands for water. Mapmakers often use different colors to show separate states or countries.

Mapmakers use a **map key** to explain their symbols. (A key is also called a legend.) The map key tells what each symbol stands for. Look at the maps on this page. What does the star stand for?

scale a diagram that shows the relationship between distances on a map and real distances on Earth

map key an explanation of what the symbols on a map stand for

2.4 Lines of Latitude

Suppose you want to describe the exact location of a place on Earth. To help you do this, mapmakers invented a system of imaginary lines around the globe. Some of these lines run east and west around the globe. They are called **lines of latitude**. Lines of latitude are also known as parallels because they are always the same distance apart.

Lines of latitude tell us how far north or south of the equator a place on Earth is. The equator is a line of latitude. It divides Earth into two halves. They are called the Northern Hemisphere and the Southern Hemisphere. Because the United States lies north of the equator, it is in the Northern Hemisphere.

North Pole

75°N
60°N
45°N
30°N
15°N
0° Equator
15°S
30°S
45°S
60°S

South Pole

The equator is the starting point for measuring latitude. It is labeled 0°, or zero degrees. Parallels north of the equator are labeled N. The North Pole is 90° N. Parallels south of the equator are labeled S. The South Pole is 90° S. Lines of latitude measure between 0° and 90° N or 90° S. The closer a parallel is to the equator, the smaller its number of degrees. The closer it is to one of the poles, the greater its number of degrees.

A boat's location on the ocean can be pinpointed using latitude and longitude.

2.5 Lines of Longitude

Lines of longitude tell us how far to the east or west we need to go to locate a place. Look at the map on this page. It shows lines circling Earth. They are called lines of longitude. Lines of longitude are also called meridians.

Unlike lines of latitude, meridians are not parallel to each other. All meridians meet at the North Pole and the South Pole. The distance between meridians is greatest at the equator. That distance shrinks as you move from the equator to the poles.

Can you find the line that is labeled *prime meridian* on the map? This imaginary line divides the world into the Eastern Hemisphere and the Western Hemisphere. Because the United States lies west of the prime meridian, it is in the Western Hemisphere.

The longitude of the prime meridian is 0°. Lines of longitude west of the prime meridian are labeled W. Meridians east of the prime meridian are labeled E.

Lines of longitude measure between 0° and 180°. The closer a meridian is to the prime meridian, the smaller its number of degrees. The farther it is from the prime meridian, the greater its number of degrees.

line of longitude an imaginary line that runs around the globe between the North and South Poles; also called a meridian

North Pole

South Pole

global grid the grid formed by crisscrossing lines of latitude and longitude on a map

2.6 The Global Grid

Mapmakers combine lines of latitude and longitude to form a grid. A grid is a set of crisscrossing lines. The grid you see on the map below is called a **global grid** because it covers all of Earth.

Using the lines of latitude and longitude on the global grid, you can locate places anywhere in the world. For example, suppose you want to locate New Orleans on the map below. It is 30 degrees north of the equator, or 30° N. It is also 90 degrees west of the prime meridian, or 90° W. When locating places on a map, latitude is stated first, then longitude. So the location of New Orleans is 30° N, 90° W.

The city of Uíge, Angola, is located at 8° S, 15° E. To find this location, put your finger on the map where the equator and the prime meridian meet. Move your finger east to the 15° E meridian. So far, so good.

Now you have a problem. The 8° S parallel is not marked on this map. You know, though, that 8° S must lie between the equator and 15° S. If you move your finger along the 15° E meridian to the spot halfway between these two parallels, you will find the city you are looking for.

North Pole

South Pole

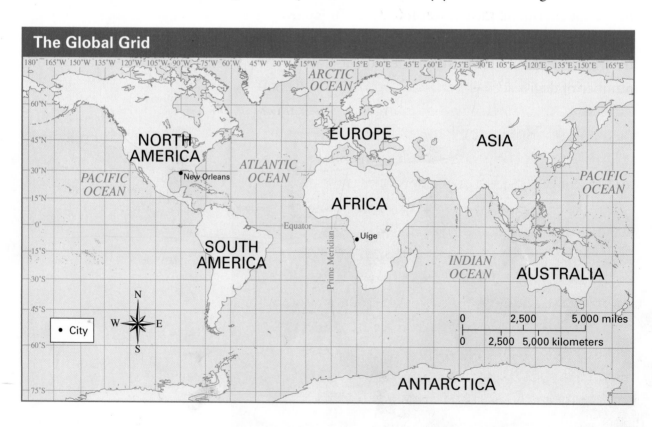

The Global Grid

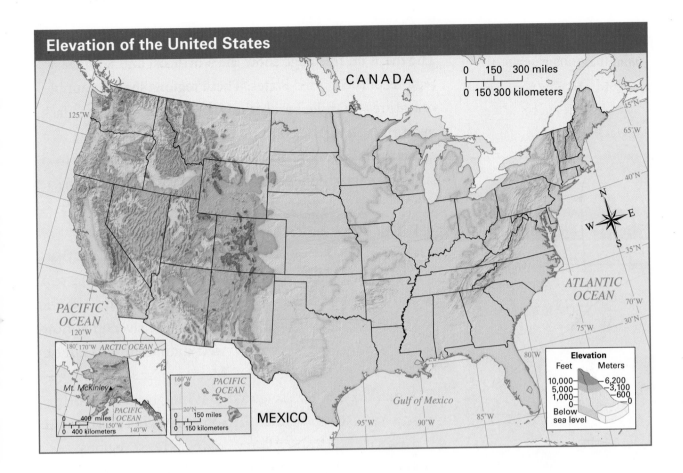

Elevation of the United States

2.7 Kinds of Maps

Geographers make different kinds of maps for different purposes. Maps that show natural features are called physical maps. Physical maps show landforms, such as mountains, valleys, and plains. Physical maps also show bodies of water, such as rivers, lakes, and oceans. Other maps show human features. For example, a political map shows cities, capitals, states, and countries.

Special-purpose maps show just one kind of information. Rainfall maps, for example, show how much rain falls in different parts of the world. Population maps show how many people live in different areas. Language maps show what languages people speak in different places.

The special-purpose map above is an elevation map of the United States. Elevation is the height of the land above the ocean. The surface of the ocean, called sea level, is at zero elevation. The highest point in North America is Mt. McKinley in Alaska. Its elevation is 20,320 feet. What does the map show about your state's elevation?

special-purpose map
a map that shows just one kind of information, such as rainfall or elevation

2.8 The Northeast and Southeast

The maps on this page show the Northeast and Southeast regions of the United States. These regions share a number of features. Both lie beside the Atlantic Ocean. A low, flat plain runs along the coast in both regions. It is known as a **coastal plain**.

The Appalachian mountain range also runs through both of these regions. Large rivers flow out of these mountains. The rivers that flow east cut across the coastal plain to the Atlantic Ocean. The rivers that flow west drain into the Gulf of Mexico.

While they are alike in some ways, the Northeast and Southeast regions have different climates. The climate of a place is the kind of weather it has over time. It includes temperature, rainfall, and wind conditions.

In the Northeast region, winters are long and cold. Snowstorms are common. Summers are warm and sometimes can be hot.

The Southeast region has a mild winter climate. Winters are usually warmer than in the Northeast. Summers are hot and humid. Humid means damp or moist.

The Northeast

0   150   300 miles
0   150   300 kilometers

CANADA

Maine
Vermont
Lake Ontario
New York
New Hampshire
Massachusetts
Lake Erie
Pennsylvania
Rhode Island
Connecticut
New Jersey
Maryland
Delaware
Potòmac River
APPALACHIAN MTS.
Hudson River
Susquehanna River
Connecticut R.
COASTAL PLAIN
ATLANTIC OCEAN
65°W
40°N
75°W
70°W

N E S W

Elevation

Feet	Meters
10,000	6,200
5,000	3,100
1,000	600
0	0
Below sea level	

The Southeast

West Virginia
Potomac River
Virginia
Ohio River
Kentucky
North Carolina
Arkansas
Tennessee
South Carolina
Arkansas River
Mississippi River
Tennessee R.
Savannah River
Georgia
Alabama
Mississippi
Mobile River
Louisiana
Red River
Florida
Gulf of Mexico
APPALACHIAN MTS.
COASTAL PLAIN
ATLANTIC OCEAN
35°N
75°W
30°N
90°W
85°W
80°W

N E S W

0   150   300 miles
0   150   300 kilometers

Elevation

Feet	Meters
10,000	6,200
5,000	3,100
1,000	600
0	0
Below sea level	

2.9 The Midwest and Southwest

The map on this page shows the Midwest and Southwest regions of the United States. These two regions lie in the center of our country.

The Midwest is an **inland** region. It does not border any ocean. However, the Great Lakes form part of the Midwest's northern border. These lakes are so large that they hold one-fifth of all the fresh water on Earth.

Most of the Midwest is flat plains. The Central Plains and Great Plains are covered with some of the best soil on Earth. That soil makes the Midwest an important farming region.

The Mississippi River runs through the Central Plains. It is the largest river in the United States. It is also a busy water highway used by boats and barges.

Plains also cover the eastern part of the Southwest. Farther west, the land rises to form the Colorado Plateau. A **plateau** is a high, flat landform that rises steeply from the land around it.

Most of the Colorado Plateau is fairly level. But it is crisscrossed by many deep canyons. The largest and most famous is the Grand Canyon.

inland not bordering an ocean

plateau a high, flat landform that rises steeply from the land around it

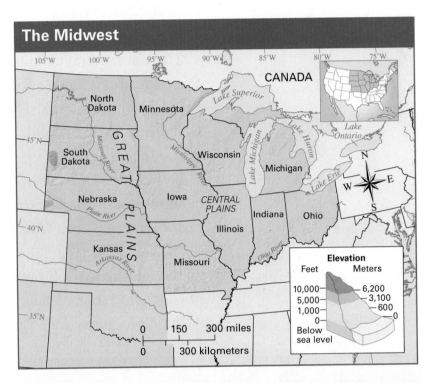

The Midwest

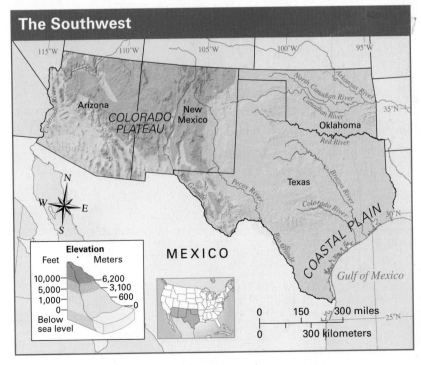

The Southwest

2.10 The West

Mountain ranges stretch across much of the West. The Rocky Mountains begin far to the north, in Alaska. From there they stretch south through Canada, Montana, Idaho, Wyoming, and Colorado.

The Great Basin lies to the west of the Rockies. A **basin** is a bowl-shaped landform that is lower than the land around it. Small ranges of mountains circle around the Great Basin.

There are several mountain ranges along the Pacific coast. The Coast Ranges are low hills that seem to rise right out of the Pacific Ocean. The Cascade Range and the Sierra Nevada are further inland. (*Sierra Nevada* means "snowy range" in Spanish.)

Between the Coast Range mountains and the inland mountains are two rich farming valleys. One is California's Central Valley. The other is Oregon's Willamette Valley.

Hawaii is also mountainous. Volcanoes formed its islands long ago. A volcano is an opening in Earth's surface through which hot, melted rock and ash may pour out. As the liquid rock cools, it forms a cone-shaped mountain.

basin a bowl-shaped landform that is lower than the surrounding land

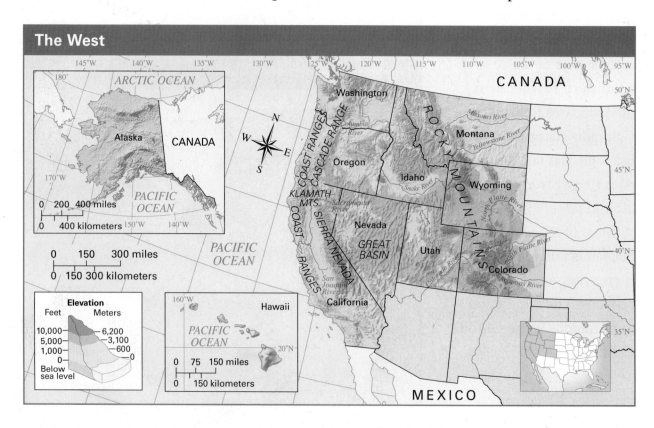

The West

Summary

As you have just read, each region of the United States is different. Did you remember to think like a geographer as you looked at the maps of each region?

You now know that there are different kinds of maps. Some maps show locations of places around the world. Lines of latitude and longitude help us find exact locations of places and measure distances north to south and east to west. Map scales also help us measure distances from place to place.

As you read about each region of the United States, you looked at physical maps. There are many other kinds of maps, including special-purpose maps. To compare climates around the country, you might use a climate map. A product map might show what each region grows or manufactures.

Each region also has its own history and culture. People in different regions eat different foods. They celebrate different holidays. They wear different kinds of clothing. They tell particular stories and honor special heroes.

Often part of what gives a region its special character is an important natural feature—an ocean, a chain of mountains, a desert, a series of lakes, or a great river.

The Mighty Mississippi

The Mississippi River—the largest river in the United States—runs down the middle of the United States. It flows through ten states. But the Mississippi influences many more. Why do geographers call it one of the most important rivers in the nation?

Mark Twain's *The Adventures of Tom Sawyer* was published in 1876. Ever since, Americans have enjoyed reading about Tom and Huck's adventures.

It was dark. But Tom Sawyer and Huck Finn could hear the great river drifting along in front of them. They continued to their raft, untied it, and then pushed it from shore. Then they climbed on. In his book *The Adventures of Tom Sawyer*, Mark Twain tells what happens next:

Mark Twain

"The raft drew beyond the middle of the river; the boys pointed her head right, and then lay on their oars. . . . They came near to letting the current drift them out of the range of the island. But they discovered the danger in time. . . ."

The boys were off on an adventure down the great Mississippi River. Although Tom and Huck are made-up characters, the Mississippi is a real river. It is just as remarkable as the two friends soon discovered.

Many readers enjoyed Twain's story. He soon followed it up with *The Adventures of Huckleberry Finn*. This book, too, featured the Mississippi River. Twain's writings brought the river into the minds of a great many Americans.

Life on the Mississippi Long Ago

Mark Twain's real name was Samuel Clemens. He based Tom and Huck's adventures on his own life growing up in a small town on the Mississippi.

To the young boy, one of the most exciting sounds in the world was the cry "S-t-e-a-m-boat a-comin'!" The steamboats brought interesting people and new things—like goods for the store or letters from faraway places.

In 1859, Twain became a steamboat pilot. Standing behind the wheel of his boat, he learned to avoid dangers in the muddy waters. He took his name as a writer from the calls the boatmen made to tell the pilot how deep—and safe— the water was: "M-a-r-k three! . . . Half twain! . . . M-a-r-k twain!"

In Twain's time, the Mississippi was like a great highway. People could travel down smaller rivers and then into the Mississippi, all the way from Minnesota to the Gulf of Mexico.

People used rafts and boats to carry goods down the Mississippi to the busy port at New Orleans. After the invention of the steamboat, people could send goods up the river as well as down it.

As a boy, Mark Twain loved to watch steamboats like these travel down the Mississippi River.

The Mississippi River

Changing the River

People depended on the Mississippi River. But they could never quite rely on it to be safe. At low water, its sandbars made travel dangerous for boats, which could run aground. In the spring and during very rainy times, the river sometimes overflowed. Mark Twain remembered that during one flood, the river became 70 *miles* wide.

So people began to change the river. First, they built **levees** to stop the river from flooding farms and towns. The levees did their job well some of the time. At other times, the river seemed to have a mind of its own. It pushed right through the levees. Then people fixed the levees and built more of them. They hoped the new ones would hold better.

People also changed the river to improve travel. They built bridges across the river. They dug mud out of the river bottom to make it deeper so that large boats could travel the river more easily.

levee a wall, typically made of dirt, built along a river to keep it from flooding

In 1882, the Mississippi flooded people out of their homes.

The River Today

The changes people made to the river have made it easier to use. If Mark Twain visited the river today, he would see huge barges. These barges carry millions of tons of goods up and down the river each year.

But changing the river does not mean people control it. In 2005, a hurricane called Katrina hit the city of New Orleans and proved that. Huge winds and heavy rains from the storm made the Mississippi overflow. One by one, the levees failed. Most of the city was under water. Lots of people climbed onto roofs to get away from the water. But many did not get away and died. Thousands of people lost their homes and their businesses. The storm and the flood cost billions of dollars. It was one of the greatest disasters in our nation's history.

Since that time, people have worked hard to rebuild New Orleans. They have looked to geographers for help. Geographers study the river and the ways human changes influence it. Their knowledge helps people plan well for the future.

Today the Mississippi is still a major water highway. Barges carrying goods regularly travel down the river.

The Peopling of the United States

3

How have different groups contributed to the United States?

3.1 Introduction

In the last chapter, you learned about the geography of the United States. But a nation is more than its land. A nation is a place where people live together under one government.

Americans are not all alike. Look around your school. Do the students you see all have the same color hair or skin? Do they all speak the same language at home? Do their families all share the same **culture,** or way of life? For many schools, the answer is no.

The United States is a **diverse** nation. This means that people from many different backgrounds live here. In this chapter, you will learn about people from five parts of the world who came to our country. And you will see how each group has contributed to our country in a special way.

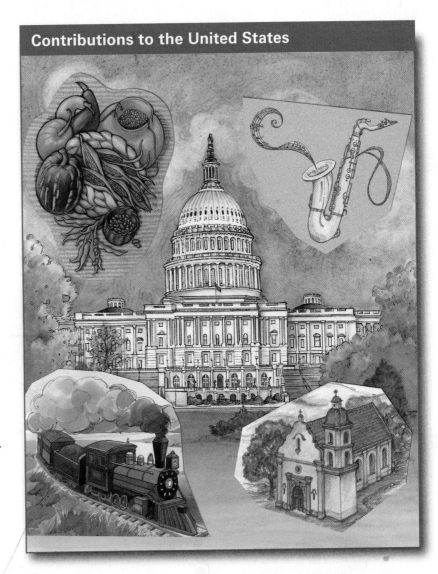

Contributions to the United States

3.2 The First Americans Arrive

Scientists agree that the first Americans arrived long ago. But they have different ideas about exactly how and when people came to North America.

For many years, most scientists believed that the first people in **the Americas** came from the continent of Asia about 11,500 years ago.

At that time, Earth's climate was much colder than it is today. Much of Earth's surface was covered with ice. This long cold period is known as the ice age. During the ice age, snow piled up in huge sheets of ice called glaciers.

Because so much water was in the form of ice, the level of the oceans went down. A narrow strip of ocean between Asia and North America disappeared. This left a bridge of land between the two continents.

Scientists believed that herds of animals wandered onto this land bridge, looking for food. Hunters from Asia may have followed them and crossed the land bridge to North America. Years later, the ocean once again covered up the land bridge.

the Americas
the landmasses and islands of North America and South America

Possible Early Routes to the Americas

More recent discoveries have led some scientists to think that people may have arrived in the Americas even earlier. About 12,500 years ago, people with boats may have moved along the Pacific coast of Alaska and northwestern Canada and then south.

Over time, people spread throughout North and South America. **American Indians** are the descendants of these first Americans. A descendant is someone who is related to a particular person or group from the past.

American Indian
someone who is a descendant of the first people to live in North and South America

3.3 Contributions of American Indians

American Indians have affected American life in many ways. One important contribution has been their respect for nature. Native peoples used the land they lived on. But they seldom harmed it.

Today, we still use the names they chose for many rivers. We've also named some of our states with the American Indian words for those areas.

You may be able to see other contributions in your kitchen at home. American Indians were the first to grow many of the foods we eat today. Two of the most popular foods they grew are corn and potatoes. In the different areas where they settled, American Indians also grew such fruits and vegetables as beans, squash, and pineapples. In some areas, they raised cocoa beans that they used to make a bitter liquid form of chocolate.

Here are even more American Indian contributions to American life:

- Foods: vanilla, jerky
- Words: tepee, tomahawk, hammock, skunk, tomato, avocado
- Cool stuff: moccasins, parkas, toboggans, pottery, jewelry, baskets, beadwork
- Other gifts: powwows, legends and myths, dogsleds

American Indians lived in tribes. Each tribe developed its own language and customs.

3.4 The Spanish Settle the Americas

In 1492, an explorer named Christopher Columbus left Spain with a crew in three small ships. Columbus believed that by sailing west across the Atlantic Ocean, he would reach Asia. Instead, he landed on a Caribbean island.

Columbus returned to Spain to tell what he had found. But he left some men behind to start a **colony** for Spain.

More Spanish people followed Columbus's route to the Americas. Some Spaniards began colonies on islands in the Caribbean Sea. Others built colonies in North and South America, often near where American Indians lived.

One of the largest Spanish colonies was in Mexico. From Mexico, settlers moved into what is now the United States. They built towns, churches, and forts in the areas we know as Texas, New Mexico, Arizona, California, and Florida.

Today, Mexico and all the countries to its south are called Latin America. People who were born in Latin America or whose ancestors were born there are called **Latinos**. An ancestor is a relative from a past generation.

Some Latinos have lived in the United States for many years, while others have just arrived. They have come from Mexico, Cuba, Puerto Rico, and the rest of Latin America.

colony a settlement that is ruled by another country

Latino someone who was born in Latin America or is a descendant of someone born in Latin America

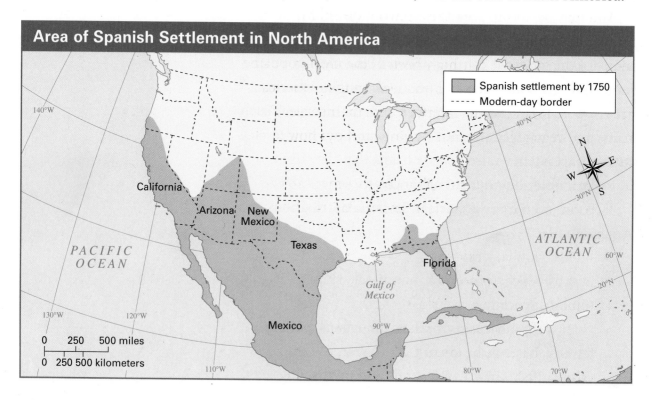

Area of Spanish Settlement in North America

Spanish settlement by 1750
- - - - Modern-day border

California
Arizona
New Mexico
Texas
Florida
PACIFIC OCEAN
ATLANTIC OCEAN
Gulf of Mexico
Mexico

0   250   500 miles
0 250 500 kilometers

3.5 The Contributions of Latinos

Latinos have made many contributions to American life. One is their skill at mining. In 1848, a sawmill worker discovered gold in California. Thousands of people went to California hoping to become rich, including many experienced miners from Chile. Wealthy Americans hired many people from Chile to dig tunnels to help them mine for gold.

Another contribution is Latinos' skill at desert farming. Latinos have shown Americans how to turn the dry Southwest into a rich farming region. Many crops, such as oranges, that are grown in this region today were first brought by Spanish settlers to Mexico and then from Mexico to the United States.

You may have seen another contribution on television: the cowboy. Everything about cowboys came to the United States from Mexico—even the cows, which originally came from Spain. Mexican settlers brought cattle to the Southwest. They then built cattle ranches. And they introduced the Mexican cowboy, called a *vaquero* (vah-KEHR-oh).

Americans learned how to be cowboys from Mexican vaqueros. Their wide-brimmed cowboy hats came from Mexican *sombreros*. Their high-heeled cowboy boots came from Mexican *botas*. Mexican vaqueros taught Americans how to use *la riata*, or the lariat, to rope their cattle. The vaqueros even taught the first singing cowboys how to play the Spanish guitar.

Here are more Latino contributions to American life:

- Foods: tacos, chili, burritos, enchiladas, tamales, salsa, tortillas
- Words: barbecue, tornado, canyon, patio, hurricane, ranch, coyote, mosquito
- Cool stuff: ponchos, western saddles, guitars, Spanish-style buildings, lassos
- Other gifts: rodeos, tango and mambo dances, Spanish folk songs

Mexican vaqueros, or cowboys, wear large-brimmed hats to protect them from the sun.

3.6 More Europeans Come to America

The Spanish were the first Europeans to colonize North America. Other Europeans soon followed. The French started a colony in Canada. Russians began a colony in Alaska. Dutch settlers built a colony in what is now New York.

Settlers from England began colonies on the eastern shore of North America. Between 1607 and 1733, the English built 13 colonies in America. These colonies hugged the Atlantic Coast from Maine to Georgia.

The 13 American colonies attracted settlers from many parts of Europe. Many of these people were poor. They came to find land or work. Others were searching for freedom to follow their religion. All hoped to start new lives in a new land.

In 1776, the American colonies broke away from England. Together, they formed a new nation called the United States of America.

The new nation welcomed immigrants from Europe. An **immigrant** is a person who comes from some other place to live in a country. **European Americans** are immigrants from Europe or descendants of European immigrants.

At first, most of the immigrants came from western Europe. Later, others came from eastern and southern Europe as well. Each group added to America's diversity, or mix of peoples.

immigrant someone who comes from another place to live in a country

European American someone who is an immigrant from Europe or a descendant of a European immigrant

Some people came to America so they could freely practice their religion.

3.7 The Contributions of European Americans

European Americans have played a large part in shaping American life. One significant contribution is the English language. Americans speak English today in part because so many English colonists settled in the American colonies. This was because early in American history, the British won the French and Indian War. The victory over France meant that English became the primary language spoken in the American colonies.

A number of European Americans were inventors. Their inventions included the telephone, the radio, and electric lights. The American government is another contribution of European Americans. The United States is the world's oldest **democracy**. Democracy has its roots in the governments of ancient Greece and Rome.

democracy a form of government in which people vote for their leaders

The colonists from Europe eventually tired of being told what to do by an English king. They wanted to govern, or rule, themselves. The king of England did not want to give American colonists this freedom. He sent troops to America to keep the colonies under his control.

The colonists decided to fight for their freedom. The war they fought is known as the American Revolution.

Here are even more European American contributions to American life:

- Foods: hamburgers, spaghetti, pizza, waffles, bagels
- Words: poodle, dock, dollar, kindergarten, denim, garage
- Cool stuff: skis, trains, radios, bikes, cars, pianos, telephones
- Other gifts: ballet, opera, plays, classical music, poetry, paintings

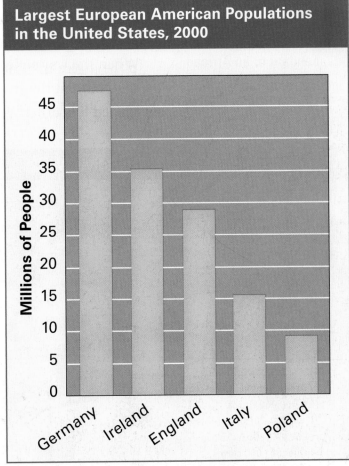

Largest European American Populations in the United States, 2000

Source: U.S. Census Bureau, Census 2000 special tabulation

3.8 Africans Arrive in America

In 1619, a Dutch trading ship arrived in the colony of Virginia. The ship's captain made a deal with the colonists. He traded 20 Africans—taken by force from their homes— for food. These Africans became servants. Within a few decades, people brought from Africa were forced to be slaves. A slave is a person who is owned by another person.

Today, we know that slavery is very wrong. But in 1619, the practice of buying and selling people was common in much of the world. In Africa, for example, people who were captured in raids were often sold as slaves.

For almost 200 years, traders used force to bring many Africans to this country. Most Africans were sold as slaves. They worked on farms raising tobacco, rice, and cotton. For this work, slaves received no pay. Slave owners viewed their slaves as property, rather than as people who worked for them. They often treated the slaves very harshly.

Slavery became part of life in the American South. But outside the South, many people opposed slavery. The fight over slavery finally led to the American Civil War in 1861. When the war ended in 1865, the practice of slavery was stopped. But the struggle by **African Americans** to be treated like other Americans was just beginning.

African American
someone who is an African immigrant or a descendant of an African immigrant or slave

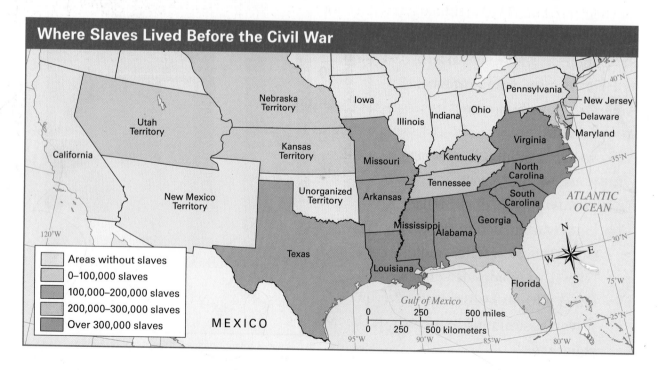

Where Slaves Lived Before the Civil War

Legend:
- Areas without slaves
- 0–100,000 slaves
- 100,000–200,000 slaves
- 200,000–300,000 slaves
- Over 300,000 slaves

3.9 The Contributions of African Americans

African Americans have made many contributions to American life. In Africa, telling stories is an honored art. African slaves brought that art to America. We enjoy it today in books, plays, and poetry.

African Americans also created new styles of music. They introduced gospel, jazz, and blues. They helped create rock and roll. Rap and hip-hop are more recent music contributions.

Another very important contribution has been the fight for equal rights. Rights are freedoms that belong to all people. The American Civil War ended slavery in 1865, but it did not end prejudice against African Americans. Prejudice is the use of skin color, cultural background, or religion to form an unfair opinion about other people.

Martin Luther King Jr. led the movement for equal rights in the 1960s.

Because of prejudice, whites often denied African Americans the same rights that whites enjoyed. In some states, white people made laws to keep African Americans separate from them— in restaurants and in schools. Separate also meant not equal. Often the rules to keep the two groups separate were less fair to African Americans.

African Americans fought long and hard for equal rights. Some Americans were killed in that struggle. Others were sent to jail. Laws were finally passed to end the unfair treatment.

Today, all Americans—no matter what their skin color— are equal under the law. We all have equal rights because African Americans refused to accept anything less.

Here are even more African American contributions to American life:

- Foods: corn bread, black-eyed peas, collard greens, yams
- Words: jazz, voodoo, tote
- Cool stuff: banjos, drums, proverbs
- Other gifts: ragtime music, spirituals, folktales, dance styles

3.10 Asians Come to America

In 1848, a worker discovered gold in California. News of this discovery attracted the first Chinese immigrants to the United States. Not all Americans welcomed the Chinese gold-seekers. But many admired how hard they worked.

As Americans moved west in the late 1800s, they had big dreams. They wanted railroads to cross the country. They wanted to build new farms and factories. But to make these dreams come true, Americans needed workers. So the word went out across Asia: send workers!

Between 1850 and 1882, many Chinese came to the United States to work. Some saved their money and later returned to China. But others stayed in the United States for good.

Next came immigrants from Japan, Korea, and the Philippine Islands. Some immigrants went to Hawaii to work in the sugar fields. Others worked on farms and in factories on the West Coast. One Japanese immigrant wrote this poem about going to the United States:

Many Chinese helped build our railroad system. This train trestle, or bridge, is in the Sierra Nevada, a western mountain range.

> Huge dreams of fortune
> Go with me to foreign lands
> Across the ocean.

Instead of finding fortune, however, most of the Asian immigrants found hard lives. They worked long hours for little pay. Their bosses often treated them roughly. Still, most of the immigrants stayed in their adopted land. They were the first **Asian Americans**.

Asian American
someone who is an Asian immigrant or a descendant of an Asian immigrant

3.11 The Contributions of Asian Americans

Asian Americans form one of the most diverse groups in the United States. Today, this group includes people from China, Japan, the Philippines, North Korea and South Korea, Vietnam, Cambodia, Laos, Thailand, India, and the countries of the Pacific Islands.

Asian Americans have made many contributions to American life. One is their way of preparing food. Asian immigrants brought new foods to the United States. They also brought new ways of cooking. As a result, today Americans enjoy many kinds of Asian foods, such as sushi and stir-fried dishes.

Another contribution is Asian Americans' respect for learning. Education has great value in Asian cultures. Asian Americans have continued that tradition.

Here are even more Asian American contributions to American life:

- Foods: chow mein, ramen, curry, tofu, pot stickers
- Words: jungle, shampoo, bamboo, rattan, gingham, lei, samurai, tattoo, kimono
- Cool stuff: chopsticks, woks, hot tubs, rice cookers, acupuncture, surfboards
- Other gifts: origami, Japanese gardens, yoga, martial arts

Asian American Populations in the United States, 2000

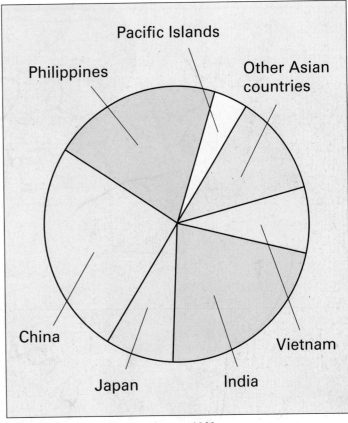

Source: U.S. Census Bureau, Census 2000

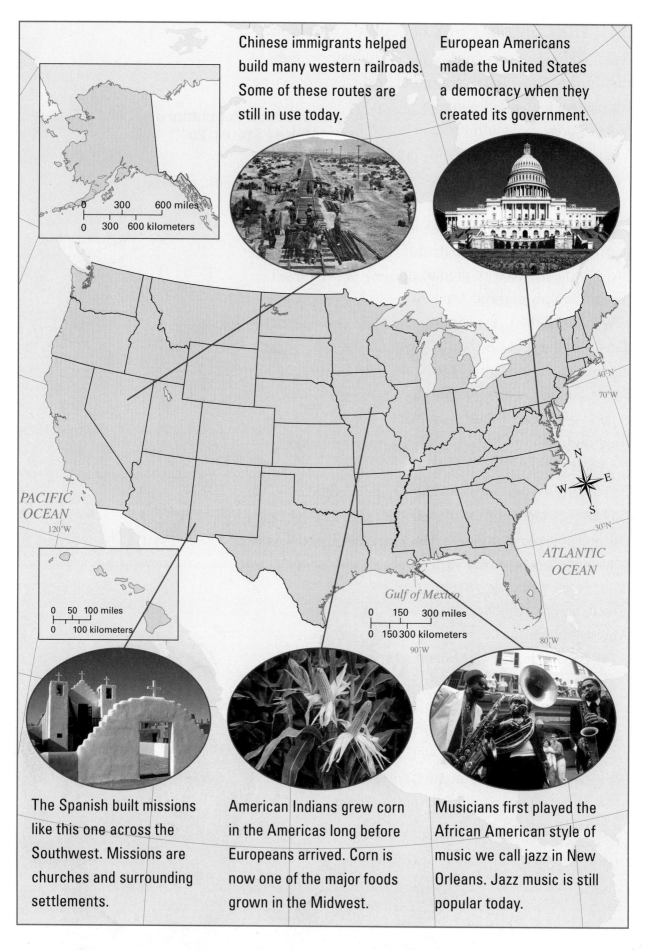

Chinese immigrants helped build many western railroads. Some of these routes are still in use today.

European Americans made the United States a democracy when they created its government.

PACIFIC OCEAN

120°W

ATLANTIC OCEAN

Gulf of Mexico

40°N
70°W

30°N

80°W

90°W

0   300   600 miles
0   300   600 kilometers

0   50   100 miles
0   100 kilometers

0   150   300 miles
0   150 300 kilometers

The Spanish built missions like this one across the Southwest. Missions are churches and surrounding settlements.

American Indians grew corn in the Americas long before Europeans arrived. Corn is now one of the major foods grown in the Midwest.

Musicians first played the African American style of music we call jazz in New Orleans. Jazz music is still popular today.

Summary

Sooner or later, you will hear someone describe the United States as a nation of immigrants. It's true. All of us came to this land from some other place. Some made the journey thousands of years ago. Others arrived just yesterday.

Each group came for its own reasons. Ancestors of American Indians may have followed the animals they hunted to a new land. The Spanish were looking for a route to Asia. The English came seeking freedom and opportunity. Other Europeans were fleeing war and hunger. Asians originally crossed the ocean to find gold and work. The first Africans were brought to America against their will.

Immigrants are still traveling to America. Most of these new immigrants come from countries in Latin America and Asia. But people also come from many other parts of the world.

The contributions of each group of people have changed and strengthened the United States. Without any one group and its contributions, the United States would not be as richly varied as it is today.

These three girls have something in common. They are all Americans.

Reading Further

3

New York City: Layers of the Past

Stand on any corner in New York City. You'll see people from many backgrounds walking past. The same thing has been true for hundreds of years. How have different groups of people made New York City what it is today?

Welcome to Corlears Hook Park. You are on New York City's Lower East Side. Can you hear the loud moan of the riverboat horn? There are children laughing and running in the park today. Listen and you can hear them speak in Spanish and Chinese, as well as English, as they play.

About 100 years ago, on this very same spot, children also played—when they were not working. Those children spoke Dutch, English, French, German, and Yiddish.

Some 300 years before that, the children here were American Indians, from the Lenape tribe. There were no streets then, only paths through the woods and fields. The children helped their parents to fish, grow corn, or trap animals. Stand in Corlears Hook Park today, and you stand on layers and layers of American history. Each group of people that lived in this place left its mark. Who were these people? What were their traditions? How did they shape the New York City of today?

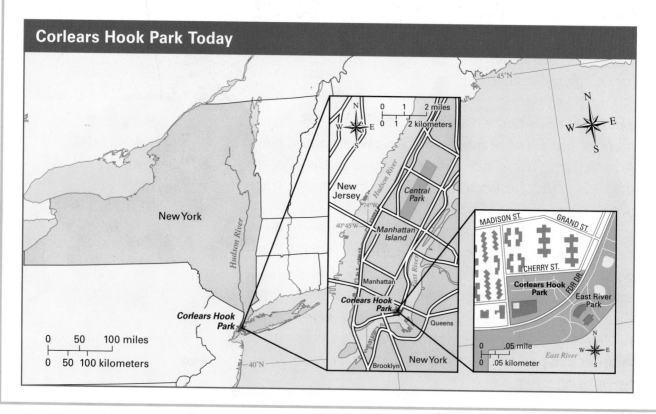

Corlears Hook Park Today

A Meeting of Three Worlds

Manhattan Island was first settled by American Indians more than 10,000 years ago. Thousands of Lenapes lived on the island they called Mana-hatta, "the hilly island." They fished, grew corn, and trapped animals such as beavers. Those beavers would eventually change life on Mana-hatta forever.

In 1609, a Dutch ship sailed into the harbor of Mana-hatta. It was the *Half Moon*, Henry Hudson's ship. The Dutch were looking for places to settle and for people to trade with. They especially wanted furs. And the Lenapes had lots of furs.

A few years later, the Dutch sent a free black sailor named Juan Rodrigues to Mana-hatta. It was his job to trade Dutch furs with American Indians. He was the first black man to live on Manhattan Island.

In 1624, the Dutch fur company sent 30 families to start a colony. Their settle-

The Granger Collection, New York

The Lenapes meet Henry Hudson and his crew of twenty men.

ment at the tip of Manhattan Island was named New Amsterdam. The Dutch made changes to the island as they built their new town. They cut down trees, laid out streets, and built homes.

As more and more people arrived, three worlds came together. First were the American Indians. Then people came from Holland and, later, France, Ireland, and other European countries. Africans such as Juan Rodrigues were part of the story, too. In 1644, a visitor to New Amsterdam said that he heard 18 different languages spoken on the streets! It was a diverse town even then.

Waves of Immigrants Come to New York

Since the 1600s, when the Dutch first settled there, New York City has attracted immigrants by the millions. In 1664, the English took over New Amsterdam. They renamed the city New York.

In the 1800s and early 1900s, most immigrants to the United States came from Europe by ship. They traveled past the Statue of Liberty into New York Harbor and landed at Ellis Island. In the year 1907, more than 1 million new Americans came through Ellis Island.

tenement a four- to six-story building with many small apartments

Many immigrants settled on the Lower East Side. The neighborhood around Corlears Hook was crowded with families. They came from Italy and Russia and other parts of Europe. Everyone—even children—worked hard to start a new life in their new country.

Many immigrant families lived in **tenements**. Sometimes, twenty families or more lived in one tenement. Each floor had several small apartments and only one bathroom. The apartments did not have much fresh air or good light. Rats and cockroaches added to the poor living conditions.

Tenement apartments were often very crowded. A lot of living happened in the street.

The Confino family lived in a tenement located at 97 Orchard Street. Ten people lived in their small apartment. Like other families, the Confinos brought their traditions with them. They worshipped as Jews. They ate foods like those they had eaten in Italy. They also brought their dreams to the United States. In time, they became Americans.

New York City Today

The Lower East Side is still crowded. It is still a place where many new Americans first live. And it is still a place where you can see signs of the past. An Italian bakery or a Jewish delicatessen reminds New Yorkers of the Lower East Side that the Confinos knew.

Today, though, you hear different languages on the streets. In Little Italy, you once heard Italian everywhere. Now, you are more likely to hear Chinese or Spanish as you walk through the neighborhood. In fact, New York City's Chinatown is the largest Chinatown in the United States.

The Lower East Side celebrates its history all year long. It has been home to a mix of people since Juan Rodrigues first arrived. People in all groups that have come to New York City have changed the place in some way.

People celebrate the Feast of San Gennaro in Little Italy. For eleven days each year they honor Italian traditions.

In Chinatown, dragons dance in the street. People come from many places to welcome the Chinese New Year.

NEW YORK CITY

A Train Tour of the Northeast

4

What are different parts of the Northeast like?

4.1 Introduction

Welcome to our train tour of the historic Northeast. My name is Ms. Mariner. I will be your guide for the next few days. When not leading tours, I work in my town's local history center. So you'll hear a lot from me about the past as we go.

Our tour will take you to many different places. Each one has a story to tell about the Northeast and its people.

As we visit these places, I want you to look for answers to three questions. First, why do we call the Northeast the "birthplace of our nation"? Next, why did our nation's first factories start here? And finally, what large cities are found in the Northeast? You'll hear and see clues to the answers to these questions as we travel along.

Watch your step as you climb aboard. Our first stop will be in the beautiful state of Maine.

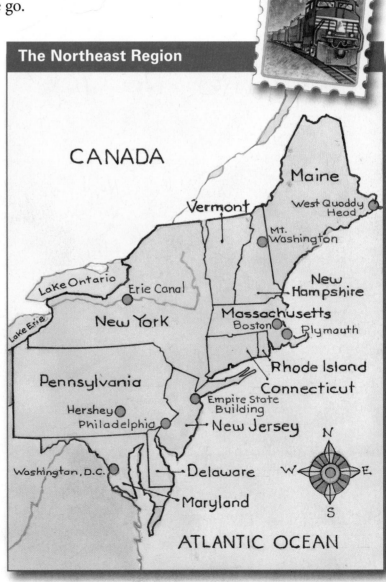

The Northeast Region

The Northeast Region

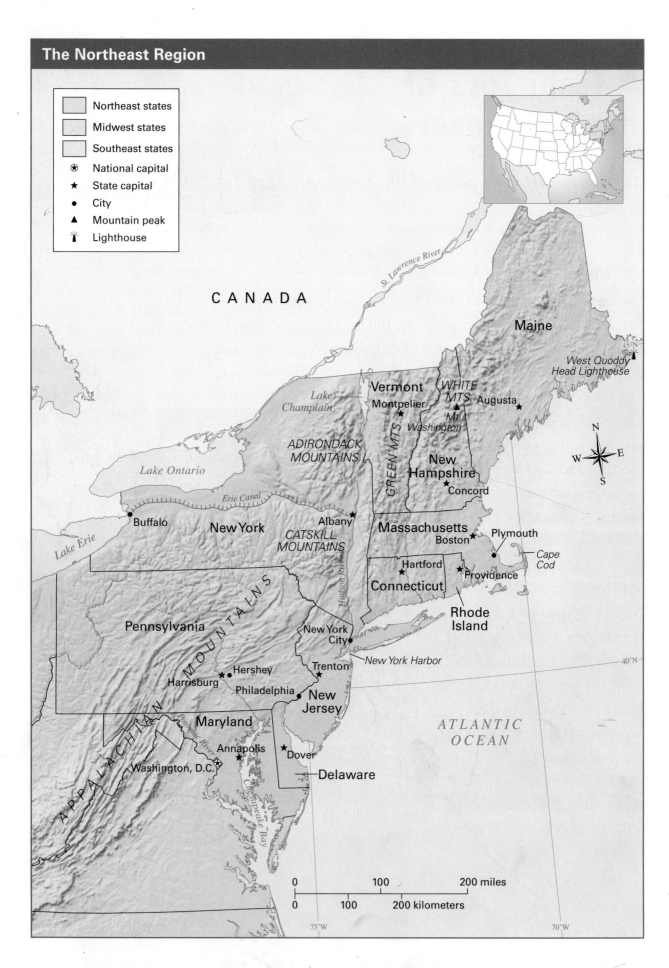

Northeast states
Midwest states
Southeast states
⊛ National capital
★ State capital
● City
▲ Mountain peak
Ⴘ Lighthouse

CANADA

St. Lawrence River

Maine

West Quoddy
Head Lighthouse

Lake
Champlain

Vermont
Montpelier ★

WHITE
MTS.
Mt.
Washington

Augusta ★

ADIRONDACK
MOUNTAINS

GREEN MTS.

New
Hampshire
Concord ★

Lake Ontario

Erie Canal

Buffalo ●

New York

CATSKILL
MOUNTAINS

Albany ★

Massachusetts
Boston ★

Plymouth

Lake Erie

Hudson River

Hartford
★

Connecticut

Providence
★

Cape
Cod

Rhode
Island

Pennsylvania

APPALACHIAN MOUNTAINS

New York
City ●

New York Harbor

Trenton
●

Hershey
Harrisburg ★ ●

Philadelphia ●

New
Jersey

ATLANTIC
OCEAN

Potomac River

Maryland

Annapolis
★

● Dover

Washington, D.C. ⊛

Delaware

Chesapeake Bay

N
W   E
S

45°N

40°N

0   100   200 miles
0   100   200 kilometers

75°W   70°W

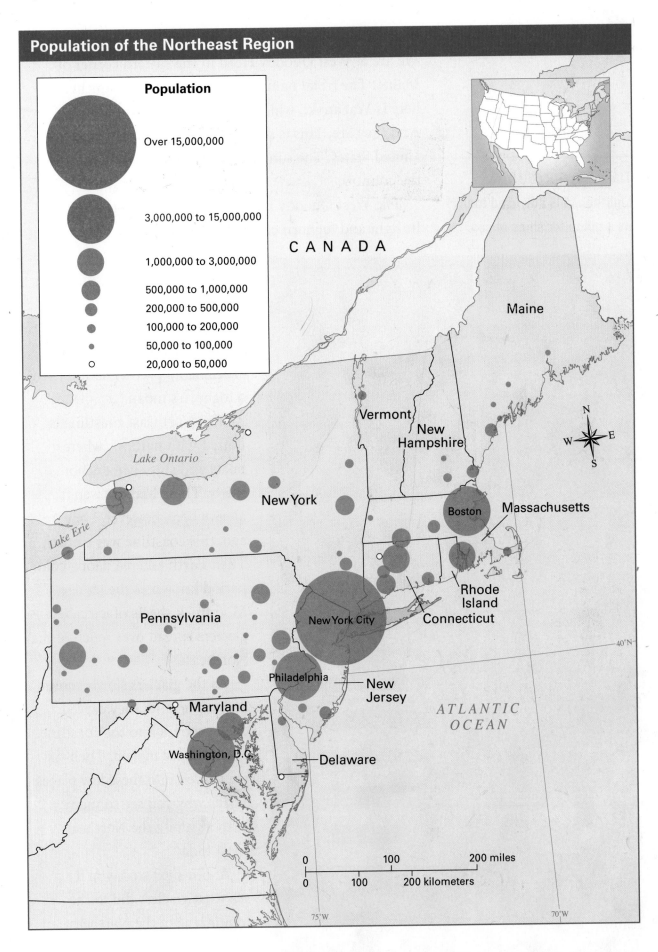

Population of the Northeast Region

Population

Over 15,000,000

3,000,000 to 15,000,000

1,000,000 to 3,000,000

500,000 to 1,000,000

200,000 to 500,000

100,000 to 200,000

50,000 to 100,000

20,000 to 50,000

CANADA

Maine

Lake Ontario

Vermont

New Hampshire

New York

Boston

Massachusetts

Lake Erie

Rhode Island

Pennsylvania

Connecticut

New York City

Philadelphia

New Jersey

ATLANTIC OCEAN

Maryland

Washington, D.C.

Delaware

45°N

40°N

N
W E
S

75°W

70°W

0   100   200 miles
0   100   200 kilometers

4.2 The Northeast Coast

We are at West Quoddy Head in the eastern corner of Maine. The tribal name of the American Indians living here is Wabanoki, which means "living at the sunrise." And they are. This is the most eastern point of land in the United States. The sun rises here before anywhere else in the country.

The West Quoddy Head Lighthouse was built in 1808. Its light and foghorn continue to keep ships from crashing into Maine's rocky shore. Some people find foghorns annoying, but my grandfather didn't. He trapped lobsters near here. "On a foggy day," he liked to say, "there is no prettier sound than a foghorn's moan."

The Northeast coastline is dotted with harbors, where boats and ships can anchor safely. These harbors weren't always here, however. Long ago, this coastline was smooth. Then Earth entered a long cold period known as the ice age. Mile-thick sheets of ice called glaciers spread over much of the Northeast.

As the glaciers slowly moved across the land, they carved deep grooves into the coastline. Later, the ice melted. Then the sea flowed into these low places. That's why you see so many harbors along the Northeast coast today.

At our next stop, you'll see what glaciers did to the mountains of the Northeast.

The West Quoddy Head Lighthouse is still used today as a guide for ships at sea.

4.3 The Mountains of the Northeast

Welcome to Mount Washington in New Hampshire. At 6,288 feet tall, Mount Washington is the highest **peak** in the Northeast. On a clear day, visitors can see for a hundred miles from its top.

Mount Washington has some of the world's most severe weather. It can snow here all year long. The peak is also one of the windiest places on Earth.

My family visited Mount Washington when I was your age. We rode the Mount Washington Cog Railway to the top. This train is the second-steepest mountain-climbing train in the world. The wind speed that day was 75 miles per hour. My mother still believes that if she hadn't held on to me, I would have blown out to sea. The highest wind speed ever recorded here was 231 miles per hour. That was in 1934.

Mount Washington sits in the White Mountains of New Hampshire. The White Mountains are part of the Appalachian mountain range. The Appalachians are one of the oldest mountain ranges in the world.

Many hikers climb Mount Washington each year.

peak the top of a mountain

4.4 Democracy Takes Root at Plymouth

This is Plymouth, Massachusetts. The Pilgrims landed here almost 400 years ago. You can visit a reproduction, or copy, of their ship, the *Mayflower*, in Plymouth Harbor.

In 1620, the *Mayflower* left England with 102 passengers aboard. All of the passengers were headed for Virginia. Less than half of them were Pilgrims in search of religious freedom. The rest simply wanted to make their home in America. The Pilgrims called these settlers "strangers."

Storms blew the *Mayflower* off course. Instead of Virginia, the ship reached New England. Sick of stormy seas, the Pilgrims decided to stop there. But they had a problem. There was no government in New England. And some of the "strangers" looked like troublemakers. What would you have done in their situation? Think about this as you leave the train to visit Plymouth.

At Plymouth, you can visit the *Mayflower II,* a copy of the Pilgrims' ship.

Welcome back. I'll tell you now how the Pilgrims solved their problem. Before going ashore, they drew up an agreement called the Mayflower Compact. It said that they would set up a government and make laws for the good of everyone. Each man signed the compact. Then the passengers elected a governor to lead the government.

Today, Americans believe that people should make their own laws and elect their own leaders. We call this form of government a democracy. During the Pilgrims' time, when kings and queens were the rulers of countries, this was a bold idea.

4.5 Boston Leads the Fight for Freedom

We are now visiting the Boston Common in Boston, Massachusetts. The Boston Common is America's first public park. And Boston is one of America's oldest cities. It is also where the fight for America's freedom from Great Britain began.

In 1775, many people in the 13 colonies did not want to live under British rule anymore. Fighting broke out between colonists and British troops near Boston. This was the beginning of a long war called the **American Revolution**. The fighting lasted for six years. The American Revolution led to the overthrow, or end, of British rule of the colonies.

Two historic trails begin at the Boston Common. The first is the Freedom Trail. This walking tour takes you to places where the fight for freedom began. The trail ends at Bunker Hill. One of the early battles of the American Revolution was fought near this hill.

The second trail is the Black Heritage Trail. On this walking tour, you will learn about the long history of African Americans in Boston. The trail ends at the African Meeting House. This meeting house is the oldest African American church building in the United States.

Which trail should you take? I recommend both. Just be sure to wear good walking shoes.

American Revolution
the war in which the American colonies won independence from Great Britain

The Old State House in Boston is one of the sights along the Freedom Trail.

Old State House
A REVOLUTIONARY WAR SITE

canal a ditch dug
across land that often
connects two waterways

lock a water elevator
used to raise and lower
boats

4.6 The Erie Canal Links the Northeast and the Midwest

Have you ever sung a song called "The Erie Canal"? You are looking at the **canal** that inspired the song. A canal is a ditch dug across land. Often canals connect one waterway with another. The Erie Canal is a 340-mile-long ditch that connects the Hudson River with the Great Lakes.

Work on the Erie Canal began in 1817. At that time, there was no good way to move goods from the Northeast to the Midwest. Moving goods by horse and wagon was slow and costly. Moving goods by boat was faster and cheaper. But there was a problem. The Appalachian Mountains lay between the Midwest and the Northeast. No river crossed the mountains.

The men who built the Erie Canal solved that problem. They dug a 40-foot-wide ditch from the Hudson River to Lake Erie. Along the way, they built 83 **locks** to help carry boats over the mountains. Locks are used to raise and lower boats in the water.

The Erie Canal opened for use in 1825. It was an instant success. Freight prices between Lake Erie and New York City dropped from $100 a ton by road to just $10 a ton by canal. New York City was soon the nation's busiest seaport.

This is just one small segment of the Erie Canal. The structure at the bottom of the picture is a lock.

4.7 New York City: Where Buildings Touch the Sky

We are in New York City. More than 8 million people live here. It is the largest city in America.

New York City has always been a city of immigrants. The Dutch were the first Europeans to settle here. People from other parts of Europe and Africa followed. Together, they made New York City a city of many cultures, or ways of life.

Today, people still come to New York City from all over the world. Just listen to people talking on the streets. You will hear English, Spanish, Chinese, Arabic, Russian, Hebrew, Italian, Korean, and many other languages.

Are you wondering how New York City finds room for all of these people? The answer is—up in the air! A hundred years ago, New Yorkers began building **skyscrapers**. People live and work in these very tall buildings.

The Empire State Building is one of New York City's most famous skyscrapers. This office building has 102 stories, or floors. Visitors can go to the very top of the building and look out at the view. You could climb the 1,860 stairs. But I suggest that you take the elevator.

On clear days, visitors to the top of the Empire State Building can see parts of New Jersey, Pennsylvania, Connecticut, and Massachusetts, as well as New York.

skyscraper a very tall building

At the chocolate factory, you can see how chocolate Kisses are made. When you leave, you can see that the streetlights are shaped like chocolate Kisses.

4.8 Hershey, Pennsylvania: A Town Built on Chocolate

One of my favorite movies is *Willy Wonka and the Chocolate Factory*. So I was very excited when my family visited Hershey, Pennsylvania. At last, I got a chance to see a real chocolate factory. Yum!

Later, I wondered why America's first factories were built in the Northeast. I think there were two main reasons. One reason was waterpower. The first factories were built alongside rivers. The rivers rushed down out of the mountains. This rushing water turned big waterwheels that made the machines in the factories run.

A second reason was people power. The Northeast was a good place for people who wanted to start businesses. Candy maker Milton Hershey was one of these people. And there were many people to work in these businesses.

More than 100 years ago, Hershey started a candy business here in Pennsylvania. He used a system called **mass production** in his factory. Mass production is a way of making very large quantities of the same product. The Hershey bar was America's first mass-produced candy bar. Today, Hershey's factory is the largest chocolate factory in the world.

We'll stop here to learn more about mass production. Enjoy your visit. And try not to eat too much chocolate.

mass production a way of making large quantities of products

4.9 Independence Hall: The Birthplace of the United States

You are looking at Independence Hall in Philadelphia, Pennsylvania. It was here that the United States was born. We celebrate our nation's birthday each year on Independence Day.

The date of our nation's birth was July 4, 1776. On that day, leaders from the 13 colonies met in Independence Hall to approve the **Declaration of Independence**. This statement told the world that the Americans had formed their own nation. They called the new country the United States of America.

Americans fought a long war to win their independence. Great Britain finally agreed that Americans should govern themselves. But how would they do that?

In 1787, some of the best thinkers in the nation met in Independence Hall to answer that question. They talked and argued for months. Then they wrote a new constitution, or plan of government, for the country. We still live under that plan today.

The **United States Constitution** is based on the idea of democracy. Under this plan of government, we, the people, choose our leaders. The Constitution also protects our rights. You have the right to say what you think. You may follow any religion you choose. You have the right to a fair trial. These and many others are rights that the Constitution provides and that Americans hold dear.

Declaration of Independence the document that declared the United States to be free from Great Britain

United States Constitution the plan of government for the United States

Today, Independence Hall is part of a national historic park.

4.10 Washington, D.C.: Our Nation's Capital

Does this building look familiar to you? It is the Capitol Building. It is one of the great landmarks of the city of Washington, D.C.

Washington is our nation's capital. It is the home of our national government. It is the place where the people who have the power to make rules and decisions for our country do their jobs.

The work of our government is important to all of us. The government creates the rules we live by. Picture what life would be like without rules. Think about it as you leave the train to visit Washington, D.C.

Welcome back. Now that you have had a chance to think about how important rules are, let me tell you a bit more about our government's rules, or laws.

Our government's laws help to make sure that each person's rights are protected. Our rights include the right to life, liberty, property, and the pursuit of happiness.

The government also works for the common good. This means that the government tries to act in ways that serve all people, not just a few. Our government seeks to provide an equal chance for all people. It tries to treat all people fairly.

Our government is based on the idea of democracy. The word *democracy* means "rule by the people." One way in which the people in the United States rule is by choosing their leaders. People choose leaders in elections. Voting in elections is a key part of being a good citizen.

The Capitol Building is where Congress meets to make our nation's laws.

4.11 Our Government Buildings

The national government of the United States has three branches, or parts. Each branch has a different role. Each helps promote the common good and protect people's basic rights. And each has a special building it calls home.

Congress is the legislative branch. It makes laws for our country. Voters in each state elect lawmakers to represent them in Congress. Congress works in the Capitol Building.

The president of the United States is the head of the executive branch. The president's main job is to make sure that laws passed by Congress are carried out. The president is also elected. The president lives and works in the White House.

The judicial branch is the third branch of government. It is made up of the nation's courts. This branch guarantees that the laws passed by Congress are obeyed. The courts also seek truth and justice. They decide questions and disagreements about our laws. For example, courts decide whether someone has broken a law.

The highest court is the Supreme Court. Its home is also in Washington, D.C.—in the Supreme Court Building. One of the Supreme Court's jobs is to make sure that laws passed by Congress follow the United States Constitution. The Constitution explains what the U.S. government and its leaders can and cannot do. The Supreme Court also helps make sure that government treats all people fairly.

The president of the United States lives and works in the White House.

The top court in the United States meets in the Supreme Court Building.

The Washington Monument (at left) and the Jefferson Memorial (at right) are both located in Washington, D.C.

4.12 Our National Monuments

Washington, D.C., is more than a home to government. It also has many famous landmarks. You have visited the Capitol Building and have seen the White House and the Supreme Court Building. Other buildings honor the ideas and the people that have helped make our country great. Still others hold some of our national treasures.

Washington, D.C., has many monuments. These are buildings that help us remember important people or events. The Washington Monument celebrates the first president of the United States. His name was George Washington. The Jefferson Memorial honors Thomas Jefferson. He was our third president. Jefferson also wrote the Declaration of Independence. This document says, "All men are created equal." It gives some of the main ideas that have shaped our government.

In Washington, D.C., you can see the signed copy of the Declaration of Independence. It is at one of the city's great museums—the National Archives. Also in the National Archives are the U.S. Constitution and the Bill of Rights. The Bill of Rights was added to the Constitution in 1791. It lists our most cherished freedoms. Thanks to the Bill of Rights, we have the freedom of speech. We can speak out if we are unhappy with our government. The Bill of Rights also promises us freedom of religion. These are just two examples.

As you have learned, there is much to see and do in Washington, D.C. You can find out about our nation's history. You can learn about the ideas that are important to our country. You can celebrate our past. I hope you have enjoyed your visit!

Summary

Do you remember the questions I asked you when we began our journey?

The first question was why we call the Northeast the "birthplace of our nation." After visiting Boston and Philadelphia, you should know the answer. Boston is where the American Revolution began. And Philadelphia is where Americans first declared their independence from Great Britain.

I also asked you why the nation's first factories were built in the Northeast. We talked about two reasons. The Northeast had a lot of waterpower for running factories. And it had people who enjoyed the challenge of starting new businesses, as well as people who wanted to work in them.

Also, new methods of transportation encouraged people to build factories here. Canals and railroads lowered the cost of moving goods to customers.

My last question was what large cities are found here. You visited some of the largest cities in the Northeast: Boston, New York City, Philadelphia, and Washington, D.C.. You also stopped at two smaller towns, Plymouth and Hershey. Which city or town would you most like to visit again?

Our tour of the Northeast is ending now. I hope you enjoyed your trip as much as I enjoyed being your guide.

Vermont bursts into a blaze of color in autumn.

Lowell, Massachusetts: Factory Life

In the early 1800s, the Northeast filled with factories. Many of them made just one item—cotton cloth. People around the world wanted cotton goods. In Lowell, Massachusetts, thousands of women took jobs to make these goods. What was it like to work in Lowell's cotton mills?

mill a factory in which people make products out of raw materials

Many girls spent their childhoods in the massive mill buildings.

In the still dark just before dawn, loud bells awoke the New England town. Sleepy young women and girls—some only 10 years old—dressed quickly.

It was 4:30 A.M. They had to arrive at work in 30 minutes. If they got there even one minute late, they might lose their jobs. They would surely receive an unpleasant scolding.

The girls hurried the few blocks across town. They were headed to the textile **mills** of Lowell, Massachusetts.

Gate

Canal

Water Pipe

Gear

Turbine Gear

Loom

Power House   Mill

Cotton, Cotton, Cotton!

Lowell was established in 1822. Mill owners in the Northeast had wanted to expand to make more cotton thread and cloth—and more money. So they looked carefully for a place to build a new mill town.

They chose the area where the Merrimack and Concord rivers meet. This was the perfect location. Water brought the factories to life. It turned the mill's turbines. These were wheels with blades that used the power of the flowing water to turn the gears that powered the machines inside the mill.

With waterpower, the Lowell mills produced millions of yards of cloth in a year.

More than 5 miles of canals carried river water through Lowell. This water turned large wheels that powered the machines inside the mills.

The Lowell mills grew quickly. Factory buildings lined a mile of the Merrimack River.

Workers Needed

The mill owners needed many workers to produce so much cotton thread and cloth. And because new mills continued to be built, new workers were needed to fill them, too. Clever business owners knew just how they could fill all of those jobs. They could hire women—thousands of them.

In the early 1800s, many Americans felt that women should not work. The thought of women doing factory work shocked them.

But the hum of the mill cities attracted young women and girls from all over the Northeast. Most came from farms. Workers also arrived from Canada and parts of Europe. And men eagerly took jobs in the mills, too.

Still, most of the workers were women. They soon became known as "mill girls."

Lowell quickly became one of the most important factory towns in the United States. By 1850, 40 large mill buildings stood side by side for a mile along the Merrimack River. And the mills had hired 10,000 women, girls, and men to work in them.

Why Did They Come?

In the early 1800s, women could hold only a few types of jobs outside of the home. For example, they could be servants or they could sew clothes. But these jobs did not pay much. Harriet Robinson, who worked in one of the Lowell mills from age 10 to 23, described the other options:

> "If she [a woman] worked out as servant, or 'help,' her wages were from 50 cents to $1.00 a week; or if she went from house to house by the day to spin and weave, or do tailoress [sewing] work, she could get but 75 cents a week and her meals."

At $2.00 a week, the factories offered good, steady pay. That was hard for many mill girls to ignore. They saw a mill job as a way to a better life.

At the mills, women could earn their own living. They could be independent. Some used their earnings to help pay for a brother's education or a family debt. The girls had more options than they might have had otherwise.

One mill girl, named Ann Swett Appleton, explained, "The thought that I am living on no one is a happy one, indeed."

Women could earn more money at the mills than they might otherwise. This gave them some independence.

Long, Hard Days

But life in the factories was tough. Women often ran the spinning machines or weaving looms. Spinning machines turned strands of cotton into thread. Looms turned thread into cloth. The work was tiring and often boring. Workers repeated the same tasks for 13 or 14 hours a day.

Today, there are laws that prevent children from working. In the 1800s, there were not. Even young teens worked from 5 A.M. until the bell announced the end of the workday at 7 P.M. And the mill girls were allowed only two half-hour breaks each day— for breakfast and dinner.

Inside the mills, the noise was deafening. Hundreds of machines screamed and squealed all day long.

And many factory owners kept all windows shut, even in summer. They wanted the air inside to stay warm and moist. That kept the thread from breaking easily. Sometimes workers fainted from the heat.

At times, the stomach-turning smell of burning whale oil filled the air. The oil burned in lamps that lit the dim factories in the dark days of winter.

Often, workers left their jobs because they were unhappy with the working conditions. Others left to return to their families or get married. But many stayed, day after day, for several years. Some even stayed as long as 15 years.

Some women ran the spinning machines. Others, like these, worked the weaving looms.

Women Speak Out

Mill owners ran crowded boarding houses where mill girls had to live. In 1836, the owners decided to charge women more for their rooms. The owners also lowered **wages,** saying that they had to because the country was facing hard times. Mills were losing money.

Many mill girls could not afford to lose that much pay. About 1,500 women walked out on their jobs to protest. Harriet Robinson described the day:

> "One of the girls stood on a pump and [stated] the feelings of her companions in a neat speech. . . . This was the first time a woman had spoken in public in Lowell."

Unfortunately, the factory owners did not change their minds. Soon, the girls went back to work.

The strike did some good, though. It showed that female workers would join together to fight for better treatment. They did that again and again over the next 75 years. Eventually, mill workers won better pay and working conditions.

The Lowell mills buzzed with activity into the 1900s. But in the 1920s, many of the factories began moving south. By 1955, Lowell's noisy mills had fallen silent. Yet the strong voices of Lowell's mill girls have not been forgotten.

This photograph shows the women who lived in one boarding house in Lowell in 1800. Mill owners required that mill girls live in the boarding houses.

wage a payment of money for work

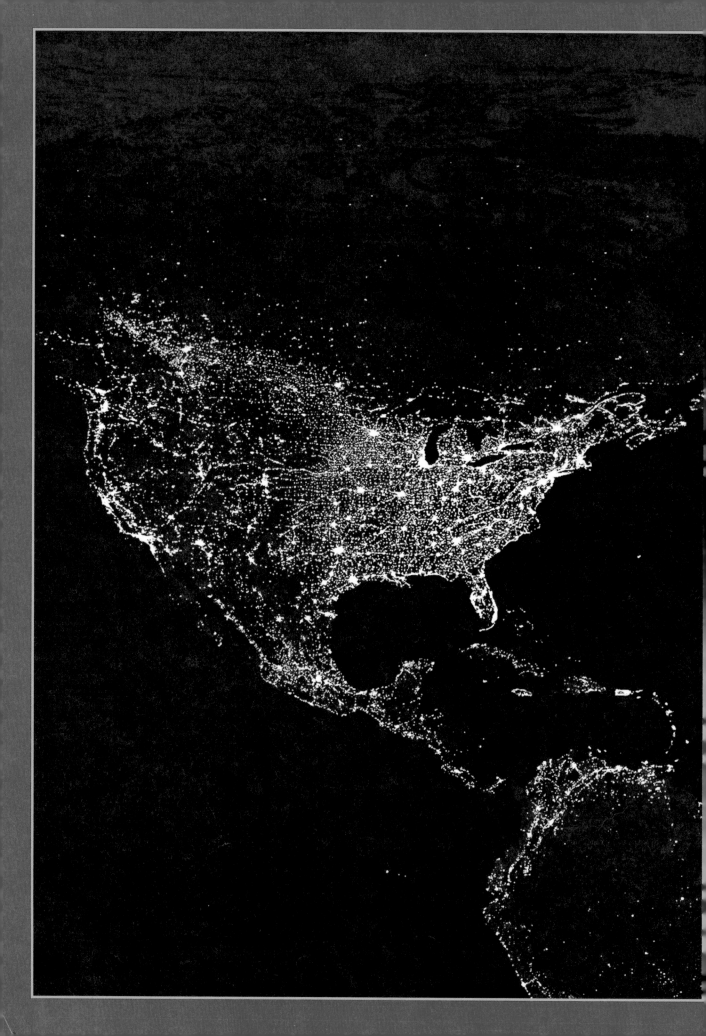

Population Density and Life in the Northeast

How do people live in the Northeast?

5

5.1 Introduction

The photograph to the left shows the United States at night. Some areas look like bright dots of lights. Other areas are darker. The bright areas are where lots of people live. These are the more populated areas. People live close together in towns and cities there.

The dark areas are where fewer people live. These are less populated areas. People live far apart there.

Look at the Northeast region in the photograph. Do you see the long, brightly lit area? This is the Northeast **megalopolis**. The word *megalopolis* means "great city." It is a string of towns and cities where many people live. The Northeast megalopolis stretches 500 miles from southern Maine to southern Virginia. People sometimes call this area "Boswash."

In this chapter, you will read about how the number of people in the Northeast affects daily life there.

Cities and Small Towns in the Northeast

New York City has more than 27,000 people per square mile. Small towns in the Northeast are much less crowded.

population density

a measure of the average number of people living in one unit of area

5.2 Living in the Northeast

Where do you live? In a big city? In a medium-sized suburb? In a small town? In a rural area? Each of these places has a different **population density**. Population density is a measure of how many people live in a given amount of land. It is often shown as the number of people per square mile of land. The word *per* means "for each." A square mile is a square piece of land measuring one mile on each side.

Population density affects how people live. Rural areas have fewer than 1,000 people per square mile. This means that there are, on average, fewer than 1,000 people living on each square mile of land. Urban areas have more than 1,000 people per square mile.

There are good things about living in both rural and urban areas. In small towns, people can get to know each other more easily. Neighbors often help each other. Life can be quiet and peaceful there.

Cities may not seem as friendly as small towns. But cities offer people more choices. There are many places to shop. Restaurants serve food from many places around the world. And there are many exciting things to do in a city.

5.3 Reading a Population Density Map

Maps can show many things about a place. The map on this page shows the population density of the Northeast. It shows how many people per square mile live in different parts of the region.

Look at the map key. Each color stands for a different number of people per square mile. Which color shows the least densely populated, or rural, areas? Which color shows the most densely populated, or urban, areas?

Can you find the megalopolis Boswash on the map? It stretches from Massachusetts south through parts of Rhode Island, Connecticut, New York, New Jersey, Pennsylvania, Delaware, and Maryland. What do you notice about the population density of this area?

Now look at the states of Vermont, New Hampshire, and Maine on the map. How is the population density of these states different from that of Boswash?

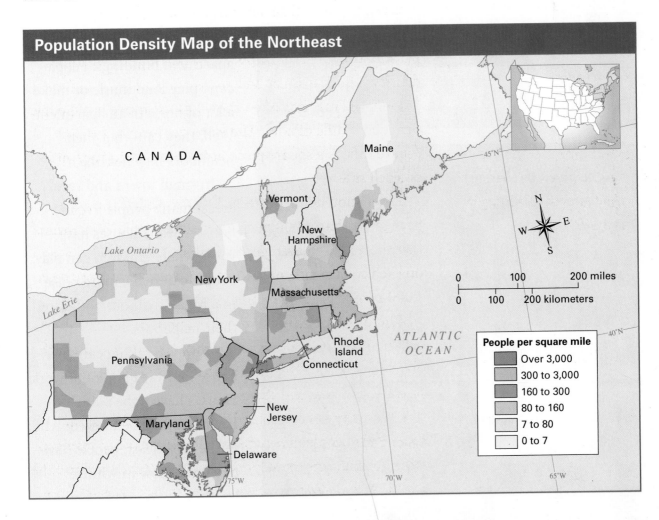

Population Density Map of the Northeast

People per square mile
- Over 3,000
- 300 to 3,000
- 160 to 300
- 80 to 160
- 7 to 80
- 0 to 7

5.4 Places to Live

Population density affects people's daily lives in many ways. One way it affects people is in the kinds of homes available to them.

In densely populated cities, many of the people live in apartment buildings. Apartments are usually stacked on top of each other and side by side. Some apartment buildings are towering skyscrapers. Others are just a few stories high.

Thousands of people may live on one city block. Just one family may live on several acres in the country.

Many people like living in apartment buildings. They may like having lots of neighbors. They may also like living near shops and restaurants.

On the other hand, at times neighbors can be noisy. People live close to each other in apartment buildings. People can't play loud music or make a lot of noise in an apartment. Well, they can—but their neighbors may not like it!

In small towns and rural areas, many people live in houses. Many houses have yards where children can play. People can make more noise in a house, without bothering their neighbors.

However, taking care of a house and yard is a lot of work. Houses have to be painted. Lawns have to be mowed. And in the Northeast, people have to shovel snow in winter.

5.5 Making a Living

Population density also affects the kind of work people do. There are many more jobs in cities than in rural areas.

Small towns and rural areas have fewer businesses. Some people may work on a farm. Others may work in stores or provide services that people need. Often, there are only a few kinds of jobs in a small town. That is one reason why some people move to cities.

There are lots of different kinds of jobs in cities. Many people work in offices. Others work in restaurants, stores, and hotels.

Newspapers and television stations have offices in cities. These businesses create jobs for writers, photographers, and designers.

Cities are also centers for the arts. They attract people who want to work as actors, musicians, or artists.

Large hospitals and health care centers are located in cities. They create jobs for doctors, nurses, and many other health care workers.

Many people like to visit cities. Tourism is the business of taking care of tourists, or visitors. Tourism creates jobs for tour guides, hotel workers, taxicab drivers, and others.

Small towns often have one general store and few other businesses. In big cities, people may build new buildings for businesses every day.

In New York City, taxicabs are easy to find. You might not see many taxis in a small town.

5.6 Getting Around

Population density affects what types of transportation people use. Getting from place to place in a densely populated area can be difficult. Driving a car is usually the worst way to get around in big northeastern cities. Many of these cities' streets are narrow. Others are wide but crowded. Think of all the cars, buses, trucks, and taxis that fill city streets today. They cause traffic to move slowly.

It's not easy to find a place to park a car in a large city. Parking garages help solve this problem. But they can be expensive. Bicycles fit well on narrow city streets. But riding a bike in city traffic can be dangerous.

Because city streets are often crowded, many people walk wherever they want to go. For longer trips within cities, people often need to use public buses, taxis, or subways.

In rural areas, it can be hard to get around without a car. Driving is much easier in small towns than in big cities. Traffic is not a problem. Parking is usually free. And country roads are usually safe for both cars and bikes.

In less populated areas, many small towns have no public bus or taxi service. This can be a problem for people who don't drive or own a car.

5.7 People and Pollution

Population density also affects **pollution**. Pollution is anything that makes our air, water, or soil dirty or unsafe to use.

Many things people do cause pollution. When we toss trash on the ground, we pollute the land. When we drive cars, we pollute the air. When we dump waste into rivers, we pollute the water.

Pollution is a big problem in urban areas. People living in cities throw away mountains of trash each day. Some of the trash can be recycled. The rest must be carried off to landfills. If left on the streets, trash attracts insects and rats. These pests often carry harmful diseases.

Air pollution is a problem as well. Smoke from cars, factories, and homes can hover over cities. This dirty air can cause our eyes to burn. It can also damage our health.

Dirty water from city streets and sewers may run into rivers and lakes. The result is water pollution. Polluted water is not safe to drink or swim in.

In rural areas, there are fewer people to cause big pollution problems. Air and water are generally cleaner there than in cities. At night, people can look up and see thousands of stars.

pollution any substance that makes air, water, or soil dirty or unsafe to use

The hazy color of the sky in the top picture comes from air pollution. Rural areas tend to have much cleaner air.

5.8 Finding Fun Things to Do

What do you do for fun on weekends? Your answer may depend partly on where you live.

People living in rural areas often enjoy outdoor activities year-round. Many people may live close to good places to go hiking or fishing in summer. In winter, they may go skiing or ice skating for fun. In both winter and summer, they may go in to town to see a movie or meet with friends at a restaurant.

In cities, people find many things to do close to home. Cities in the Northeast have lots of activities to do. On a sunny summer Saturday in New York City, you might

- go to a Yankees or Mets baseball game.
- tour an aircraft carrier or an old submarine.
- walk through a rainforest at the Bronx Zoo.
- plant a garden at the New York Botanical Garden.
- ride the roller coaster at Coney Island.

On a rainy Saturday in New York City, you might

- climb the Statue of Liberty.
- create a puppet at the Children's Museum of the Arts.
- try indoor soccer or rock climbing at Chelsea Piers.
- make a movie at the American Museum of the Moving Image.
- see a circus or a play just for kids.

People who live in small towns might choose to go to a city for a day of fun. And people who live in cities sometimes travel to the country for fun.

Many people like to skate or sled in wintertime—in the country and in the city.

Summary

In this chapter, you learned how population density shapes people's daily lives. In the Northeast, many people live in very densely populated areas. Others live in less densely populated areas. Life in a city is very different from life in a small town.

You saw how the density of people living in an area affects the kinds of homes people choose. People in cities often live in apartments. People in rural areas often live in homes with yards.

You saw how population density affects the work people do. In rural areas, there are fewer people and fewer jobs. In cities, there are many more people and kinds of jobs.

You saw how population density affects types of transportation. People in cities often walk or use public transportation to get around. In rural areas, people depend on cars to get from place to place.

You saw how population density affects pollution. Cities often face serious pollution problems because of their large populations.

And you saw how population density affects what people do for fun.

It is clear that life in a city is very different from life in a small town. How did the modern city come to be the way it is today? And what might inventors and inventions have to do with city life? Keep reading to find out.

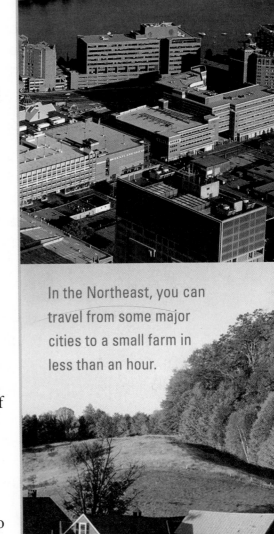

In the Northeast, you can travel from some major cities to a small farm in less than an hour.

Inventing New Ways of Living

The Northeast is known for its big cities. And big cities are known for their bright lights, towering buildings, and crowded streets. Whom do we have to thank for the inventions that helped make modern cities possible?

It was just one little light bulb. It glowed for only 13 hours. Then it burned out. Yet those who saw the experiment were amazed. They could see the great power of electricity. Soon, that power would change the way people lived.

The 1879 light bulb experiment was the work of Thomas Edison. The famous inventor had his own laboratory in Menlo Park, New Jersey. There, he and his team performed amazing work. Making a safe, usable light bulb was just one example.

In 1882, Edison built the nation's first electric power plant in New York City. The plant made enough electricity to light all the houses for several blocks.

The late 1800s were an exciting time to live in a city. People were constructing taller and taller buildings. And they built streetcars to take people around the city. Daily life was changing very rapidly. What were some of the new inventions that helped make life feel modern? Who invented them? How have those inventions helped create the cities of today?

Advertisements are a way to introduce new inventions to people. Today, old ads are a way to learn about the past.

ELECTRIC NOVELTIES make USEFUL PRESENTS.

Nickle Cycle Lamp, 3/6.

2 to 4 Volt Lamps, 6½d.

COMPLETE SET OF
ELECTRIC BELL PARTS
AND LECLANCHÉ BATTERY
INSTRUCTIONS

Flash Lamps, 9½d. to 5/6.
Torches, 1/2 to 8/6.
Watch Stands, 2/6 to 12/6.
Hand Lamps, 3/6 to 7/6.
Use our "Brytlite" Refill.

Our Batteries and Bulbs are the BEST and thoroughly RELIABLE.

Stand and Lamp, 1/3.

Motors from 1/-. Shocking Coils, 2/3 to 10/6. Dynamos from 10/6. Lighting Sets from 1/6. Electric Tram Set, 5/-

Electric Motor Parts, 1/-, 1/6.
Electro Plating Set, 2/6.
Large Variety Working Models.
Bichromate Battery, 1/-.

Large Assortment of Electric Scarf Pins and Hair Ornaments.
Ask for our ILLUSTRATED LIST

Building Higher and Stronger

When you think of cities, you may picture tall buildings. The first skyscraper was built in the late 1800s. Before that time, most buildings had only a few floors.

Two inventions helped make skyscrapers possible. One was a new way of making steel. Steel is a strong but lightweight metal. It can support a tall, thin building. In the 1850s, Henry Bessemer found an easier and cheaper way to make the metal. Builders could now buy the large amounts of steel needed for skyscrapers. They could build structures with ten floors or more.

Another new invention that helped people build skyscrapers was the passenger elevator. Before elevators, few people wanted to live or work more than a few stories above the ground. Think of all the stairs they would have to climb! Building owners had trouble renting out these spaces. No one wanted to build tall buildings.

Elisha Otis, of Vermont, helped solve this problem. In 1854, he found a way to make elevators safer. He invented a special kind of brake. It kept elevator cars from falling if their cables broke. People felt safe riding in these elevators.

Builders began putting elevators in their buildings. Now, people wanted to live and work high above the city streets. It was quieter and cleaner there. One by one, skyscrapers began to appear on city streets.

This skyscraper was built in 1897. Look at the steel beams at the very top.

In New York City, Elisha Otis demonstrated how his elevator worked.

Moving People Here to There

Cities grew quickly in the late 1800s. Thousands of Americans moved from farms to cities. Many more people came from Europe. They crossed the ocean in boats. Many of them settled in the big cities of the Northeast. New York City's population grew more than three times bigger between 1890 and 1920. Other cities also grew.

Transportation was a challenge in the big cities. People had to get to work. Each day, millions of workers traveled over large areas. More and more people crowded the streets. Many of them rode in streetcars. These were horse-drawn carriages that ran on rails. The rails helped the streetcars roll easily. It took fewer horses to pull more people. Fewer horses meant less crowding. It also meant less of a smelly mess on the streets.

In the late 1880s, streetcars began to run on electricity. The electric streetcars were called trolleys. A man named Granville Woods invented a system that used overhead wires to power the trolleys.

Later, some cities built subways. Subways ran underground. Boston built the first subway in 1897. Within 10 years, New York City and Philadelphia had subways, too.

Before New York City had subways, people often rode trains that ran on elevated tracks.

Many trolleys had no windows or walls.

Early Road Travel

People made many improvements to cities in the late 1800s. For example, in 1870, people in Newark, New Jersey, used asphalt to pave a road. Asphalt is a tar-like material. It can be pressed down to make smooth, hard surfaces. It makes an excellent road surface.

In the early 1900s, a new invention appeared on the road—the car. The new machines quickly became popular. Few people had cars in 1900. But by 1920, cars filled the streets.

Trolleys and cars changed people's lives. They also changed city life forever. They made it possible for people to live far away but work in the city. Many city people moved to homes outside the city center. The new settlements were called suburbs. Over time, suburbs grew. They filled with people. New suburbs formed, even farther out from the cities. The area of dense population spread.

Today, we can see the effects of this spread on the East Coast. The area known as Boswash shows how a dense settlement of towns and cities can stretch for hundreds of miles.

Before cars, people used horse-drawn carriages. The first cars were built more like these carriages than like cars made today. They were much slower and simpler than modern cars.

A Boat and Bus Tour of the Southeast

6

What factors have shaped the culture of the Southeast?

6.1 Introduction

Hello, I'm Mr. Davis. You can probably tell from my uniform that I'm a park ranger. As part of my job, I get to take groups like yours on tours.

Usually I lead short walking tours. This trip is special. Over the next few days, we will use a bus and three different kinds of boats to tour the Southeast. We will sail on a fishing trawler, from Florida to Virginia. From there, we'll take a big bus and cross the Appalachian Mountains. Then we'll board an old-time riverboat and sail down the Mississippi River to the port of New Orleans. A port is a place where ships load and unload their goods. We'll take a short motorboat ride to an oil rig in the middle of the Gulf of Mexico. Then it's back on board the bus for our final two stops.

As we travel, keep your eyes, ears, and minds wide open. Notice the land and how it is used in different ways. Listen for the sounds and music of this region. Think about how the Southeast has changed over time.

The captain says he's ready. So put on your life jackets, and let's go.

The Southeast Region

The Southeast Region

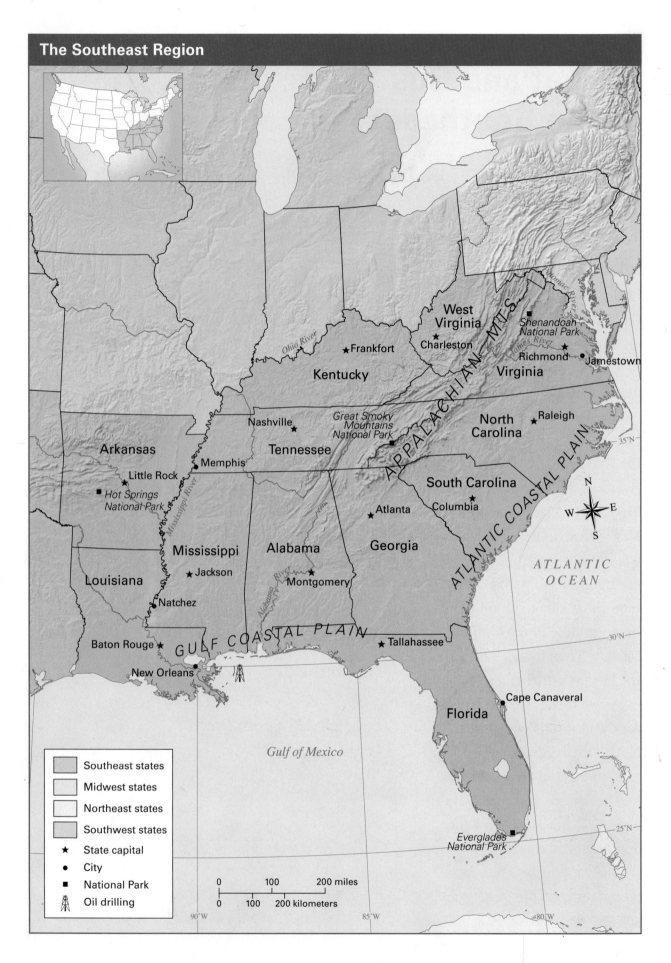

West Virginia

★ Charleston

Shenandoah National Park

James River

★ Richmond

• Jamestown

Potomac River

★ Frankfort

Kentucky

Ohio River

Virginia

Nashville ★

Tennessee

Great Smoky Mountains National Park

APPALACHIAN MTS.

North Carolina

★ Raleigh

35°N

Arkansas

Memphis

Little Rock ★

■ Hot Springs National Park

South Carolina

Columbia ★

• Atlanta

ATLANTIC COASTAL PLAIN

N
W ★ E
S

Mississippi River

Mississippi

★ Jackson

Alabama

Alabama River

Georgia

ATLANTIC OCEAN

Louisiana

Natchez

★ Montgomery

Baton Rouge ★

GULF COASTAL PLAIN

★ Tallahassee

30°N

New Orleans

Cape Canaveral •

Florida

Gulf of Mexico

Everglades National Park

25°N

	Southeast states
	Midwest states
	Northeast states
	Southwest states
★	State capital
•	City
■	National Park
⊕	Oil drilling

0   100   200 miles

0   100   200 kilometers

90°W   85°W   80°W

Important Ports in the Southeast Region

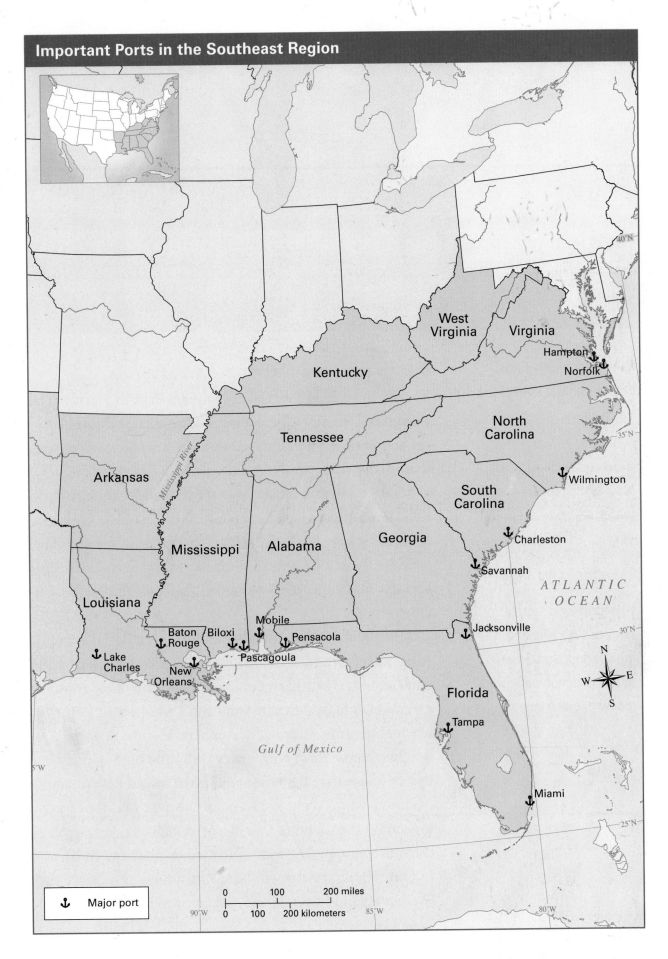

West Virginia

Virginia

Hampton

Norfolk

Kentucky

North Carolina

Tennessee

Arkansas

Mississippi River

Wilmington

South Carolina

Charleston

Mississippi

Alabama

Georgia

Savannah

ATLANTIC OCEAN

Louisiana

Jacksonville

Baton Rouge

Biloxi

Mobile

Pensacola

Lake Charles

Pascagoula

New Orleans

Florida

Tampa

N

W   E

S

Gulf of Mexico

Miami

| | Major port |

0   100   200 miles

0   100   200 kilometers

Many waterways flow through the flat land of the Everglades.

swamp a low area of land that is covered by water at least part of the year

savanna a flat grassland

hurricane a storm, with heavy rains and high winds, that develops over the ocean and often moves toward land

6.2 Everglades National Park, Florida

You are looking at Everglades National Park in Florida. The Everglades is a vast area of swamp, savanna, and forest at the southern tip of Florida. A **swamp** is an area of low land that is covered by water. A **savanna** is a flat grassland.

My first job as a ranger was in Everglades National Park. I had studied geography in college and wanted to work in a real live swamp. But I had no idea just how alive it would be!

More than 300 kinds of birds live in the Everglades. I get up early many mornings to record their calls on my pocket tape recorder.

I like to record the sounds that the animals make too. Alligators, crocodiles, turtles, and snakes live in the park. So do deer, bears, panthers, bobcats, otters, and other animals.

The park looks peaceful now. But I was here in 1992 when Hurricane Andrew hit southern Florida. A **hurricane** is a dangerous storm with heavy rains and high winds that develops over the ocean and often moves toward land. Andrew's winds damaged some of the park's visitor center. I recorded the sound of that storm at its worst. Whenever I listen to that tape, the roar of the winds gives me chills.

Our fishing trawler will head north now, as we leave the Everglades and travel up the east coast of Florida toward Cape Canaveral.

6.3 The John F. Kennedy Space Center at Cape Canaveral, Florida

Rockets blast the space shuttle off its launch pad.

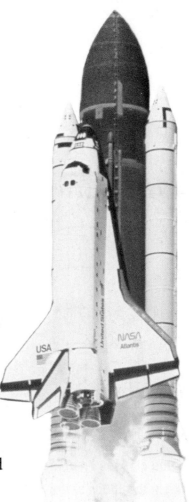

Florida is in a part of the United States called the Sunbelt. The Sunbelt stretches across the country from Florida to California. States in the Sunbelt have a mild climate all year long. A mild climate means that it is usually warm and sunny there.

Florida's sunny climate makes it a popular place to visit. People from all over the world travel to Florida for vacations. People who travel for fun are called tourists.

Many tourists visit Florida every year. Some come to enjoy the sunshine and the beaches. Places such as Disney World and Cypress Gardens attract 40 million visitors every year.

I like to visit the John F. Kennedy Space Center at Cape Canaveral. In 1961, the people at the space center launched Alan Shepard into space in a rocket-propelled ship. He was the first American to travel in space. Today, Cape Canaveral is home to our nation's space shuttles.

Visitors to the Kennedy Space Center learn all about space exploration. They may even see a shuttle launch. I saw a launch last year and recorded the sound on my recorder. The blast from the rockets was so loud that the ground shook under my feet.

6.4 Jamestown, Virginia: England's First American Colony

We have traveled quite a distance along the east coast of the United States. We are now in Virginia. You are looking at the site of Jamestown, Virginia. Jamestown was the first permanent English settlement in America.

In the spring of 1607, settlers from England chose this spot on the James River to build a colony. John Smith, one of their leaders, called it "a very fit place." Wrong! The land was swampy. Mosquitoes made life miserable. They also carried a disease called malaria.

By summer, many people were sick. They were also hungry. The forests around Jamestown were full of food. But the colonists didn't know how to find it. By fall, many of the colonists were dead. For many years, the pattern continued—new colonists arrived each spring; by winter, most had died.

But in 1612, things started to get better. The colonists found a crop that grew well in this area. It was tobacco. Virginia tobacco sold well in England. The colony began to make money.

As you learned in Chapter 3, a Dutch trading ship arrived in the Virginia colony in 1619. Its cargo included 20 Africans. They had been taken from Africa by force and were sold as workers. By the mid-1600s, Africans were being sold as slaves in the American colonies.

My ancestors were Africans. They were brought to the Americas in the late 1600s. They were forced to work as slaves on large farms.

It is time to leave the trawler now and get on a bus for the next part of our journey.

Today, you can see what life was like in the 1600s at the Jamestown settlement.

6.5 A Coal Mine in Appalachia

Welcome to Appalachia. This mountain area is located in the southern part of the Appalachian mountain range. Appalachia has no exact borders. It covers most of West Virginia and parts of several other states, including North Carolina, South Carolina, and Georgia. A bus is a good way to travel through these mountains.

Appalachia is too hilly for large-scale farming. But it is rich in **minerals**. Minerals are natural substances found in rocks. One important mineral is coal. Coal is used to heat homes and produce electricity.

There are underground coal mines in Appalachia. Miners have dug tunnels into the mountains to get at the coal hidden inside. Some coal also comes from **strip mines** like the one you see here. Strip mines are surface mines. Miners use heavy machinery to strip away the dirt and rocks covering the coal. Then they use giant shovels to dig the coal out of the mountain.

Last fall, I went to a bluegrass music festival near this mine. Bluegrass is the traditional music of Appalachia. It is played on banjos, guitars, and fiddles. I recorded a lot of old songs. The fast beat of this music always makes me feel good. Let's get back on the bus to learn more about the music of the Southeast.

Miners dig coal out of strip mines such as this one.

mineral a natural material found in rock

strip mine a place where minerals are scraped from the ground

Riverboats still tour the Mississippi River.

delta a triangle-shaped area of land at the end of a river

6.6 Musical Memphis, Tennessee

We've reached Memphis, Tennessee. From here, we'll be traveling on a riverboat like the one you see here.

Memphis is in the center of the Mississippi Delta region. A **delta** is a triangle-shaped area at the end of a river. Soil carried downstream by the river builds up to make a delta. Delta soil is fertile and good for farming.

The Mississippi Delta is a large area of land. It starts in lower Illinois and stretches from Kentucky, Missouri, Arkansas, Tennessee, and Mississippi through Louisiana to the mouth of the Mississippi River. A river's mouth is where it empties into the ocean.

In the early 1800s, the delta's rich soil attracted cotton planters to this region. At that time, cotton was a valuable crop. Many planters brought slaves with them. Slaves did most of the work of planting and picking cotton.

Slaves led hard lives. They worked from sunrise until sundown most days of the year. They were given no right to choose what they wanted to do. They could be bought and sold like animals.

Slaves would sometimes sing about their sorrows. These sad songs contributed to a musical style that became known as the blues. In 1912, an African American songwriter in Memphis wrote the first popular blues song. He called it "Memphis Blues." Today, Memphis is famous around the world as one of the birthplaces of the blues.

6.7 The French Quarter in New Orleans, Louisiana

Welcome to New Orleans, the largest city in Louisiana. French colonists built the city. It is near the mouth of the Mississippi River. Here, in the French Quarter, you can still see homes similar to those the original colonists built.

You may recall from Chapter 2 that in 2005 Hurricane Katrina did serious damage to many parts of New Orleans when it caused the Mississippi River to overflow. Today, the people of New Orleans continue to work hard to restore the city.

Ships from all over the world come to New Orleans. It is an important port in the United States.

New Orleans is also the birthplace of jazz. African American musicians living in the area created this new style of music. One of the most famous jazz musicians of all time was Louis Armstrong, known for his great trumpet playing. There are many kinds of jazz. One of the oldest is called Dixieland. You can hear great Dixieland jazz right here in the French Quarter.

Louisiana's nickname is the Bayou State. A **bayou** is a stream flowing through swampy land. In the 1700s, French colonists from Canada settled along Louisiana's bayous. They called themselves Acadians. Over time, the name was shortened to Cajuns.

Cajuns and their way of life used to be hidden away in the bayous. Not anymore! Cajun food is all the rage in New Orleans. It's hot, spicy, and delicious. Cajun music is even more popular. It's as spicy as Cajun food—and it makes your toes tap!

We will leave our riverboat and board a motorboat for the short journey to an oil rig in the Gulf of Mexico.

The French Quarter is the oldest neighborhood in New Orleans. It is the part of the city that most tourists visit.

bayou a stream that flows through a swamp

petroleum a thick, black liquid found underground

6.8 An Oil Rig in the Gulf of Mexico

Many people who live near the Gulf Coast are oil workers. Another name for oil is **petroleum**. The state of Louisiana has more than 20,000 wells that pump petroleum out of the ground.

Petroleum is a thick, black liquid that is found deep in the soil and under the ocean floor. Drilling for oil under the ocean is not easy. Oil workers build huge platforms, called rigs, to hold their machinery. Then they drill down under the sea until they find oil.

Once the oil is pumped out of the earth, it is sent to a factory. This factory is called a refinery. It turns petroleum into useful products. The product you probably know best is gasoline for cars.

Oil is also used to make petrochemicals, a big word that means "chemicals made from oil." Petrochemicals are used in all kinds of products, from medicines to plastics. I'll bet you're wearing a petrochemical product right now. It might be a button, a zipper, or the soles of your running shoes.

Let's take the motorboat back to New Orleans. We still have two more places to visit by bus on our journey through the Southeast.

From shore, you can see oil rigs like this one all along the Gulf of Mexico.

6.9 A Cotton Plantation in Natchez, Mississippi

Our bus has brought us back to Natchez, Mississippi. You are looking at a cotton **plantation** home. A plantation is a large farm.

plantation a large farm, usually worked by many laborers

In the early 1800s, cotton planters settled this area. Many of them became very rich growing cotton. They spent their wealth building big homes like this one. Then they filled their homes with the best things money could buy.

In the mid-1800s, many planters wanted to start new plantations on western lands that belonged to the United States. They wanted to use slave labor. Other people felt that slavery should not spread into new areas. Who had the right to decide—the federal government or the Southern slave owners?

It took a war to settle this argument. Divided into North and South, Americans fought the American Civil War for four long years. Much of the Southeast was damaged in the fighting. More than 600,000 people died.

One good thing came out of this terrible war. Slavery was ended forever. I wonder how my slave ancestors felt when they heard they were free. It must have been an amazing feeling.

Natchez escaped most of the fighting. Many of its beautiful homes were not damaged in the war. Today, they are the city's main tourist attraction. We get on our bus for one last trip.

This plantation home is in Natchez, Mississippi.

..UNTIL JUSTICE ROLLS DOWN LIKE WATER AND RIGHTEOUSNESS LIKE A MIGHTY STREAM

The Civil Rights Memorial shows the names of all the people known to have been killed during the civil rights movement.

segregation the separation of people because of race, religion, or gender

6.10 Montgomery, Alabama: Birthplace of the Civil Rights Movement

You are looking at the Civil Rights Memorial in Montgomery, Alabama. This memorial honors 40 Americans who were killed during the civil rights movement.

After the American Civil War, blacks in the South were free. But they were denied many of the rights other citizens had. At the same time, **segregation** became a way of life. Segregation is the separation of people because of race, religion, or gender. African Americans could not go to school with whites. They could not eat at white lunch counters. They could not sit beside white people on a bus.

Montgomery was home to an important milestone in the struggle to achieve racial equality. In 1955, a minister named Martin Luther King Jr. led a protest against segregation on buses. African Americans in Montgomery refused to ride the buses until they were treated the same as whites.

Most African Americans back then did not have cars. My grandma walked to work every day for a year rather than ride on a segregated bus. But finally, bus segregation was ended in Montgomery.

When I was little, I asked my grandma how her feet held up during the protest. "Child," she said, "my feet were tired, but my soul was rested."

Summary

Do you remember what I said to you when we began our journey? I asked you to keep your eyes, ears, and minds wide open. Now I'll tell you why.

I wanted you to use your eyes to see the different ways in which the land is used in the Southeast. In Everglades National Park, for example, you saw land that people are working to preserve. But, in Appalachia, you saw a mountain that is being torn apart for the coal it contains.

You also saw four settlements built beside rivers. Three of them grew into cities. One did not. Can you figure out why?

I wanted you to use your ears to hear some of the sounds of the Southeast. As a park ranger, I enjoy the sounds of nature—even the roar of a hurricane. But most of all, I love the music of this region. From bluegrass to jazz, the Southeast has given this country a lot of great music.

Finally, I wanted you to learn how the Southeast has changed over time. Slavery and segregation are part of this region's past—but not its future. As my grandma likes to say, "Times have changed, child, and they've changed for the better."

The Quilters of Gee's Bend

Gee's Bend is a small, out-of-the-way town in Alabama. But its people have created a great tradition of art. For many years, the women of Gee's Bend have made quilts of great beauty. How has the isolated location of the town helped shape this art?

Not too long ago, most women in Gee's Bend hardly ever left their community. After all, it took about an hour to travel by road to the nearest town.

But times have changed. In recent years, women such as Arlonzia Pettway have done a lot of traveling. They have visited big cities, like New York City and Houston, Texas. In those cities, they have gone to fine art museums. They have made these trips to see their own art. For Arlonzia Pettway and the women of Gee's Bend are now famous artists. The quilts they have made are considered great treasures.

"I felt so good," said Pettway, when she saw her quilt in a museum exhibit. "I had the happiest time I had in my life to see our quilts hanging on the wall, and peoples just praising our quilts, and everybody's eyes full of water."

The quilts of Gee's Bend certainly are beautiful. They also help tell the story of an amazing place.

GEE'S BEND QUILT 39 USA 2006

GEE'S BEND QUILT 39 USA 2006

GEE'S BEND QUILT 39 USA 2006

GEE'S BEND QUILT 39 USA 2006

To many people, the quilts of Gee's Bend are great treasures. In 2006, the U.S. Postal Service celebrated the women who created them. It created a set of stamps that show their quilts.

An Out-of-the-Way Place to Live

Gee's Bend is located on a small piece of land only 5 miles wide and 8 miles long. It is almost an island. The muddy Alabama River bends around—and nearly surrounds—the community. To get to Gee's Bend, you must take a ferry or travel the one road into town.

That makes Gee's Bend an isolated place to live. An isolated place is a long way from large towns and might be difficult to reach.

The community is named for its first white owner. His name was Joseph Gee. The land later passed to another white man, named Mark Pettway. Around 1850, Pettway brought his family and 100 slaves to Gee's Bend. After the American Civil War ended, the slaves in Gee's Bend were free men and women.

Over time, all the white people in Gee's Bend left. The African Americans, however, stayed and continued to farm the land.

For most of the people of Gee's Bend, life was hard in the late 1800s and early 1900s. Even though they were free, they struggled to make a living. Most of them were very poor.

The women of Gee's Bend learned to make use of every little thing they had. They learned not to throw out pieces of old fabric. For example, scraps of worn-out work pants and dresses or bits of burlap sack could all be used again. They could be used to make quilts, which would help keep a person warm at night.

This old photograph shows the ferry that people used to take to get to Gee's Bend. In recent years, the ferry has been re-opened.

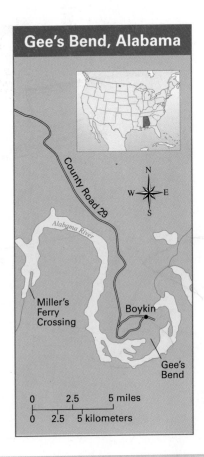

Gee's Bend, Alabama

Arlonzia Pettway (far right) is not the only woman in her family who makes quilts. All the quilters shown here with their quilts are her relatives.

From Parent to Child

Quilting was a way of making something useful out of worn-out fabric. But it was also a way of making something beautiful. The quilters of Gee's Bend never thought that they were making art. But they did work hard to make something that would please the eye.

The making of quilts is an old tradition in Gee's Bend. For as long as anyone there can remember, the women of Gee's Bend have been gathering in groups to piece together bits of fabric. They have been sharing ideas about new designs. They have been telling each other stories about their lives.

They have also been teaching their children. In this way, the craft of quilting has been passed down from parent to child, on and on over the decades. Stories and memories have also been kept alive.

However, for a long time, the only people who enjoyed these quilts were the people of Gee's Bend. Few people from outside the community ever visited there. And few of Gee's Bend's residents ever left the community.

That changed in the 1960s. Civil rights workers came to visit Gee's Bend. They noticed the fantastic quilts drying on the clotheslines. They saw the vibrant colors and the exciting designs. The quilters of Gee's Bend had been discovered.

Sharing Their Talent with the World

What makes the quilts of Gee's Bend so special? Of course, the bright colors are beautiful. The skill of the quilters is outstanding. Each quilt has been sewn with great care. But it is the startling designs of the quilts that make them so remarkable.

Usually, quilts follow a rigid pattern. Lines are straight, and the shapes repeat in an orderly way. But the Gee's Bend quilts are different. The patterns shift and change. The lines are not straight. Each quilt is unique. Yet, certain styles keep coming up in quilt after quilt. You can see how ideas were shared by the quilters, changed a bit, and then passed on to others.

Some experts think that the Gee's Bend quilts look like modern art. The quilts seem to have simple designs. But they are very complex. In fact, they have **abstract** designs. Something is considered abstract if it makes use of shapes and patterns, rather than showing people or things as they actually are.

abstract making use of shapes and patterns, rather than showing people or things as they actually are

When people outside the community of Gee's Bend saw the quilts, they wanted to buy them. Museums wanted to put them on display. The quilters of Gee's Bend began their own business to make and sell their quilts. The business helped improve their lives. And the quilters were happy to share their work with the rest of the world.

This style of quilting is found only in Gee's Bend. But now, the rest of the world can enjoy these works of art.

Gee's Bend quilts have traveled the country, stopping at museums in New York City; Boston; Washington, D.C.; Houston; Atlanta; and other large cities.

The Effects of Geography on Life in the Southeast

How has geography helped shape daily life in the Southeast?

7.1 Introduction

If you brought your lunch to school today, what did you bring? For some of you, the answer may be "a bit of the Southeast."

Start with the lunch bag itself. It may be made of paper that came from a southern pine tree. Papermaking is an important industry in the Southeast.

What's in the bag? A peanut butter and jelly sandwich? Orange juice? A piece of fruit? Much of the contents of a typical lunch could have come from the Southeast. Georgia grows more peanuts than any other state. Florida grows four out of five of our nation's oranges. Even the plastic wrap on the sandwich may have been made from oil found in the Southeast.

In this chapter, you will find out why so much of the Southeast is found in your lunch bag. At the same time, you will see how geography has shaped life in the Southeast long ago and today.

Geographic Features of the Southeast

Low tide shows the lowlands near the coastal city of Savannah, Georgia.

foothills a hilly region at the base of a mountain range

Fog rolls through the Appalachian Mountains in North Carolina.

7.2 Elevation: Lowlands and Highlands

The Southeast is a region of lowlands and highlands. The low Coastal Plain stretches along the southeastern coast from Virginia to Louisiana. The water level in rivers and swamps rises and falls with the ocean tide each day. When the ocean rises at high tide, seawater flows into this lowland area. When the tide pulls back, water levels drop.

The Coastal Plain ends at the **foothills** of the Appalachian Mountains. Southerners call this area of low, rolling hills the Piedmont. Piedmont, in French, means "foot of the mountains." Beyond the Piedmont rise the Appalachian Mountains. Some of the peaks in this mountain chain are more than 6,000 feet high.

Elevation affects life here in many ways. For example, elevation affects climate. The higher the elevation of a place, the colder it is. Plants that grow well in the warm lowland freeze in the cool highland. Elevation also affects soil. Lowland soil is rich and good for farming. Highland soil is rocky and not easy to farm.

Elevation also affects travel. Travel in the lowlands is faster and easier. Travel in the highlands is slower and more difficult. People from the mountains sometimes joke that the only way to get to some of the tiny Appalachian towns is to be born there!

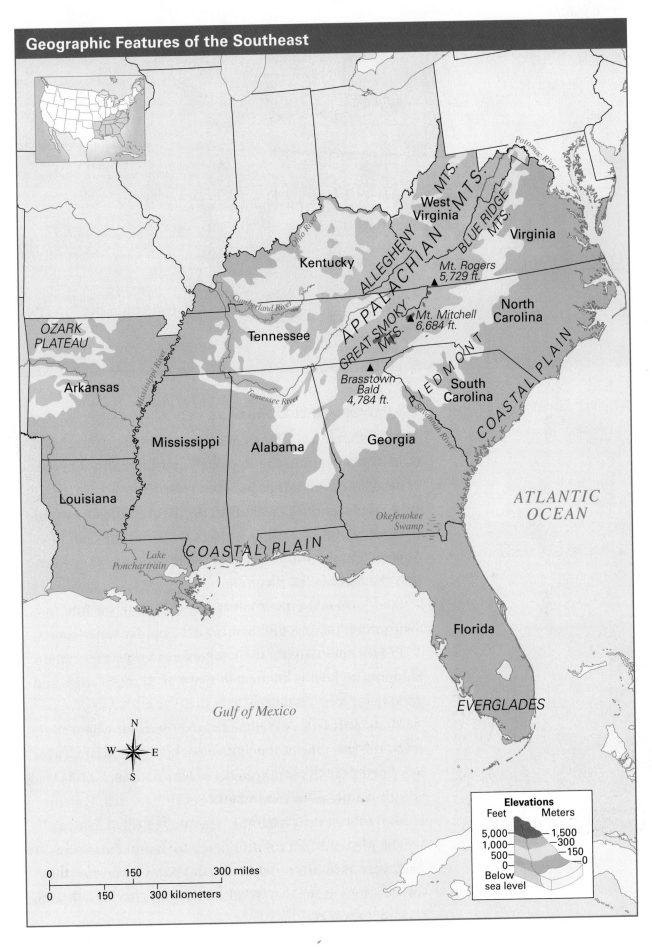

Geographic Features of the Southeast

West Virginia

ALLEGHENY MTS.

BLUE RIDGE MTS.

Virginia

Potomac River

Ohio River

Kentucky

APPALACHIAN MTS.

Mt. Rogers
5,729 ft.

Cumberland River

OZARK PLATEAU

Tennessee

GREAT SMOKY MTS.

Mt. Mitchell
6,684 ft.

North Carolina

PIEDMONT

Mississippi River

Arkansas

Tennessee River

Brasstown Bald
4,784 ft.

South Carolina

COASTAL PLAIN

Savannah River

Mississippi

Alabama

Georgia

Okefenokee Swamp

ATLANTIC OCEAN

Louisiana

Lake Ponchartrain

COASTAL PLAIN

Florida

Gulf of Mexico

EVERGLADES

N
W   E
S

0   150   300 miles
0   150   300 kilometers

Elevations

Feet		Meters
5,000		1,500
1,000		300
500		150
0		0
Below sea level		

A tanker carries oil along the Mississippi River.

7.3 Rivers and Ocean

The Southeast has a long coastline and many rivers. Most of its rivers begin in the Appalachian Mountains. On the eastern side of the Appalachians, rivers flow across the Piedmont and the Coastal Plain to the Atlantic Ocean. In the southern Appalachians, rivers flow into the Gulf of Mexico. On the western side of the mountains, they flow into the Mississippi River.

Southerners use their rivers and the ocean for fun. Swimming, fishing, and boating are popular water sports.

People here also use their waterways for transportation. Shipping by boat is an inexpensive way to move crops and goods over long distances.

Many port cities developed along the coast where rivers reach the sea. One of the busiest port cities is Miami, which is located near the southern tip of Florida. Much of its trade is with countries in Central and South America. For this reason, Miami calls itself the "Gateway of the Americas."

The port of Miami is also home to many cruise ships. Each year, millions of people leave Miami on cruise ships for vacations at sea. No wonder Miami is also known as the "Cruise Capital of the World."

7.4 The Fall Line

Many of the rivers that cross the Coastal Plain are **navigable**. A navigable river is one that is both deep and wide enough for ships to use. But when ships reach the Piedmont, they stop. The place where they stop is called the **fall line**. A fall line is an imaginary line at the point where rivers drop from higher land to lower land.

In this case, the fall line is where the Piedmont meets the Coastal Plain. The edge of the Piedmont drops sharply at this point. As rivers flow over this drop, they form waterfalls. Ships cannot continue to sail upstream beyond these falls.

For early settlers in the Southeast, the fall line was a problem. Settlers on the Coastal Plain depended on rivers to send their crops to market. But when settlers moved up to the Piedmont, they had no good way to ship their crops to the coast.

Some people saw this problem as an opportunity. Traders set up trading posts right on the fall line. Goods that arrived by boat from the coast could be traded for meat and crops raised in the highlands.

Other people settled on the fall line because they knew how to use falling water to run machines. They built sawmills, flour mills, and workshops that ran on waterpower.

Many fall-line towns—like Richmond, Virginia; Raleigh, North Carolina; and Macon, Georgia—grew into large cities.

navigable deep enough and wide enough for ships to use

fall line an imaginary line, marked by rapids and waterfalls, where rivers start to drop from higher land to lower land

This powerful waterfall on the Potomac River shows the presence of a fall line.

natural resource a resource supplied by nature

industry an organized economic activity connected with the production, manufacture, or construction of a particular product or range of products

7.5 Natural Resources

The Southeast is rich in **natural resources**. Natural resources include land, oceans, forests, minerals, and fuels.

Land was the first natural resource that attracted people to the Southeast. Growing crops and raising animals were two of the largest **industries** for many years. An industry is all the businesses that produce one kind of good or provide one kind of service.

Today, many industries are important to the economy of the region. On your tour of the Southeast, you learned about two industries that developed from resources hidden under the ground. One is the coal-mining industry. Another is the oil industry.

The Southeast's steel industry is built on another hidden resource. In the 1800s, iron ore was found at Red Mountain in Alabama. Iron ore is used to make steel. Built at the foot of Red Mountain, Birmingham, Alabama, became a steelmaking center.

Some industries are based on the Southeast's large forests. Sawmills cut trees into lumber. Paper mills grind wood into gooey wood pulp. This pulp is then used to make paper. Furniture makers turn trees into tables and chairs. Right now, you may be sitting on a chair that was made in the Southeast.

Forests, like this one in South Carolina, are an important natural resource in the Southeast.

7.6 A Long Growing Season

The business of growing crops and raising animals is called **agriculture**. It is an important part of the economy of the Southeast. For farmers to succeed in this business, they need three things from nature: good soil, plenty of rain, and a long growing season. The Southeast has all three.

Many crops grow well in the Southeast. Cotton is a good example. Cotton plants need plenty of water and six months of warm weather. The Southeast meets these needs perfectly.

In the 1800s, cotton was the main crop grown in the Southeast. Then disaster struck. A little bug called the boll weevil invaded cotton fields. The boll weevil destroyed the cotton before it was ready for harvest. Many farmers were ruined. Those who survived learned a hard lesson. No longer could they depend on just one crop.

Today, the Southeast is a region of mixed agriculture. Farmers on the Coastal Plain grow rice, cotton, peanuts, and other warm-weather crops. Orange groves cover large parts of Florida. Piedmont farmers raise dairy cattle, peaches, and tobacco. Farmers in Appalachia grow corn and apples in mountain valleys.

Citrus fruits and cotton are important crops in the Southeast.

agriculture the business of growing crops and raising animals

floodplain the low, flat land along a river that may be underwater during a flood

tornado a violent windstorm whose center is a cloud in the shape of a funnel

7.7 Dangerous Weather

Not every day is sunny in the Southeast. Rain falls all year long. Sometimes, too much rain comes down. The result can be a flood.

Most rivers flood from time to time. During a flood, a river fills with more water than it can hold. The extra water flows over the river's banks onto its **floodplain**. A floodplain is low, flat land along a river.

Floods become dangerous when people live and work on floodplains. Then floods do much more than cover the floodplain with muddy water. They destroy homes, crops, and people's lives.

The most dangerous storms are hurricanes. Hurricanes are powerful storms with winds of 74 miles per hour or more. Hurricanes form over warm water. As a hurricane grows, it produces heavy rain and high waves. Almost every year, at least one hurricane strikes the Southeast.

Tornados are another threat to the Southeast. A tornado is a violent windstorm whose center is a cloud in the shape of a funnel. Tornados form over land.

It is hard for scientists to predict the paths of hurricanes and tornados. These types of storms can damage property and hurt people.

A tornado touches down in Florida.

Summary

Suppose that you could visit any town in the Southeast. And suppose that you could ask the people living there just how important the geography of their area is to their town. What do you think they would say?

If you were in Miami, Florida, people might talk about the importance of the ocean. Miami's beaches attract tourists to the city. Many jobs in Miami depend on the ocean.

In Dawson, Georgia, you might hear about the importance of a long growing season. Making peanut butter is a large industry in Dawson. People here know that peanuts need four to five months of warm weather to grow.

In New Iberia, Louisiana, people might talk about dangerous weather. You might hear some scary stories about floods and hurricanes.

In High Point, North Carolina, people might mention the importance of forests. This town depends on wood from Southeast forests. High Point's main industry is making furniture.

In other towns, you would hear different answers. But no matter where you went in the Southeast, you would find that geography helps shape how people live in the region.

Next, you will find out how one of the worst storms to ever hit the United States affected Florida.

The flat land and central location of Atlanta, Georgia made it a good location for railroads in the 1830s. Today it is one of the Southeast's largest cities.

Hurricane Andrew

Hurricanes are a fact of life in the Southeast. But Hurricane Andrew was different. It was one of the worst disasters in the history of the United States. How did Hurricane Andrew affect daily life in Florida?

On August 24, 1992, Hurricane Andrew hit south Florida. The howling winds sounded almost hungry to some people.

David Fisher turned on his television to find out what was happening. The news reporter said that the instruments measuring the wind had just blown off the roof of the National Hurricane Center. Then the lights—and the television—went out in the Fisher house.

Dan Sanabria also remembers the noise. He thought that it sounded like a jet plane taking off. He will also never forget what the storm did to his house. "When the eye of [the storm] passed over, I went out for a look, and we had no roof."

After Hurricane Andrew, the Shropshire family had only one thing left. It was the bed that Pearlie Shropshire and her son, Travis, were hiding under. Everything else was gone.

This picture was taken about one day before Hurricane Andrew hit Florida. The dot on this satellite photograph shows the eye, or center, of the storm.

A Storm Is Coming

One week before Hurricane Andrew hit Florida, a small notice appeared on the back page of the *Miami Herald* newspaper. It said that the first tropical storm of 1992 was moving slowly toward the United States. It had winds of about 50 miles per hour, which meant that it was already a stronger storm than most. However, not many people paid attention because many storms and hurricanes occur in Florida every year.

The warm, sunny climate is one of the main reasons why so many people go to Florida—to visit and to live. In fact, Florida is one of the fastest-growing states in the country. More than 5,000 people move to Florida every week.

The number of hurricanes that threaten Florida each year varies. An average year might have about three big hurricanes. But not all of them hit land. In 2004, four hurricanes hit Florida. That was more than in any other year on record. In 2006, not one hurricane hit the state.

Hurricanes like Andrew are rare. But three-fourths of all people in Florida live on or near the coasts. So, when a storm like Andrew hits, it creates problems for most people in the state.

More than 13 million people live along Florida's coasts. They live in small towns and in big cities like Miami, above.

The Storm Hits

As Andrew came closer to the United States, its winds grew stronger and stronger. Now people began to pay attention.

Television and radio announcers urged people to leave the area. A million people did. Highways going north were jammed solid with cars. But millions of other people stayed.

According to scientist David Fisher, "the scariest place on Earth is directly in the path of an onrushing hurricane." Others have compared the energy of a hurricane to that of a very powerful bomb exploding.

Andrew was 60 miles wide before it touched land. As hurricanes go, it wasn't large, but it was very strong. Its winds reached 175 miles an hour. That is strong enough to tear buildings apart, blow big trees down, and pick up cars and people as if they were toys.

Scientists choose a number from 1 to 5 to describe the force of a hurricane. Category 1 is the mildest. Hurricane Andrew was named a Category 5 hurricane.

Path of Hurricane Andrew

Mississippi Alabama Georgia South Carolina

Louisiana Texas

Gulf of Mexico

Florida

Miami

FLORIDA KEYS

30°N

25°N

80°W

95°W 90°W 85°W

0 150 300 miles
0 150 300 kilometers

← Path of Hurricane Andrew

N W E S

Hurricane Andrew brought violent winds and flooding rains to Florida and other states.

After the Storm

Eventually, Andrew moved on into the Gulf of Mexico toward Louisiana. But it left behind a huge disaster in Florida.

Forty people were dead. More than 250,000 people were homeless. Thousands of houses were completely destroyed. Many businesses were gone. The damage to homes, businesses, and land eventually cost more than 30 *billion* dollars.

People's lives were changed forever. "I went to bed with two jobs and a home," Charles Wilson said. "I woke up with no jobs and a piece of a home."

Many people went back to Florida to rebuild their homes and communities. But 100,000 people left one heavily populated south Florida county, Dade County, for good.

For a long time after the storm, whenever Dan Sanabria walked outside, he would look around for places he could take shelter in a storm. For Dan and for all those people who lived through Hurricane Andrew, the memory of that fierce storm is hard to forget.

Hurrican Andrew devastated Florida's communities. Still, people worked together to help others find food, clothing, and shelter.

COLUMBUS

A Crop Duster Tour of the Midwest

Why do we call the Midwest "America's Heartland"?

8.1 Introduction

Hi. My name is Mr. Ortiz. I'll be your guide as we explore the Midwest. I'm an economist at a bank in Chicago. My job is to study how people make, use, and manage goods and services. I wanted to lead your tour for several reasons. I want you to learn about the economy of the Midwest. I also want to show you the geography of this region and tell you about its colorful history. And I love to travel.

We will visit nine of my favorite places in the Midwest. Along the way, look for answers to this question: How did this one region earn these two very different nicknames—"America's Breadbasket" and "America's Heartland"?

We will be touring in little planes called crop dusters. Most of the time, these planes are used to spray chemicals on crops. Because of their small size, crop dusters can fly close to the ground. We should get some great views.

Fasten your seat belts for takeoff. Our first stop will be in Missouri, nicknamed the "Show Me State."

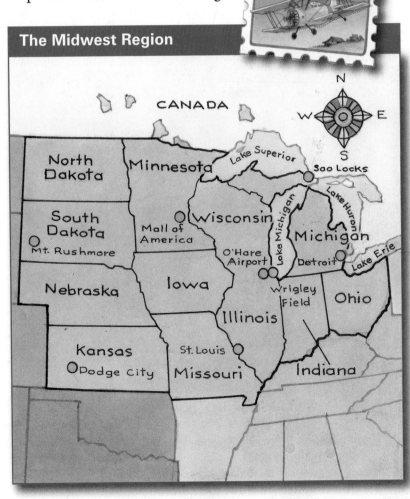

The Midwest Region

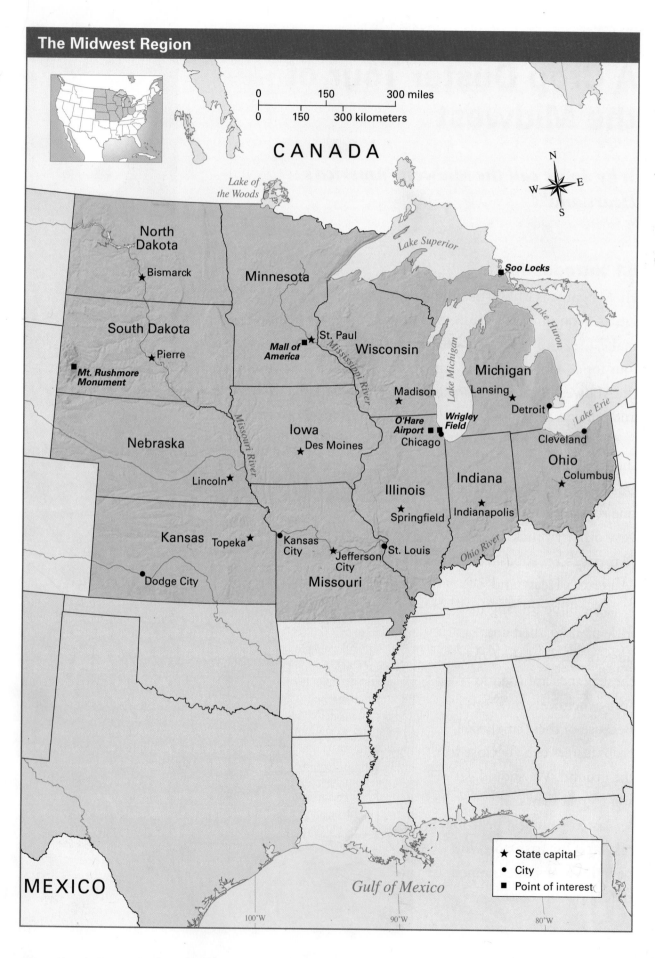

The Midwest Region

CANADA

0   150   300 miles
0   150   300 kilometers

Lake of the Woods

Lake Superior

Soo Locks

N
W   E
S

North Dakota
★ Bismarck

Minnesota

South Dakota
★ Pierre

■ Mt. Rushmore Monument

Mall of America ■

St. Paul ★

Wisconsin

Mississippi River

Madison ★

Lake Michigan

Lake Huron

Michigan
Lansing ★

Detroit ●

Lake Erie

Wrigley Field

O'Hare Airport ■

Nebraska

Missouri River

Iowa
Des Moines ★

Cleveland ●

Chicago ●

Ohio
Columbus ★

Lincoln ★

Illinois
Springfield ★

Indiana
Indianapolis ★

Kansas
Topeka ★

Kansas City ●

Jefferson City ★

St. Louis ●

Ohio River

Dodge City ●

Missouri

★ State capital
● City
■ Point of interest

MEXICO

Gulf of Mexico

100°W   90°W   80°W

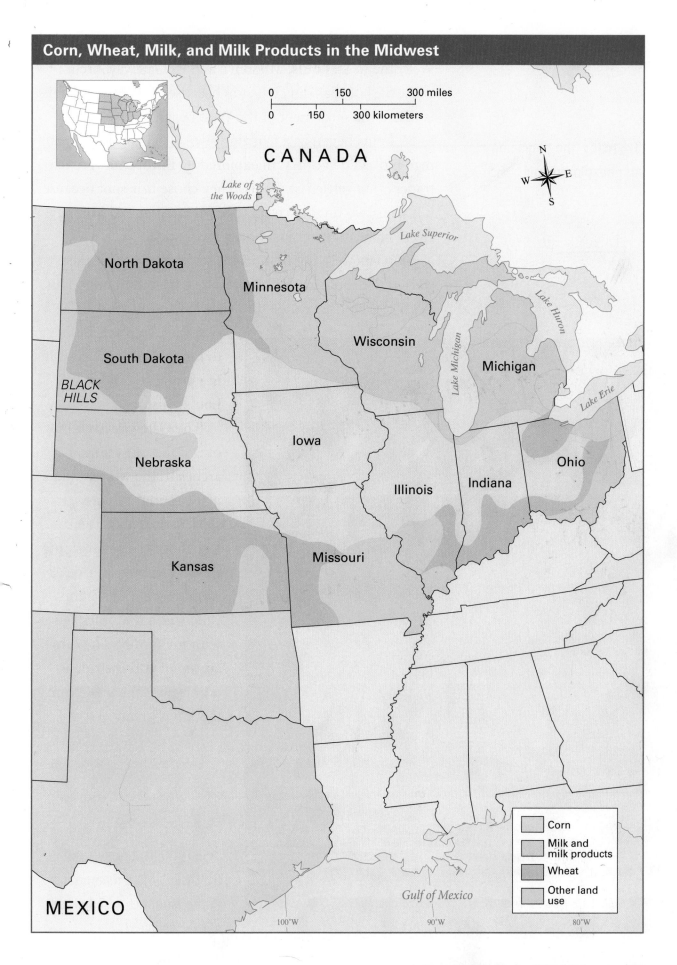

Corn, Wheat, Milk, and Milk Products in the Midwest

CANADA

0   150   300 miles
0   150   300 kilometers

Lake of the Woods

Lake Superior

Lake Huron

North Dakota

Minnesota

Wisconsin

Lake Michigan

Michigan

South Dakota

BLACK HILLS

Iowa

Lake Erie

Nebraska

Ohio

Illinois

Indiana

Kansas

Missouri

MEXICO

Gulf of Mexico

100°W   90°W   80°W

Corn

Milk and milk products

Wheat

Other land use

8.2 St. Louis, Missouri: Gateway to the West

Welcome to St. Louis, Missouri, and its Gateway Arch. I chose St. Louis as our first stop because of its history. This is where the settlement of the West began.

frontier the beginning of unexplored land

St. Louis began as a **frontier** town. The frontier was a region of wild country, unexplored by Europeans. French traders first settled St. Louis. They chose this spot because it is near two mighty rivers. The Mississippi and Missouri rivers come together just north of St. Louis.

Pioneers were the first people to settle the West. They started their journey by heading west from St. Louis. This is why St. Louis is called the "Gateway to the West." The Gateway Arch was built to honor those pioneers. It is a proud reminder of St. Louis's history.

The Gateway Arch is one of the most famous arches in the world. Made of gleaming stainless steel, it rises about 630 feet above the Mississippi River. Visitors can ride a tram inside it to the top. I did this a few years ago with my family. The cars are small and the ride is bumpy, but the view from the top is great.

This is the Gateway Arch in St. Louis. It is a memorial to the pioneers who helped settle the West.

8.3 The Farm State of Iowa

If you wanted to invent a farming state, you couldn't do much better than Iowa. That's what my best friend from college said. He grew up on an Iowa farm that looks a lot like the one you see here.

"First," he said, "you would want your farm state to be mostly flat." Iowa began as **prairie** land. A prairie is an area of flat or rolling land covered mostly with tall grasses. Later on, farmers planted crops on the prairie.

Next, you would want **fertile** soil. The word *fertile* means "able to produce good crops." Iowa has so much fertile soil that farms cover almost all of the state.

Finally, you would want good transportation. Iowa lies between the Mississippi and Missouri rivers. Before there were trains, Iowa farmers used these rivers to send their crops to market.

Today, Iowa farms produce huge crops of corn, soybeans, oats, and hay. Much of this harvest is fed to **livestock.** Livestock are animals raised on farms, such as cattle, hogs, and chickens. Iowa farm products are used in all kinds of foods. The chances are good that the next bag of popcorn you pop was grown on an Iowa farm just like this one.

The state of Iowa has fertile soil for its many farms.

prairie a flat or gently rolling land that is covered with tall grasses and wildflowers

fertile soil that is able to produce good crops

livestock animals that are raised on farms, such as cattle, hogs, and chickens

8.4 Dodge City, Kansas: Where the Cattle Once Roamed

Welcome to Dodge City, Kansas. Kansas—a land of flat plains—has long been famous for wheat and cowboys.

The plains of Kansas make it a wonderful place to grow wheat. Travel through Kansas in the early summer and you will see mile after mile of golden wheat. Kansas produces more wheat than any other state.

Back in the 1870s, cowboys from Texas used to herd cattle across the Great Plains to Dodge City. Herding cattle is hot, dusty, smelly work. Those cattle drives took weeks and sometimes months. When the cattle finally reached Dodge City, they were loaded onto trains and shipped east for sale.

Today, fewer cattle graze on the plains. Cattle are mostly raised on **feedlots**. Feedlots are areas or buildings where livestock are kept while being fattened for slaughter. Dodge City is home to one of the biggest **meatpacking** plants in the country. Meatpacking is the preparing of meat for sale. It's an important industry in the Midwest.

When I was your age, I wanted to be a cowboy—or, as my dad would say in Spanish, a vaquero. Some people still work as cowboys today. But they are likely to leave their horses at work at the end of the day. We'll stop here to learn more about cowboys from long ago.

feedlot an area or a building where livestock are kept while being fattened for slaughter

meatpacking the preparing of meat for sale

Dodge City's streets were once filled with horses, wagons, and cattle. Today the streets look much different.

8.5 South Dakota's Heroes

Two huge monuments are carved into the Black Hills of
South Dakota. The first is Mount Rushmore National
Memorial. It shows the faces of four American presidents:
George Washington, Thomas Jefferson, Theodore Roosevelt,
and Abraham Lincoln. Each head is six stories tall.

The second monument honors an American Indian
named Crazy Horse, who was chief of the Sioux tribe. It is
still being carved into the Black Hills. When it is finished,
Crazy Horse Memorial will be the world's largest statue.

The Black Hills are sacred to the Sioux and other
American Indians. When white settlers moved into this
area, they began pushing American Indian tribes off
this land. American Indians fought back to keep their
homeland. This struggle led to war with the United States.

During that war, an American general named George
Custer attacked a group of Sioux who were camping by
Little Bighorn River in Montana. Crazy Horse led his
warriors into battle, yelling, "It is a good day to die!" In
minutes, Custer and his men were dead.

Despite this victory, the Sioux lost most of their land
over time. Like many other American Indian tribes, the
Sioux were pushed by white settlers onto **reservations,** or
special areas set aside for American Indian tribes to live.

Mount Rushmore National
Memorial honors four
American presidents.

The Crazy Horse Memorial
honors the Sioux chief
Crazy Horse.

reservation public
land set aside by the
government for use by
American Indians

The back gates open and the ship enters the lock. Then the gates close.

Water is taken out of or released into the lock to lower or raise the ship.

The front gates open and the ship leaves the lock.

In Lake Superior, a ship approaches the Soo Locks. The water in Lake Superior is higher than the water in Lake Huron. The Soo Locks will lower the ship to Lake Huron. The diagram shows how the lock raises and lowers ships between the two lakes.

8.6 Michigan's Soo Locks: Linking the Great Lakes

You are looking down on one of my favorite sights: the Soo Locks. The Soo Locks are the two longest locks in the world. They can raise and lower ships that are up to 1,000 feet in length.

The Great Lakes are part of a water highway that stretches from the Midwest to the Atlantic Ocean. Ships move from lake to lake along canals. Because the lakes are at different water levels, locks are used to lift and lower ships from one lake to the next. The Soo Locks raise or lower ships the 21 feet between Lake Huron and Lake Superior.

Many ships pass through the Soo Locks each day. Some are small passenger boats. Others are oceangoing ships filled with iron ore, coal, grain, or other cargo. People call these ships "salties" because they have journeyed from the Atlantic Ocean.

8.7 Detroit, Michigan: America's Motor City

In 1896, a Michigan farm boy named Henry Ford built his first car. At that time, automobiles were very expensive to buy. People saw cars as toys for the rich.

But Ford had different ideas. He dreamed of building cars that most people could afford. Ford's dream gave birth to the American automobile industry.

In 1908, Ford started an automobile factory in Detroit, Michigan. He needed a way to keep his costs down. In the past, workers could build only one car at a time. So Ford installed a moving **assembly line**. A moving belt carried unfinished cars past workers. Each worker did one task. One worker might install a windshield. Another might screw on a door handle. The time needed to assemble a car dropped from 12 hours to just 93 minutes. The assembly line lowered the cost of each car by reducing the time it took to make it.

Ford's success brought other carmakers to Detroit. Detroit became known as "Motor City," or "Motown" for short. The automobile industry attracted many other businesses to the Midwest, too.

Today, Midwest industries continue to look for better ways to manufacture goods. One example is the invention and use of robots, or computer-controlled mechanical devices, to speed up assembly lines.

We'll stop here and learn more about Ford's original assembly line.

assembly line a process in which each worker assembles one part of a product before passing it to the next worker down the line

These cars, called Model T's, were built on Ford's assembly line in the early 1900s.

8.8 O'Hare International Airport: The Midwest's Transportation Hub

You are looking at O'Hare International Airport in Chicago, Illinois. It is one of the busiest airports in the United States. Hundreds of thousands of people pass through O'Hare each day. That adds up to millions of airplane passengers a year.

transportation hub
a city that serves as a center for moving goods and people

Chicago has always been a **transportation hub,** or a center for moving goods and people. In the 1800s, railroad tracks fanned out from Chicago across the Midwest. Trains left Chicago every day, carrying goods from factories to small farming towns. The trains returned loaded with corn, wheat, and livestock for the big cities.

Today, railroads, highways, airports, rivers, and lakes move more people and goods into and out of Chicago than they do in any other American city. Moving all these people and goods is a big business. O'Hare International Airport, by itself, employs 50,000 workers.

As an economist, I know how important transportation is to the economy of the Midwest. Last year, for example, my college friend from Iowa sold his entire soybean crop to a buyer in Japan. Without a good transportation system, how could my farmer friend move his crop halfway around the world?

Products from the Midwest ship all over the world. Many of them leave from O'Hare International Airport.

8.9 Chicago's Wrigley Field

For me, this is one of the best views in the world. You are looking down at Wrigley Field, home of the Chicago Cubs.

Sports are popular in the Midwest. The first professional baseball team played not far from here, in the city of Cincinnati, Ohio.

As a kid, I listened on the radio to the Cubs play baseball. The Cubs never won a championship. But I still became a big fan. Now that I live in Chicago, I love watching the Cubs play at Wrigley Field.

Wrigley Field is a special place for people who like baseball. It is the second-oldest baseball park in America. A lot of historic events have happened here. The most famous one may be Babe Ruth's "called shot," during Game 3 of the 1932 World Series. As the story goes, when Ruth came up to bat, he pointed to the bleachers. Then, on the next pitch, he hit a home run to that very spot. I wish I'd been there to see it.

Baseball is a popular sport in the Midwest. Many famous games have been played at Chicago's Wrigley Field.

People from all over the world come to the Midwest to visit the Mall of America.

8.10 Minnesota's Mall of America

Our last stop is the Mall of America, in Bloomington, Minnesota. This is the largest indoor shopping mall in the United States. The Mall of America was built in 1992.

The nation's first mall covered by a roof was built in 1956. Its purpose was to make shopping a more pleasant experience by proctecting shoppers from bad weather.

People in the Midwest have to pay a lot of attention to the weather. In winter, storms called blizzards bring heavy snow and freezing winds. Spring brings hailstorms that drop hailstones, or lumps of ice, instead of rain. Spring is also when tornado season begins.

Because of these types of weather, indoor malls are a good way to protect shoppers. These malls also offer customers lots of choices about what to buy.

The Mall of America has more than 520 stores. If you spent just 10 minutes in each one, it would take you four days and three nights to visit the entire mall. And that time doesn't include your eating in any of the 50 restaurants, visiting any of the 14 movie theaters, or playing in the amusement park.

Summary

When we began, I asked you why the Midwest is called "America's Breadbasket." Midwestern farmers grow a lot of the wheat we use to make bread. Kansas grows the most wheat. North Dakota, South Dakota, Minnesota, Ohio, Illinois, and Nebraska also produce large wheat crops. You will learn more about agriculture, and why the Midwest earned this nickname, in the next chapter.

Why do we also call the Midwest "America's Heartland"? There are many answers to this question. One answer looks at geography. The Midwest lies at the heart, or center, of the United States.

Another answer looks at history. The Midwest is the point where pioneers began their westward journeys. It is where American Indians fought bravely to defend their lands. And the first professional baseball team played in the Midwest.

A third answer looks at economics. The Midwest is a center for both farming and industry. From popcorn to cars, many products you use every day come from America's economic heartland.

Our crop dusters are about to land. Thank you very much for coming on my tour. Your next journey will be a bit different. It will take you back in time—to learn about Detroit, Michigan, during World War II.

This machine harvests snap beans. One mechanical harvester can pick the same amount of beans as 100 people picking by hand.

Detroit During World War II

Detroit was already an important center of industry in 1941. That year, when the United States entered World War II, this city became even more important. People looked to Detroit to build the tanks and planes needed for the war. How did wartime change one Midwestern city?

Louise Thompson, an African American woman, already had a job. But in 1941, she heard that one of Detroit's factories was looking for workers. The factory made planes for the United States to use in World War II. And it was paying high wages. Louise was interested.

In the early 1940s, there were few good jobs open to African American women. But wartime was changing many things. Factories needed thousands of workers. Many men were away fighting the war. This meant that more jobs were open to women. Thompson decided to train for one of the factory jobs. It was a great opportunity. And she could help her country.

Mr. and Mrs. Castle also saw an opportunity. Before the war, they had run a small business in their home, about 150 miles outside Detroit. When the war started, they closed their business and moved to Detroit. Both of them found jobs at the airplane factory near the city. But they had to live in a tiny trailer near the factory. It was a difficult change for the Castles. But they, too, wanted to help their country and themselves.

These women learned a new job—assembling planes.

Changes in Industry

Before World War II, Detroit had been home to the nation's auto industry. Many people worked to make cars in Detroit. Most of the workers were men.

In 1939, several countries went to war in Europe. Before long, countries in many parts of the world became involved. The United States entered World War II in December 1941.

The war brought many changes to the auto industry in Detroit. The country no longer needed new cars. People could make do with old cars during wartime. So the auto factories stopped making cars. Instead, some auto companies made tanks. Some made ship engines. And others made airplanes.

Henry Ford built a new factory called Willow Run. This factory made a special kind of airplane. It was called the B-24 bomber. The new factory was huge. The people who ran it used many of the same ideas that Ford had introduced to make cars. They decided to use an assembly line to make planes.

It was a new idea for building planes. And the results were amazing. Before the war, it took 200,000 worker hours to build a plane. At Willow Run, workers could build one in 18,000 hours. At one point, thousands of workers were completing a new bomber every hour.

Willow Run workers built thousands of planes during World War II.

At Willow Run, many workers lived in dirty and unsafe conditions.

Changes in Everyday Life

It took many workers to keep Willow Run's assembly lines moving. By June 1943, more than 42,000 people worked at the factory. The large number of new workers created some changes for Detroit.

Workers needed to live near the factories. But at Willow Run and other factories, there were not enough houses for all the new workers. Many people, like the Castles, lived in small trailers. Some families even moved into old chicken coops. A lot of people were willing to accept such hardships to have a good job.

There were also shortages of many things. Goods such as gasoline and rubber were needed for the war. So the government put a limit on how much of these products people could use at home.

The Castles had trouble finding bottled gas for cooking. Once, they had to drive 150 miles to fill their bottles. They also had to pay high prices for things like restaurant meals. With so many new customers coming in, restaurants could charge more money for their food.

African Americans like Louise Thompson had to face similar problems, and more. Even though Thompson had been trained to work in a war factory, she had trouble finding a job. Even during wartime, some factories would not hire African Americans.

Conflict and Opportunity

In wartime Detroit, people faced many new challenges. They had to build new factories. They had to make new products. They had to learn new skills.

Detroit suddenly had thousands of new residents. Some longtime residents were unhappy to see their communities changing. Some newcomers were made to feel unwelcome.

Occasionally, these stresses and challenges led some people to become violent. In 1943, conflict between white and black Americans led to fighting in the streets of Detroit. Thirty-four people died before the fight was over. Hundreds were hurt.

But there were also many times when the people of Detroit worked together to meet the challenges of war. Workers at Willow Run made 8,685 airplanes. The Chrysler Company made 25,000 tanks. General Motors also made tanks. Other auto factories made engines for planes and ships. The people and the factories of Detroit played a key role in helping the United States win the war.

The war created many opportunities for individuals and families. Many people entered the workforce for the first time. Women had a wider range of jobs open to them. Different groups of people met and worked together for an important cause.

People in Detroit worked together in new ways to support the war effort.

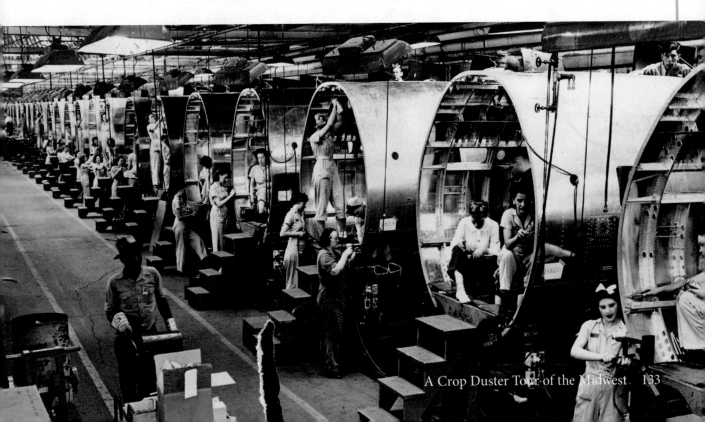

Agricultural Changes in the Midwest

How has farming changed in the Midwest over time?

9.1 Introduction

"Tickle the land with a hoe," boasted a Midwestern farmer in the 1800s, "and the crop will laugh to the harvest."

Midwesterners liked to brag about their farms. They bragged about the farm boy who got stuck on top of a cornstalk because the corn grew faster than he could climb. They boasted about pumpkins so large that cows could live inside them. They even told stories about giant watermelons. These melons were so big that they had to be pulled out of fields on sleds.

This much is true: the Midwest has some of the richest soil anywhere. And many crops grow well in the climate there.

Still, farming in the Midwest has never been as easy as tickling the land with a hoe. The first farmers to settle there struggled to overcome hardships. Farming has changed a lot since then. But Midwestern farmers still have to work hard to survive.

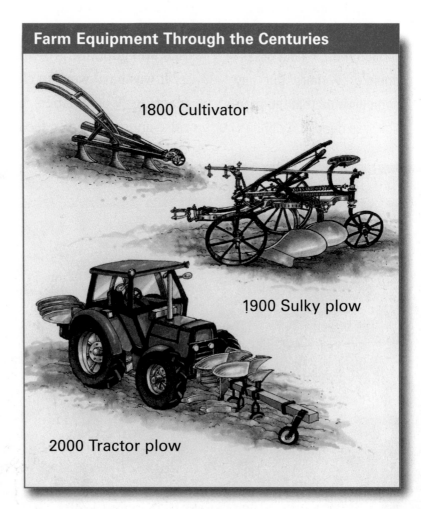

Farm Equipment Through the Centuries

1800 Cultivator

1900 Sulky plow

2000 Tractor plow

9.2 Farming in the Midwest in 1800

In 1800, almost all Americans lived on farms. About 90 out of every 100 people in America lived on a farm. Most farms had only as much land as one family could plow and plant in a year. This was about 50 acres.

Most of these farms were east of the Appalachian Mountains. However, settlers had begun to cross the mountains looking for new land to farm. By 1810, more than a million Americans lived west of the Appalachians.

People settled first in Ohio, Michigan, and Indiana. These areas were covered with forests. Before farmers could plant anything, they had to chop down the trees to clear the land.

As people moved further west into Illinois and Wisconsin, they found land where the forest grew thinner. Here there were patches of prairie covered with grasses and wildflowers. But farmers avoided these prairies because prairie grass has deep, tangled roots. Farmers did not think that they could clear the land to get anything else to grow there. But they soon learned that prairie soil was deep and rich and good for growing crops.

It was hard work to clear forests and prairies for planting. Most farmers felt that they were doing well just to raise enough food to feed their families.

At first, farmers avoided these grassy areas. They thought nothing but grass could grow there. But they soon learned that the prairie soil was deep and rich.

9.3 Farm Tools in 1800

The tools farmers used in 1800 were simple ones. Farmers used axes to cut down trees. Saws were then used to cut the trees into logs to build log cabins. Wood from trees was also used to make fences and furniture.

A plow with an iron blade was used to prepare soil for planting. As this blade was dragged across a field, it dug a long groove called a furrow.

If farmers were lucky, they would have had a team of oxen to pull these plows. Even then, plowing was slow work. The thick prairie soil stuck to the iron blades. Farmers had to stop every few steps to scrape dirt from their plows.

Farmers planted their crops by hand. They walked up and down their fields, dropping seeds into the fresh furrows. They hoped the seeds would take root in this loose soil.

Farmers used a scythe, a curved knife on a long handle, to harvest their grain crops. Later on, they threshed the grain by beating it with a tool called a flail. Threshing separates the seeds of the grain from the rest of the plant.

With these tools, a farmer had to work about 300 hours to raise 100 bushels of wheat. For this amount of wheat, he had to plow, plant, and harvest five acres of land.

Farmers often hired a team of men to help harvest fields of wheat. Here, men use scythes to cut the wheat.

9.4 The Family Farm in 1800

The first farmhouse most families built was a log cabin. The typical cabin had one main room and perhaps a sleeping loft. There was a stone fireplace for cooking and heating. The main room was furnished with a table and a few stools.

Cabins were gloomy inside. Glass was expensive to buy, so people used greased paper to cover their small windows. At night, the only light in the cabin came from the fire and the smelly lamps that burned grease. Farm families went to bed early. Family members slept under quilts made from scraps of cloth, on mattresses stuffed with oak leaves.

A farmyard in 1800 was a busy, noisy place.

Farm families raised almost all of their own food. They planted vegetable gardens and fruit orchards. They kept cows for milk, butter, and cheese. They raised chickens for eggs and hogs for meat. They raised sheep for wool that was used to make clothes.

Farm families faced many hardships, some of which prevented families from getting enough to eat. Wolves attacked farm animals like chickens and hogs. Rabbits and deer raided their gardens. Squirrels and raccoons stole corn from the cornfields.

Disease could strike family members at any time. Injuries were common as well. Women hurt themselves cooking over open fires. Men hurt themselves working in the fields. With no doctors nearby, farm families did their best to care for themselves.

9.5 Farming in the Midwest in 1900

In the year 1900, less than half of all Americans lived on farms. About 40 out of every 100 people in America lived on a farm. Most farms were three times the size of farms 100 years earlier. The average farm was about 150 acres.

The first farmers on the prairie had worked hard to be **self-sufficient**. Being self-sufficient means doing everything necessary to take care of yourself on your own. These farmers had raised their own food and made their own clothes. They hadn't made much money. But they hadn't needed much money, either.

By 1900, farms covered the Midwest. Farmers on the Central Plains raised corn, pigs, and cows. On the Great Plains, they raised wheat, cattle, and sheep.

No longer did farmers plant crops on just enough land to feed their families. Instead, farmers raised large crops of grain and great herds of animals. These crops and livestock were sold for cash. Some farmers had **dairies**. A dairy is a farm that produces milk and milk products that can also be sold for cash.

With more money in their pockets, farmers could buy more land. They could purchase machines to help them work that land. And they could buy the useful new goods coming out of American factories—such as iron stoves, sewing machines, and telephones.

self-sufficient doing everything necessary to take care of yourself on your own

dairy a farm that produces milk and milk products

A country store in 1900 sold just about everything a farmer might need.

9.6 Farm Tools in 1900

During the 1800s, Americans had invented many new farm tools. Many of these tools had to be pulled through fields by teams of horses.

The most important new tool for prairie farmers was the steel plow. A man named John Deere invented it in 1837. Deere's plows were made with steel blades rather than iron. Steel blades were sharper and smoother than iron blades. As a result, steel plows could cut through the thick prairie soil far more easily than the earlier iron plows.

Another new tool was a grain-cutting machine called a **reaper**. A man named Cyrus McCormick invented it in 1834. A farmer could cut much more grain with McCormick's reaper than with a scythe.

New machines also helped farmers. One machine was the horse-drawn seed drill. It planted seeds much faster than a farmer could by hand. Another machine was the horse-drawn **combine**. A combine could cut and thresh a field of grain at the same time.

These inventions helped Midwestern farmers grow more food with less effort. In 1800, a farmer had needed to spend 300 hours of labor to raise 100 bushels of wheat. By 1900, it took farmers just 50 hours to raise the same number of bushels.

reaper a machine for cutting grain

combine a machine for cutting and threshing grain

This photograph was taken in a wheat field near Moro, Oregon, in the 1890s. Notice how many horses were needed to pull the combine.

9.7 The Family Farm in 1900

Most families' first home on the prairie was a tent, a log cabin, or a soddie. Soddies were houses made of blocks of **sod,** or dirt mixed with grass roots. When it rained, soddies dripped mud. "Life is too short," wrote one farm woman, "to be spent under a sod roof."

As soon as farm families had money saved, they built houses made of wood boards. The typical farmhouse had lots of windows and a big porch. The largest room was the kitchen. Few farmhouses had bathrooms. Instead, families used an outhouse that stood behind the main house.

Only the richest farmers could afford such wonders as electricity and running water. Most farm families used candles or oil lamps for lighting. They cooked on wood-burning iron stoves. They used hand pumps to draw water from wells.

Everybody worked. Men plowed, planted, and harvested crops. Women cooked, cleaned, and cared for the children. In summer, farm women spent hours **canning** food from their gardens.

Every child had farm chores, as well. Children helped out by chopping wood, drawing water, and weeding the garden. They also gathered eggs, milked cows, and fed the animals.

This sod house was in Custer County, Nebraska. Family members are shown next to their well.

sod a mixture of dirt and roots of grass

canning preserving food by cooking and sealing it in cans or jars

Crop dusters are airplanes that fly low over a farm and spray pesticides over fields of plants.

agribusiness farming on a large scale by big companies

fertilizer a substance added to the soil to improve plant growth

pesticide a substance used on crops to kill insects and other pests

9.8 Farming in the Midwest Today

Today, very few Americans live and work on farms. Only 2 out of every 100 people in America live on a farm. Some farms are almost 10 times the size of farms 200 years earlier. The average farm is 450 acres in size.

Farming in the 21st century is a big business. If you look at the total number of farms, most are still owned and run by families. But if you look at the total amount of farm acres, most are owned by big companies. We call these companies **agribusinesses**.

Farming in the Midwest has changed in many ways over the past 100 years. Today, most farm work is done by machines. Most farmers add **fertilizers** to the soil to make plants grow better. Some fertilizers are natural products. Other fertilizers are made from chemicals. Farmers also use chemicals to kill insects and other pests that attack their crops. These products are called **pesticides**.

These changes have helped farmers grow more food than ever before. But they have also created new problems. Chemicals used on crops can be harmful to other living things. For example, fertilizers and pesticides wash into rivers. There, they can kill fish and other wildlife.

9.9 Farm Tools Today

By the year 2000, most of the work of plowing, planting, and picking crops was done by machines. Gasoline engines supply the power for these machines.

The most important new farm tool of the last 100 years has been the tractor. Farmers can use tractors in two ways. One way is to pull heavy loads. A modern tractor can pull more weight than 100 horses can. The other way is to power other farm equipment. Farmers use tractors to pull plows, seed drills, and machines that harvest their crops.

For dairy farmers, no tool has been more useful than the milking machine. Before the invention of the milking machines, dairy farmers had to milk each cow by hand. This was slow work. Milking machines allow a farmer to milk many cows at the same time. As a result, dairy farms are much larger today than they were in 1900.

New tools have also helped Midwestern farmers grow more food on less land. In 1800, a farmer needed five acres to grow 100 bushels of wheat. By 2000, the same amount of wheat could be grown on just three acres.

New machines have also reduced the time it takes to raise 100 bushels of wheat. In 1800, it took farm workers 300 hours of labor to raise that much wheat. Today, it takes less than 4 hours to raise 100 bushels of wheat. That's a big difference.

Today, computers play an important part in farming, and even in farm machinery.

Farm auctions are like huge yard sales at which farmers sell their equipment to make money to pay the farm's bills.

9.10 The Family Farm Today

Throughout U.S. history, as the nation expanded westward, the number of farms increased. By the 1920s, there were more than 6 million farms in the United States.

But in the 1930s, hard times hit the family farm. Crop prices fell so low that farmers could not make any money. Then a long drought struck the Midwest. With no rain, fields turned to dust. Many families gave up farming.

Since then, farmers have seen some good times and some bad times. But the number of family farms has decreased year by year. Today, there are only 2.1 million farms left in the United States. Of these, 90 percent are owned by families and individuals. The rest are agribusinesses.

Farm families live like most other American families. They buy their clothes in department stores. They send their children to school. Every year, however, more families are leaving the farm way of life. Some get tired of the hard work. Others don't like the loneliness of farm life. But the most common reason why people are choosing to leave farming today is simply the day-to-day struggle to make enough money to pay their bills.

Summary

As you have seen, farming in the Midwest has changed greatly in 200 years. In 1800, farmers used only hand tools and muscle power to work the land. Most farmers were able to raise just enough food to feed their families.

Today, large agribusinesses employ workers with computer-assisted tractors and machines to farm the land. Farmers may also use fertilizers that allow more food to be grown on fewer acres of land. As a result, one farm can raise enough food to feed many families.

In 1800, farm families grew or made almost everything they needed to live. They bought very little. Today, farmers grow large amounts of crops for sale. With the money they earn from selling these crops, farm families can buy whatever goods they need in stores.

Some things have not changed much in 200 years. Farming was hard work in 1800. It is still hard work today.

One other thing has not changed in the past 200 years. Farming was a risky business in 1800. Many things could go wrong. Farming is still a risky business today. But for those who love to work the land, there is no better way of life.

Next, we will take a closer look at one Midwestern crop that has truly changed the way we live.

Corn: Key Crop of the Midwest

In the United States today, farmers grow more corn than any other crop. Midwest farmers produce more than 616 billion pounds of corn every year. Why is corn such an important crop in the Midwest?

For most people, the word *corn* brings to mind either fresh corn on the cob like people eat at summer barbecues or a crunchy snack eaten while watching television. But in Mitchell, South Dakota, people celebrate corn in every way possible. They call their town the "Corn Capital of the World." Their high school sports teams are called the Kernels (for corn kernels). The name of the radio station is KORN. And on the main street of Mitchell, you can visit the world's only corn palace. The outside of this large building has murals made with corn kernels from thousands of ears of corn.

Why would anyone care enough about something as simple as corn to build this huge structure? Why does the United States grow so much corn? And how do people use the corn we grow? Keep reading to find out.

Mitchell's first corn palace opened in 1892. It was built to show the world that South Dakota was a great place to grow corn.

Corn Long Ago

Corn has a long history in the Americas. About 7,000 years ago, the people of central Mexico developed a plant, called **maize,** from wild grass. Maize is a tall plant that produces large cobs of sweet corn.

maize a tall plant that produces large cobs of sweet corn

Corn proved to be a very useful plant. The kernels were good to eat. The leaves were good to chew. Corn could even be popped. People used corn husks to make things like baskets, shoes, masks, and bed frames. They burned dried cobs for fuel.

As American Indians moved north, over thousands of years, they took corn with them. When European settlers arrived, American Indians were growing corn throughout North America.

As European settlers grew and harvested corn, they soon realized what a valuable crop it was. They sent word of what they had learned—along with seeds—back home. Before long, people in other parts of the world were growing corn and other crops from the Americas.

These crops grew so well and fed so many people healthily that they contributed to population increases around the world. For example, in southern Europe, from 1500 to 1900, the population grew from about 15 million people to about 70 million people.

Today, people grow corn on every continent, except Antarctica.

The slippers and basket in these photographs were made by American Indians from corn husks.

Corn Today

Today, many Americans depend on corn just as the early settlers once did. The Midwestern states of Iowa, Illinois, Nebraska, and Minnesota raise more than half of the country's corn. These states are part of what we call "the Corn Belt."

The number of ways in which people use corn today might surprise you. Corn is used in about 4,000 products! Take a look at the chart below. It shows what happens to some of the corn grown in the United States.

Animal Feed
More than half of all U.S. corn goes to feed animals such as cows, pigs, and chickens, and even our dogs and cats.

Food
Corn is found in many foods, from breakfast cereals to tortilla chips. Corn adds "crunch" to foods.

Fuel
Ethanol is a fuel that can be made from corn. It can power cars. Its use helps reduce air pollution.

Cornstarch
Made from corn, cornstarch is a powder that is used in food and many paper and plastic products. Your picnic utensils might be made from corn.

Corn Sweeteners
Corn sweeteners are found in many foods, from lunch meats to salad dressing. Corn sweeteners keep frozen yogurt from turning into ice.

Dried Corn Products
Dried corn is an ingredient in many household products. The pillow you sleep on and the comforter keeping you warm could have corn in them.

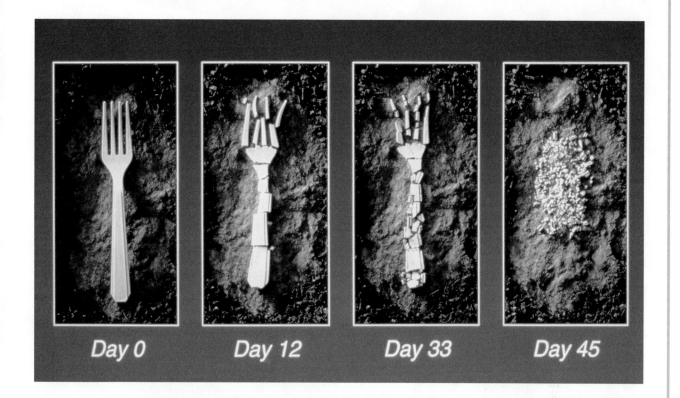

Day 0   Day 12   Day 33   Day 45

The Future of Corn

Some scientists wonder whether corn could be used to help solve some of today's environmental problems.

Can you believe that corn is being used to run cars? That may sound crazy, but a fuel called ethanol lets us do just that. Ethanol is made from corn and can be used to power automobiles. Burning ethanol creates less pollution than burning other types of fuel. And unlike the oil in gasoline, ethanol is a **renewable resource**.

And think about this the next time you use plastic plates at a picnic. When you throw the plates away, they may sit in the trash dump forever. Could we make plates out of a new material that would fall apart over time and become part of the soil? Many scientists say that this would be a good thing for the environment. They are working on ways to make just such a form of plastic out of cornstarch.

Not everyone agrees that corn is the solution to our energy problems. It takes a lot of energy to create ethanol. And both ethanol and the new form of plastic are expensive to make. But many people hope that corn will prove as useful in the future as it has in the past.

This fork is made from a corn-based plastic. It decomposes safely and quickly—in just 45 days.

renewable resource
something that renews itself, or regrows, even as people use up the original supply of it

DALLAS

HISTORIC
NEW MEXICO
U.S.
66
ROUTE

A Big Rig Tour of the Southwest

10

How have geography and history shaped life in the Southwest?

10.1 Introduction

Welcome to the Southwest. My name is Mr. Nakai. I will be your guide to this region.

Let me tell you a little about myself. I am an American Indian, from the Navajo tribe. Until I retired last year, I was a truck driver. I drove my big rig—that's what truckers call their trucks—all over the Southwest. I know this region like the back of my hand.

When I was asked to lead this tour, I thought about how I could make it really special. Then, it hit me! I'm a trucker. Why not take you on a truck tour? My big rig holds only three people. But some of my trucking buddies offered to help out. Together, we rounded up enough trucks to take your whole class.

The view from high up in a big rig can't be beat. So pick a truck, buckle your seat belt, and let's go.

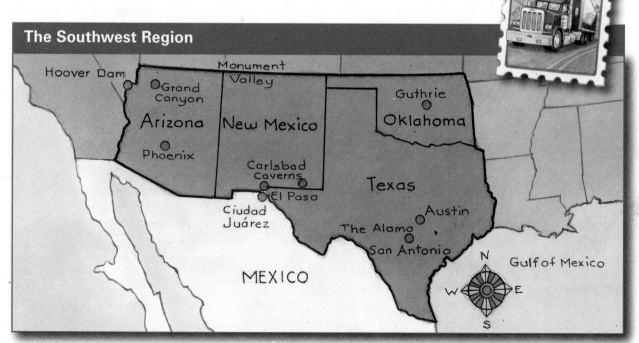

The Southwest Region

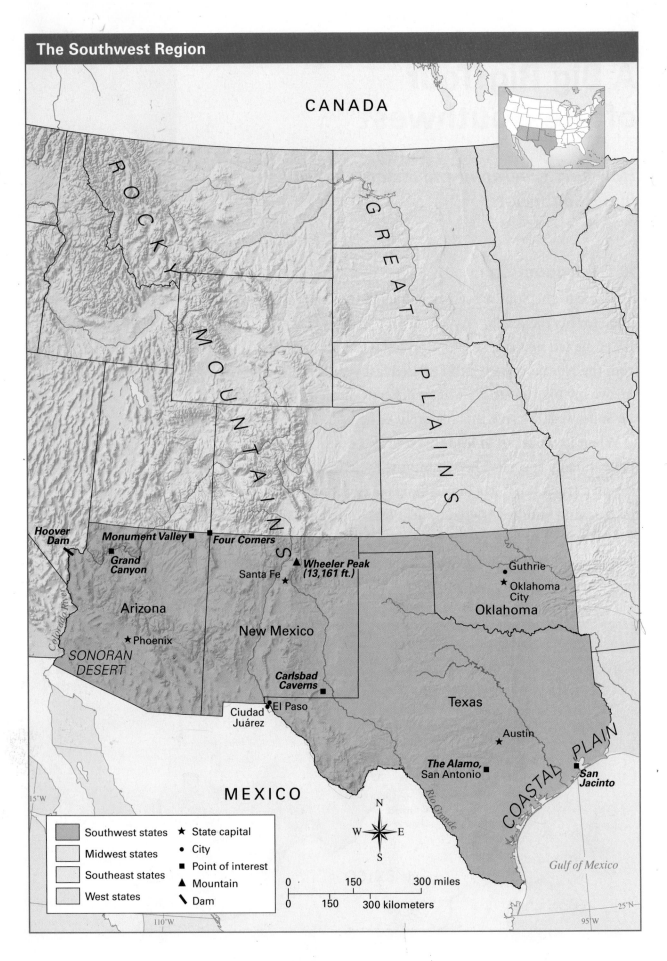

The Southwest Region

CANADA

ROCKY MOUNTAINS

GREAT PLAINS

Hoover Dam

Monument Valley ■ ■ **Four Corners**

Grand Canyon ■

▲ **Wheeler Peak (13,161 ft.)**

Santa Fe ★

• Guthrie

★ Oklahoma City

Arizona

New Mexico

Oklahoma

★ Phoenix

SONORAN DESERT

Colorado River

Carlsbad Caverns ■

Ciudad Juárez

• El Paso

Texas

Austin ★

COASTAL PLAIN

The Alamo, ■ San Antonio

■ **San Jacinto**

MEXICO

Rio Grande

Gulf of Mexico

N W E S

■ Southwest states	★ State capital
■ Midwest states	• City
■ Southeast states	■ Point of interest
■ West states	▲ Mountain
	╲ Dam

0   150   300 miles
0   150   300 kilometers

115°W   110°W   95°W   25°N

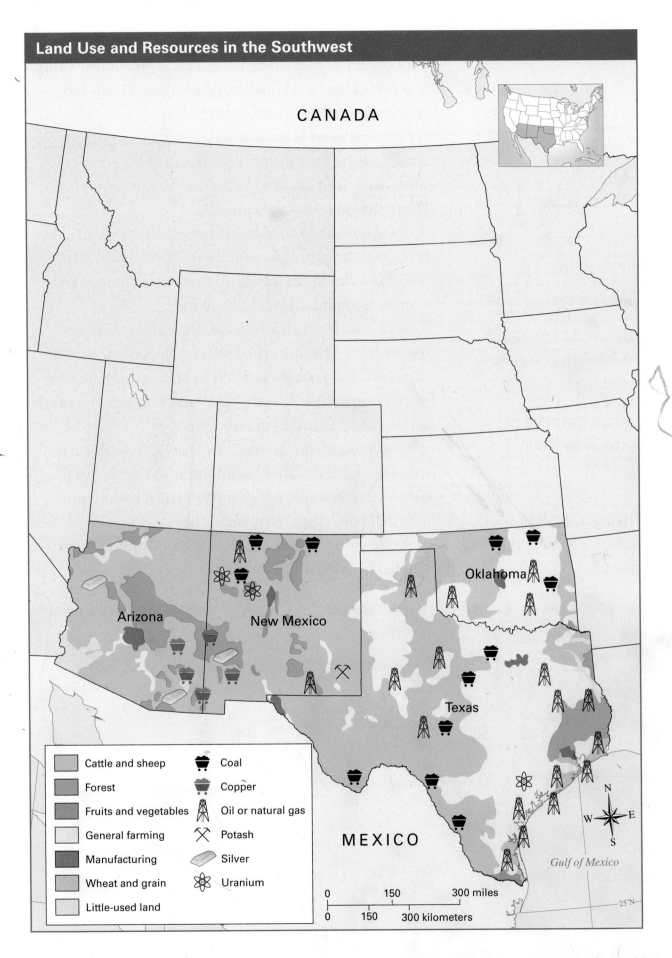

CANADA

Arizona

New Mexico

Oklahoma

Texas

MEXICO

Gulf of Mexico

Cattle and sheep

Forest

Fruits and vegetables

General farming

Manufacturing

Wheat and grain

Little-used land

Coal

Copper

Oil or natural gas

Potash

Silver

Uranium

| 0 | 150 | 300 miles |
| 0 | 150 | 300 kilometers |

N
W E
S

25°N

10.2 Monument Valley: Home of the Navajos

Let's begin our tour where I live. This is Monument Valley. It is part of the Navajo Indian Reservation. This is the largest reservation in the United States.

The Southwest is home to a large number of American Indians, more than in any other region of the country. Many American Indians live and work on reservations. Others live in towns and cities.

I was born and raised in Monument Valley. To me, this is the most beautiful place on Earth. Moviemakers also love this valley for its setting. Many western movies and television commercials are filmed here.

Look closely at this landscape. Do you see those flat-topped hills? They are called **mesas**. Notice how bare the mesas are. Not enough rain falls in Monument Valley for forests to grow. Much of the Southwest is desert. A **desert** gets less than 10 inches of rain a year.

Over time, plants, animals, and people have all adapted to living in this dry land. To **adapt** means to change to survive. The Navajos, for example, learned how to grow corn and raise sheep, even with little rainfall.

As we move on, look for other ways that people have adapted to living in the desert.

mesa a flat-topped hill

desert an area of land that receives very little rain

adapt to change in order to survive

The mesas in Monument Valley are made of shale and sandstone.

10.3 Phoenix, Arizona: America's Hottest City

This is Phoenix, Arizona, America's hottest large city. During July, temperatures here can soar to 121 degrees Fahrenheit.

A hundred years ago, Phoenix was a small town. Not many people wanted to move to Arizona in those days. Folks said that it was too hot, dry, and lonely here. What I call the three "A's" changed their minds.

The first "A" was air conditioners. These machines use electricity to cool the air in a room. Air-conditioning allows people to live in comfort no matter how hot the day is.

The second "A" was aqueducts. An **aqueduct** is a large pipe or canal that moves water over a long distance. Aqueducts are used in the Southwest to move water from lakes and rivers to farms and cities. Aqueducts make it possible to have green lawns in Phoenix.

The third "A" was automobiles. Travel in the Southwest used to be hard, and even dangerous. A traveler stuck in the desert could die of thirst.

Cars, along with good roads, made travel safer and easier. People began to come to the Phoenix area as tourists. Some liked the hot, dry weather so much that they came back here to live. Since 1940, Phoenix has grown at an amazing rate.

With a population of more than 1,461,000 people, Phoenix is the sixth-largest city in the United States.

aqueduct a pipe or canal for carrying water over a long distance

10.4 Hoover Dam: A Concrete Marvel

You are looking at one of America's greatest manufactured structures, Hoover Dam. A **dam** is a wall built across a river to stop the water from flowing.

Hoover Dam was built for two main reasons. The first reason was to control flooding on the Colorado River. The dam slows the rush of water down the river during flood times. The second reason was to store water. Water stored behind Hoover Dam flows through aqueducts to farms and cities.

Hoover Dam was built more than 70 years ago. At that time, nobody had ever built such a huge dam. Many people said it couldn't be done. Some said the Colorado River could never be stopped long enough to build a dam. Other people did not think a dam could be made strong enough to hold back so much water. My dad helped prove these people wrong! He helped build Hoover Dam.

My dad knew a great many facts about Hoover Dam. He told me that there is enough concrete in the dam to pave a road from California to New York. He said that the lake behind the dam holds enough water to flood the entire state of Pennsylvania with one foot of water. That's a lot of concrete holding back a lot of water!

Hoover Dam sits on the border of the states of Arizona and Nevada.

10.5 The Grand Canyon: Arizona's World-Famous Wonder

Wow—what a view! You are looking into the Grand Canyon. This is the most famous natural feature in the United States.

A **canyon** is a deep, narrow valley with steep sides. There are many canyons in the Southwest. But this one is the grandest of them all.

The Grand Canyon is about 277 miles long and 1 mile deep. It is so deep that the canyon's top and bottom have different weather. It can be cold here on top and hot down below. It is so deep that when I stand here on the rim, I sometimes see eagles flying below me.

The American Indian tribe known as the Havasupais live at the bottom of the Grand Canyon. According to Havasupai legend, the canyon was formed when a flood covered the world. To end the flood, a god dug a hole in the Earth. The floodwater rushed down the hole, carving out the Grand Canyon as it went.

Scientists tell a different story. They say the Grand Canyon began to form anywhere from 6 to 17 million years ago. It has been carved slowly out of the Earth by water and wind. The Grand Canyon is still growing today, even while we are here looking at it.

canyon a deep, narrow valley with steep sides

The Grand Canyon's rock walls tell us what the world was like hundreds of millions of years ago.

10.6 Carlsbad Caverns: Big Rooms and Bats in New Mexico

cave a natural underground hole

cavern a large cave

At most national parks, the big attractions are found above the ground. Not here! At Carlsbad Caverns National Park in New Mexico, the show takes place underground. About 100 caves and caverns lie beneath this park. A **cave** is a natural hole found in the Earth. A **cavern** is a large cave.

According to local legend, some cowboys, including one named Jim White, found Carlsbad Caverns. One evening, they saw what looked like a plume of smoke rising into the sky. That plume of smoke turned out to be a big cloud of bats flying out of a cave entrance.

A bat looks like a mouse with wings. Hundreds of thousands of bats sleep in the caverns during the day. At night, the bats leave in a great, whirring cloud to hunt for food. If you come to the entrance at sunset, you may see them take flight. It's a very pretty sight.

More than a half million visitors tour Carlsbad Caverns each year. One of the most popular stops is a huge chamber known as the Big Room. The Big Room is about 25 stories high and a third of a mile wide. It could hold six football fields and still have space left over.

Limestone and water created the formations in these caverns.

10.7 El Paso and Ciudad Juárez: Two Cities, Two Countries, One Border

We are at the border between the United States and Mexico. A **border** is a line that people agree on as a boundary to separate two places. The border between the United States and Mexico is a river called the Rio Grande.

The Rio Grande separates two countries. It also divides two busy cities. El Paso, Texas, an American city, lies north of the border. Ciudad Juárez, a Mexican city, lies south of the border.

Forty years ago, El Paso and Juárez were sleepy little border towns. There weren't many people or trucks here then. Today, a total of about 2 million people live in the two cities. And the area is crawling with trucks.

The reason for this change is simple. American businesses have built hundreds of factories in Juárez. Americans build factories across the border because Mexican workers will work for much lower pay than American workers. This reduces the cost of doing business. These factories, called *maquiladoras* (mah-kee-luh-DOHR-uhs), assemble all kinds of goods. The goods are then trucked across the border for sale in the United States.

Many Mexicans move close to the border to take *maquiladora* jobs.

The Rio Grande forms the border between the United States, (left) and Mexico, (right). The river begins in the mountains of Colorado.

border a boundary line that separates two places

mission a Spanish settlement built to teach Christianity in the United States

rebellion an armed fight against a government

10.8 San Antonio, Texas: Home of the Alamo

Welcome to San Antonio, Texas. San Antonio is a city famous for its Spanish missions. A **mission** is a Spanish settlement where priests once taught American Indians the Christian religion.

San Antonio's missions were built in the early 1700s. At that time, Texas was a colony of Spain. Later on, Texas became part of Mexico.

The Alamo is San Antonio's most famous mission. More than 2.5 million people visit the Alamo every year. They come to see where a small band of men fought and died so that Texas might be free.

In 1836, Americans living in Texas declared their independence from Mexican rule. A Mexican general named Antonio López de Santa Anna led 2,000 troops to Texas to crush this rebellion. A **rebellion** is an armed fight against one's government.

A band of 188 Texas freedom fighters gathered at the Alamo. Their goal was to stop the Mexican army there. Instead, the Mexican forces captured the mission and killed every one of its defenders.

News of the killings at the Alamo outraged Americans. Hundreds picked up their guns and headed to Texas to join the rebellion. Their battle cry was "Remember the Alamo!"

Texas won its independence from Mexico in 1836. For nine years, Texas was a nation. Then, in 1845, Texas joined the United States as the 28th state.

The Alamo was built mainly from adobe (bricks made of earth and straw) and stone.

10.9 Austin: The Capital of Texas

This is Austin, the capital of Texas. A **capital** is a city where the government of a country or state is located. The government of Texas is located in Austin.

Like our national government, state governments have three branches—legislative, executive, and judicial. The legislative branch is the state legislature. The Texas legislature meets in the building you see here with the large dome on top.

State legislatures make laws for all the people in a state. Most of the traffic laws in each state are passed by the state legislature. As a truck driver, I have to know and obey all these laws.

State legislatures decide how much people must pay in taxes to the state. They also decide how that money will be spent. Truckers always want state legislatures to spend more money on improving the roads.

The executive branch is headed by the state governor. It's the governor's job to make sure that all the laws passed by the state legislature are carried out.

State courts make up the judicial branch. State courts judge people who are accused of breaking state laws. If a person is found guilty of breaking a law, the courts decide how that person should be punished.

The capitol building in Austin, Texas, is the largest state capitol building in the nation.

The U.S. army held back the crowds until a bugler signaled the beginning of the land rush.

10.10 Guthrie, Oklahoma: Center of the Land Rush

Most of the Southwest was settled slowly, over time. Guthrie, Oklahoma, was settled in one day.

For many years, the U.S. government kept Oklahoma closed to everyone but American Indians. Then, in 1889, the government decided to open 2 million acres of land to new settlement. This area was to be given away in a one-day land rush. The first person to reach and claim a piece of land on that day could keep it.

On April 22, 1889, between 50,000 and 100,000 people gathered at the starting line for the land rush. Most were European Americans. Some were African Americans. Black or white, everyone wanted the same thing—free land.

At noon, a bugler blew some notes on his horn. The rush was on! People raced off in wagons, on horses, and on foot. In a few hours, every inch of land was taken.

Not everyone waited for the land rush to begin. Some settlers cheated and entered the area sooner than the government allowed. One of these "sooners" was found tending a garden full of vegetables. Oklahoma's soil was so rich, he claimed, that the plants had all sprouted up that day.

Guthrie, Oklahoma, was born during the land rush. At noon, Guthrie wasn't much more than a patch of grass. Six hours later, the town had a population of 10,000 people.

Summary

My trucking buddies and I hope that you enjoyed your big rig tour of the Southwest.

On the way back, I asked the children in my truck what words they would use to describe the Southwest. The first word they came up with was *big*. This region has big caverns, a big canyon, a big capitol building, and a big dam. Their next two words were *hot* and *dry*. Much of the Southwest is desert. Plants, animals, and people all have to adapt to its hot, dry climate to survive.

Over time, the way people adapt to the desert has changed. The Navajos came here hundreds of years ago. They adapted by learning how to grow corn and raise sheep. People coming here today adapt in different ways. They use air-conditioning, aqueducts, and automobiles to help them survive.

The last word the children chose was *beautiful*. I asked them which places seemed beautiful. "Monument Valley," they answered, "along with the Grand Canyon and Carlsbad Caverns." After thinking about this some more, one child added, "I think that the Hoover Dam is beautiful, too."

My dad would have liked that answer. He would have liked it a lot.

Hoover Dam holds back the water of the Colorado River to form Lake Mead.

Freedom—or Death

Before Texas was a state, it was the home of American Indians. It was a colony of Spain and then Mexico. And then it was an independent nation. How did one battle help shape the history of Texas?

BOOM! BOOM! The walls of the Alamo shook as the cannons fired. Hidden away in a small room near the mission's chapel, mothers and their children hugged and cried. The shouts of the men outside grew more desperate as the Mexican army advanced. No one expected to make it out of the room alive. Would this be the end of their dreams for Texas?

The date was March 6, 1836. For days, a small army of Texan soldiers had been defending the mission. They had hoped that other Texans would join them, but no help arrived.

General Santa Anna's army was outside the walls. His men flew a red flag. That meant the general would show no mercy to the Texan rebels. The Texans were determined to try to win their freedom. For Texas, they would fight until death.

Texan soldiers fought the Mexican Army at the Battle of the Alamo.

Between Two Countries

For thousands of years, American Indians lived in Texas. They hunted and farmed in the hot, dry climate. In the 1500s, Spanish settlers arrived. They built missions and towns. Spain claimed Texas as part of its Mexican colony.

In the summer of 1821, an American named Stephen Austin rode his horse through Spanish Texas. He was looking for land and liked what he saw. He decided to build a settlement between the Colorado and Brazos rivers.

The United States was not yet 50 years old, but already, Americans were pushing west. Spain let Austin settle 300 families in Texas. Each family received a large amount of land for a very low cost.

In 1821, Mexico won its independence from Spain. At first, Mexico was happy about the new settlers in Texas. To the Mexicans, U.S. settlers would be good citizens who would help protect Mexican land. To the new settlers, the colony was a chance for cheap land—and new lives.

Stephen Austin brought new settlers to Texas. Each family got more than 4,400 acres of land.

Texan soldiers dared Santa Anna to "come and take" their prized cannon. This mural is at a museum in Gonzales, Texas.

The Texas Revolution Begins

Within 10 years, thousands of Americans had settled in Texas. They were used to living in the United States. They wanted more independence than they had in Mexico. So they demanded that Texas become a separate Mexican state.

Mexican leaders were worried. Too many Americans were moving to Texas and making demands. Mexican officials said that no more Americans could move to Texas. And Mexico refused to let Texas become a state.

Stephen Austin visited Mexico to smooth things over. But the Mexican government threw him in jail. Some officials thought Austin wanted independence for Texas. Austin spent over a year in jail. When he got out, he called on Texans to fight Mexico for their freedom. He called for a Texas revolution.

In October 1835, tensions between Texas and Mexico erupted into war. Austin led 400 soldiers to San Antonio to fight. The Texans won that small battle.

In February 1836, General Santa Anna brought his army to San Antonio. The Texans were ready for him. Brave fighters, including Davy Crockett, Jim Bowie, and William Travis, stood up against Santa Anna's troops. For 13 days, the Texans and the Mexicans had a standoff at the Alamo.

Freedom for Texas

Texans declared their independence on March 2. Texas became the Republic of Texas, a free nation. But Mexico would not let Texas go.

On March 6, the Mexican army attacked the Alamo. The Texans put up a fierce fight, but the mission fell under Santa Anna's control. Only the women and children, and a few enslaved African Americans, survived the bloody fight. Stories from those who witnessed the battle enraged Americans. Many people now joined the Texan army to fight the Mexicans.

A few weeks later, a Texan general named Sam Houston defeated Santa Anna's army at the Battle of San Jacinto. Texas then declared victory. The rebels had won their independence from Mexico.

Today, the Alamo sits in downtown San Antonio, Texas. Much of the old mission is gone now. But the small chapel still stands. Its walls show scars from the fighting. People from all over the world visit the Alamo. They listen to guides describe the fighting. They learn how the Texans fought for their freedom.

For Texans, the battle at the Alamo was an important step in their battle for freedom. It led the way for Texas to become an independent nation, if only for a short time.

A memorial at the Alamo honors heroes such as Davy Crockett and William Travis, as well as other Texan heroes who defended the Alamo.

A Case Study in Water Use: The Colorado River

How do people depend on the Colorado River and share its water?

11.1 Introduction

Many rivers flow through the United States. But few of them are as important as the Colorado River.

The people who live in the West and in the Southwest depend on the Colorado River for many things. The river provides drinking water for more than 17 million people. It supplies water for more than 3 million acres of farmland. Dams on the river help produce much of the electricity used in the Southwest.

The Colorado River begins high in the Rocky Mountains. The beginning of a river is called its **source**. The Colorado wanders south and west through some of the driest parts of the country. Then it crosses into Mexico. It ends in the Gulf of California. Its journey is 1,450 miles long.

Many smaller rivers flow into the Colorado. Rivers that join other, larger rivers are called **tributaries**. Each tributary adds water and soil, called silt, to the Colorado. This silt gives parts of the river a reddish brown color.

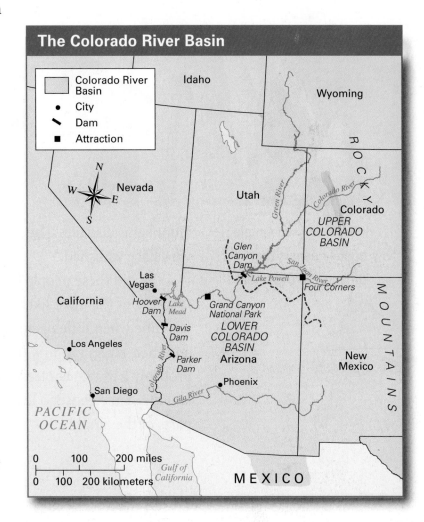

The Colorado River Basin

Legend:
- Colorado River Basin
- • City
- Dam
- ■ Attraction

11.2 The First Settlers in the Colorado River Basin

river basin the area around a river and its tributaries

drought a time when little or no rain falls

Today, millions of people live in the Colorado River Basin. A **river basin** is the area around a river and its tributaries. Not that long ago, the Colorado River Basin was an empty desert.

Two of the American Indian groups that once made their homes in this dry region were the Anasazis and the Hohokams. The Anasazis lived in the Four Corners area. This is where the states of Arizona, New Mexico, Utah, and Colorado meet today. The Hohokams lived in central Arizona.

The Hohokams used simple tools to build canals that brought water to their fields.

The Anasazis and the Hohokams were farmers. They raised corn, beans, and squash in desert fields. Not enough rain fell to water their crops. So they built canals to carry water from rivers to their fields. Some Hohokam canals were so well built that they are still used today.

Around 1350, the Anasazis left their villages. Around the same time, the Hohokams also left. The name Hohokam means "those who have vanished."

Why did these people leave their homelands? No one is sure. But the most likely answer is **drought**. A drought is a time when little or no rain falls. When no rain came and their rivers ran dry, the Anasazis and the Hohokams probably had two choices. They could leave and live, or stay and die. They chose to leave their villages to live in other parts of the Southwest.

11.3 Explorers Arrive

Spanish explorers were the first Europeans to visit the Southwest. In 1540, a Spanish soldier named Francisco Vásquez de Coronado led an army north from Mexico. Coronado hoped to find cities made of gold. Instead, he found American Indian villages built from mud and stone.

In their search for gold, some of Coronado's men came upon the Grand Canyon. From high up on the canyon rim, the river at the bottom looked like a trickling creek. The men didn't bother to give it a name.

Spanish settlers followed Coronado into the Southwest. Most lived by farming and ranching. These settlers eventually named the muddy river flowing through the Grand Canyon. They called it the Colorado. This means "reddish color" in Spanish.

In 1869, an explorer named John Wesley Powell and a crew of nine men navigated down the Colorado in small boats. These men were the first Americans to see the Grand Canyon from the bottom. The trip took three months.

In 1871, Powell made a second trip down the Colorado. He wrote a report on the Colorado River Basin. He said that the region was too dry for much settlement. He believed that there wasn't enough water for a large number of people.

During his second journey, Powell made a map of the Colorado River.

Irrigation ditches bring water to this field of lettuce in New Mexico.

irrigation a way to bring water to dry land, using water from another location

11.4 A Wave of Settlement

Powell's warning did not stop settlers from coming to the Colorado River Basin. Some of them were farmers. Like the Anasazis and the Hohokams, they found that they could grow crops in the desert. They just had to bring a lot of water to their fields.

To do this, farmers used **irrigation**. Irrigation is a way to bring water to a dry area. Some irrigation systems use canals, pipes, and ditches to carry water from one place to another. This is how farmers irrigated the Colorado River Basin.

Other settlers became cattle and sheep ranchers. Sheep and cattle could live off plants that grew wild in the Southwest. But ranchers had to find drinking water for their animals. Some ranchers also needed water to raise crops of hay for their animals.

As the number of settlers grew, towns appeared in the basin. A few—such as Las Vegas, Nevada, and Phoenix, Arizona—grew into cities. People living in these towns and cities needed water for drinking, washing, and watering their gardens.

All of these people looked to the Colorado and its tributaries for their water needs.

11.5 Sharing the Water: The Colorado River Compact

At first, the Colorado River had enough water for everyone. Water was divided up following the rule of "first in time, first in right." This meant that people who settled first were first in line to draw water from the river. Those who came last were last in line.

This way of dividing water created a problem because those settlers first in line lived mostly in California. This meant that California had the right to use almost all of the river's water. This didn't seem fair to other states in the river basin.

In 1922, the seven states in the river basin reached an agreement. It is known as the Colorado River Compact. The compact divided the basin into two parts. The Upper Basin includes Wyoming, Colorado, and parts of Utah, Arizona, and New Mexico. The Lower Basin includes Nevada, California, most of Arizona, and parts of Utah and New Mexico. The compact gave each part of the basin an equal amount of water from the Colorado River.

The Colorado River Compact said nothing about Mexico. Mexico's water users worried that there would be no water left by the time the river crossed the border. So, the United States signed a separate agreement with Mexico. In it, the United States promised to leave some water in the Colorado River for Mexico.

Representatives from the seven basin states signed the Colorado River Compact on November 24, 1922.

11.6 Taming the River with Dams

The Colorado River Compact gave each state the right to a portion of the river's flow. But turning that right into a constant water supply was not easy. In wet years, the river flooded its banks. In dry years, the river barely flowed.

The only way a state could get and keep its share of river water was to find a way to trap and store it. This meant building dams. As water backs up behind a dam, it forms a reservoir. A **reservoir** is a place where water is stored for people's use.

Since the 1930s, the states have built 20 dams on the Colorado River and its tributaries. These dams have tamed the river. In wet years, they prevent flooding by not letting too much water flow down the river at one time. In dry years, the reservoirs provide water to farms and cities.

Each dam generates electricity. Water rushing through openings in the dam causes huge machines to spin. These machines are called turbines. The spinning turbines create electricity. This electricity is sold to help pay for the dams.

reservoir an area where water is stored for people's use

The Glen Canyon Dam holds back some of the Colorado River to form Lake Powell.

11.7 The Number of Water Users Grows and Grows

The dams helped people share water from the river, but, year after year, more and more people moved to the Colorado River Basin. These people built new houses and businesses. Still, the Colorado River provided water and electricity for everyone. Who are these water users?

The largest group is made up of families. People need water to drink, shower, flush toilets, and wash clothes. Did you know that one load of laundry can use 30 to 40 gallons of water?

Farmers and ranchers are major water users, too. A farmer uses 8 gallons of water to grow one tomato. A rancher uses about 600 gallons of water to raise the beef for one hamburger.

Businesses are major water users as well. A clothing company needs 1,800 gallons of water to make one pair of jeans from cotton.

Families can save water by washing only full loads of laundry.

Miners are also major water users. Gold, iron, copper, coal, and uranium are found in the Colorado River Basin. Miners use large amounts of water to wash these valuable ores from the soil.

So far, the Colorado River has met the needs of these water users. But, as more people move into the basin, there may not be enough water for everyone.

Mayflies, trout, lizards, and owls make their homes along the Colorado. So do thousands of other animals. How might dams affect the habitats of animals that live along the river?

habitat the place where a type of animal typically lives in nature

11.8 Wildlife Water Users

People are not the only water users in the Colorado River Basin. Mammals, birds, fish, and other animals need the river, too.

The taming of the river has hurt wildlife by destroying habitats. A **habitat** is the place where a type of animal typically lives in nature. The natural habitat of fish, for example, is water.

As you know, dams built on the Colorado have turned parts of the river into reservoirs. Beavers, otters, and other animals once lived along these parts of the river. Now their habitats are deep under water.

Dams have also changed the water in the river. Before the dams were built, the river water was muddy and warm much of the year. The river's water level was at its high point in spring. Today, the water released from a dam is clear and cold. The water level is highest in summer. That is when farmers and cities need water the most. These changes have hurt fish and other wildlife.

Today, dam operators try to help wildlife by releasing more water in spring. But this change means less water for people during the summer months.

11.9 Is There Enough Water for Everyone?

The Colorado River Compact was based on the belief that about 17 million acre-feet of water flow down the river each year. An acre-foot is the amount of water it would take to cover an acre of land with one foot of water. (An acre is about the size of a football field without the end zones.)

After the United States signed an agreement with Mexico, this is how all that water was divided:

- Upper Basin states: $7\frac{1}{2}$ million acre-feet
- Lower Basin states: $7\frac{1}{2}$ million acre-feet
- Mexico: $1\frac{1}{2}$ million acre-feet
- Total: $16\frac{1}{2}$ million acre-feet

If the same amount of water flowed every year, this plan would work. But the river does not always carry this much water. In wet years, the flow may rise to more than 20 million acre-feet. In dry years, it may fall below 10 million acre-feet. And there are more dry years than wet years in the Colorado River Basin.

An acre-foot of water is about 326,000 gallons. This may sound like a lot, but it's not. A family of four uses 1 acre-foot of water each year. A farmer uses 3 acre-feet to water just one acre of land each year.

As more people settle in the Colorado River Basin, there may not be enough water for everyone.

About nine-tenths of the water used in Las Vegas and the areas around it comes from the Colorado River.

11.10 Meeting Future Water Needs

In the future, water users in the Colorado River Basin may face shortages. There are only two ways to solve this problem. One is to increase the supply of water. In the past, this was done by building dams. But most of the best places for dams have already been used. And now we know that dams hurt the natural environment.

The other solution is to use less water. This is called conservation. **Conservation** is the careful use of a resource. It sounds easy, but it's not. Using less water takes planning. It also takes new ways of thinking and new inventions.

Conservation efforts are already being made. For example, all new homes in the basin are built with low-flow toilets. These toilets use less than two gallons with each flush. Older toilets use up to seven gallons per flush.

The people of the United States are finding new ways to conserve water. For example, many cities are recycling the water that goes down the drain every day. This water is called **wastewater**. Cities collect and treat wastewater. They then use the treated wastewater to water parks and golf courses.

conservation the careful use of a resource

wastewater water that has been used

Communities across the country are finding new ways to save water. You can help, too. Report leaky faucets at school and broken sprinklers around your community.

Summary

If John Wesley Powell could see the Colorado River today, he would be amazed. The river he explored ran free from the Rocky Mountains to the Gulf of California. Today, giant dams slow the river's rush to the sea. Those dams have changed the Colorado in ways that Powell could never have imagined.

When Powell explored the river, few people lived on the land around it. Now, more than 25 million people live in the Colorado River Basin. Powell would be surprised to see so many people. He would also be surprised to find farms and cities blooming in the desert.

If Powell were here today, he might issue a new report on the Colorado River Basin. Water is precious, he might tell us. It is more precious than gold. So use the river's gift of water wisely. It is, after all, the gift of life.

It takes lots of water to keep a golf course green, especially in the desert. Many businesses in the Colorado River Basin today try to conserve water.

At Home in the Grand Canyon

For most people in the Southwest, lack of water is a problem. But the Havasupais who live in the Grand Canyon have a different challenge: flooding from Havasu Creek. How does water affect life for the Havasupais?

Chop, chop, chop. The helicopter flew through the air down into the Grand Canyon. Suddenly, the pilot saw a wall of water. It rushed toward Supai, the tiny town at the bottom of the canyon. Quickly, the pilot radioed an emergency warning.

Supai is the home of about 450 Havasupais, an American Indian tribe. In Supai, people soon saw the cascade of water coming from Havasu Creek. Many of them ran from their homes and fled up the cliffs. Two people climbed eight feet up a tree to escape the churning water.

Lester Crooke, the tribe chairman, said of the water, "It was really rushing through, bringing all kinds of big rocks and logs." Crooke and others helped people get to safety. Tourists who were hiking and camping nearby were rescued by helicopter. It was days before residents could return to the town. When they did, they found many of their belongings destroyed.

To reach Supai, you can walk or ride a mule down eight miles from the canyon rim. Or you can take a helicopter ride!

Floods in the Canyon

The flood you just read about took the Havasupais by surprise. So too had larger floods in earlier years.

Most of the time, the Havasupais have some warning about a possible flood. The floods often come after days of heavy rainfall or snowfall. At those times, water runs down the sides of the canyon rims. It fills the creeks near Supai until they overflow. The Havasupais have time to react.

Rose Marie Manakaja is an elder in the tribe. "Our parents and grandparents taught us other signs to watch out for," she explained. "For example, the animals usually know when a flood is coming. The horses and mules twitch their ears and noses in a certain way. The dogs know, too."

But sometimes, floods seem to come out of nowhere. Then the people of Supai are in great danger. Another surprise flood destroyed bridges, trails, and homes. It wrecked an irrigation system that was hundreds of years old. It washed away 43 acres of farmland. And it killed some of the farm animals. In all, it caused $2.5 million in damages.

So how *do* the Havasupais live with the threat of floods in the Grand Canyon?

These are the Havasu Falls. Every year, many thousands of tourists visit these famous waterfalls. Floods can damage the pools made by the falls.

Havasupais gather in front of a school around 1900.

Living with the Water

Manakaja explained that the people of Supai are used to these floods that come so suddenly. "We grew up here," she said. "To us, it is part of our life."

The Havasupais have lived in the canyon for hundreds of years. Their name relates to the water nearby. They are "the people of the blue-green water."

Like other American Indians in the Southwest, the early Havasupais were farmers. In spring, summer, and early fall, they lived down in the canyon. There was plenty of water from Havasu Creek. The Havasupais knew how to irrigate their fields as well as the orchards where they grew peaches.

In the Havasupai tradition, their creator, Tudjupa, said, "Here is the land where you will live. Go to the places where you find water. Mark off your land and live by the water."

However, in late fall and winter, the water in the canyon could become a threat to their village. When the floods came, the water could cause great destruction. So the Havasupais moved up to the canyon rim. It was sunnier and safer in this higher area. There, the Havasupais gathered food. They hunted deer and elk on the plateau. They roamed over thousands of acres of rich hunting grounds.

Conflict over Land

For centuries, the Havasupais lived with these cycles of nature. But the world above the canyon was changing.

By the late 1800s, thousands of Americans had moved west. Many were cattle ranchers. They fenced off the land where the Havasupais hunted. Soon, there was a conflict over who had the right to use the land. In the 1880s, the U.S. government took action. It said that the Havasupais could keep only 518 acres out of the thousands of acres they had been using. All the land that was left to them was in the Grand Canyon.

Now, without any land to go to on the canyon rim, the Havasupais could no longer leave during the flood times. So they learned to live with the water in good times and in bad.

In 1975, the government returned more than 185,000 acres of land on the canyon rim to the Havasupais. But the people of Supai stayed put. They love their land in the canyon. They want to live there, floods or not.

Some people think that the Havasupais should dam the creek to stop the flooding. To that, the Havasupais say no. They want to leave things as nature made them. So they watch carefully for floods and leave when they must. The Havasupais have been at home in the Grand Canyon for many centuries. They intend to keep it that way.

Today, the Havasupais live much as they did long ago. Here, a Havasupai man uses animals to bring supplies to Supai.

Seattle

WILSHIRE BLVD.
◄ 9500 ►

RODEO D
· 200 ►

A Van and Airplane Tour of the West

What are the features that have drawn people to the West?

12

12.1 Introduction

Aloha! My name is Ms. Yoshida. I will be your guide for our tour of the West. I was born and raised in Hawaii. As you probably can tell from my greeting, the word *aloha* is used for "hello" in the Hawaiian language. We also use it to say "good-bye."

I am a college student here on the mainland. My main interests are political science and government. Someday, I hope to win election to the United States Congress.

On school breaks, I work as a tour guide. It's a great job. I get to meet all kinds of people while seeing beautiful places. Whenever we visit someplace new, I want you to think about two questions: What first attracted people to this place? And why are people still coming here today?

For most of our tour, we will travel in vans. But we will also fly in airplanes to two stops.

Do you hear that honk? That means it's time for us to hit the road.

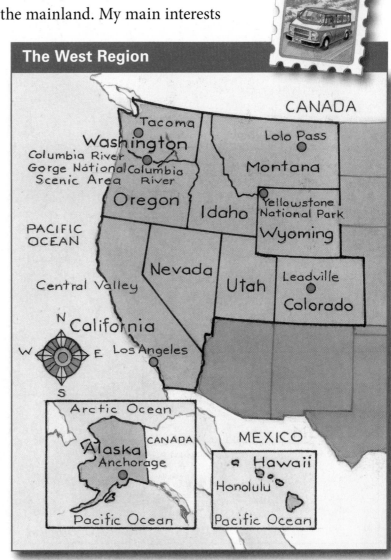

The West Region

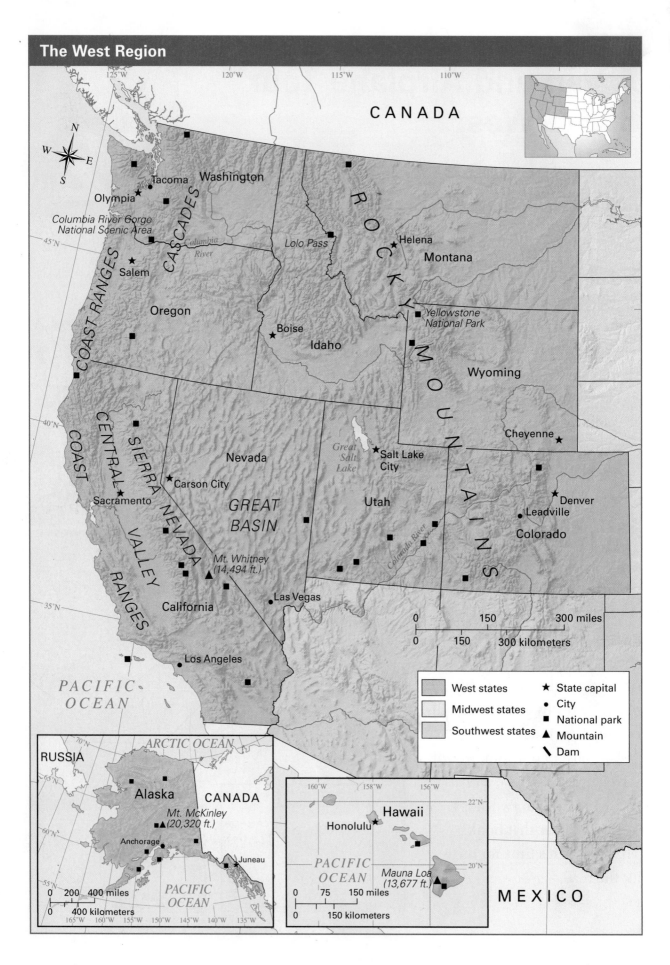

The West Region

CANADA

125°W 120°W 115°W 110°W

N
W E
S

Washington

★ Olympia
● Tacoma

COAST RANGES

CASCADES

Columbia River Gorge
National Scenic Area

Columbia River

45°N

★ Salem

Oregon

Lolo Pass

● Helena

Montana

ROCKY

● Boise

Idaho

*Yellowstone
National Park*

MOUNTAINS

Wyoming

40°N

Nevada

*Great
Salt
Lake*

★ Salt Lake
City

★ Carson City

SIERRA NEVADA

*GREAT
BASIN*

Utah

● Cheyenne ★

★ Sacramento

CENTRAL

VALLEY

COAST

Colorado River

★ Denver
● Leadville

Colorado

*Mt. Whitney
(14,494 ft.)* ▲

California

● Las Vegas

35°N

RANGES

● Los Angeles

*PACIFIC
OCEAN*

0	150	300 miles
0	150	300 kilometers

▨	West states
▢	Midwest states
▨	Southwest states
★	State capital
●	City
■	National park
▲	Mountain
◥	Dam

ARCTIC OCEAN

70°N

RUSSIA

Alaska

CANADA

65°N

*Mt. McKinley
(20,320 ft.)* ▲

● Anchorage

60°N

★ Juneau

55°N

0	200	400 miles
0	400 kilometers

*PACIFIC
OCEAN*

165°W 160°W 155°W 150°W 145°W 140°W 135°W

160°W 158°W 156°W

Hawaii

22°N

★

● Honolulu

*PACIFIC
OCEAN*

*Mauna Loa
(13,677 ft.)* ▲

20°N

0	75	150 miles
0	150 kilometers

MEXICO

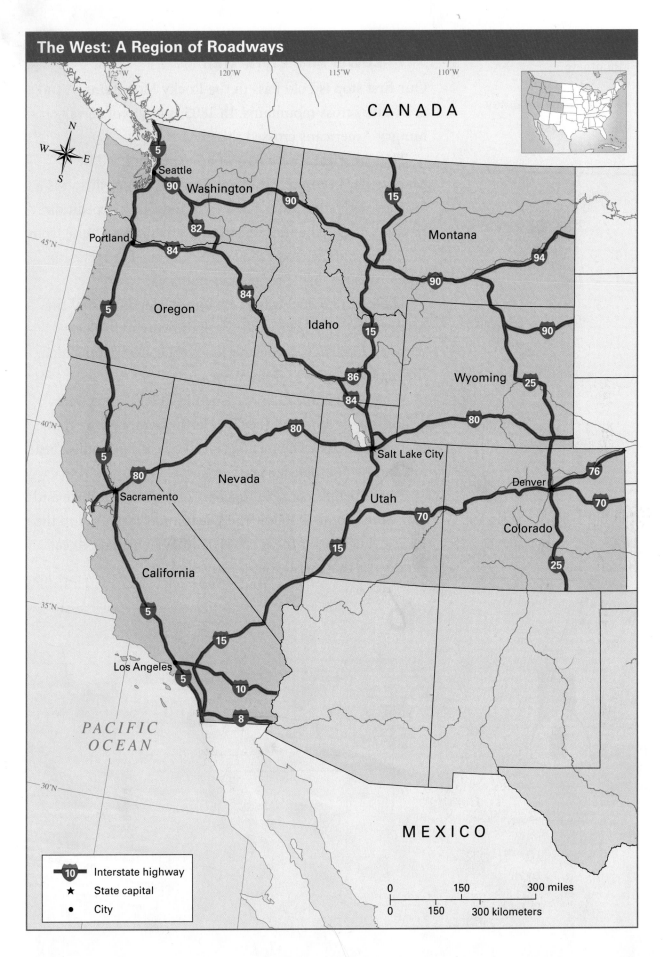

12.2 Lolo Pass, Montana: A Stop on the Lewis and Clark Trail

Our first stop is Lolo Pass in the Rocky Mountains. A **pass** is a route across mountains. In 1805, a group of 35 very hungry Americans crossed this pass.

The Americans were part of an expedition led by Meriwether Lewis and William Clark. An **expedition** is a journey with a purpose. The Lewis and Clark expedition had two goals. The first was to find an all-water route from the Mississippi River to the Pacific Ocean. The travelers failed because such a route does not exist.

Their second goal was to explore the lands west of the Mississippi. This Lewis and Clark did very well. Their maps and journals gave Americans their first good look at the region we now call the West.

When Lewis and Clark reached Lolo Pass, they were almost out of food. All they had left was a soup mix that everybody hated. The men survived by eating candles, bear oil, and two of their horses.

Today, people come to this part of Montana to hike and fish. Some come to follow the Lewis and Clark Trail to the Pacific. Luckily for these travelers, they don't have to eat candles or that awful soup to survive.

This old cabin lies along the Lewis and Clark National Historic Trail.

12.3 "Nature's Teakettles" in Wyoming's Yellowstone National Park

Lewis and Clark saw a lot of sights on their expedition. But they missed the geysers of Yellowstone National Park. A **geyser** is a spring that shoots hot water and steam into the air.

Geysers are sometimes called "nature's teakettles." Water is heated deep inside the Earth. When the water gets hot enough, it hisses and boils just like a teakettle on a stove. What happens when this boiling water reaches the Earth's surface? It shoots into the air.

There are about 10,000 hot springs, mud volcanoes, steam vents, and geysers in Yellowstone. A geyser named Old Faithful erupts in a cloud of steam every 30 to 90 minutes.

Fur trappers were some of the first Americans to see Yellowstone. No one believed their stories of steaming springs. Later on, a photographer took pictures of the geysers. People were impressed with the photographs. Many people wanted to protect the geysers and the beautiful land around them from development. In 1872, the U.S. government created Yellowstone National Park to do just that. It was the first national park in the world.

Only 300 people visited Yellowstone the year it became a park. But today, the park is very popular. Over 3 million people come to Wyoming to visit Yellowstone each year. Visitors enjoy the beauty of Yellowstone's mountains and meadows.

Each time it erupts, Old Faithful spews more than 10,000 gallons of boiling water about 170 feet skyward.

This wooden entrance leads to a mine under a hillside in Leadville, Colorado.

12.4 Leadville, Colorado: The West's Richest Silver Mining Town

Welcome to historic Leadville, Colorado. We are looking at the entrance to an old mine.

Leadville sits high in the Rocky Mountains. At 10,200 feet, it is one of our country's highest cities. In the past, it was also the West's wildest and richest silver mining town.

Miners first came to this area looking for gold. They found some, but it was hard to separate the gold from the local sand. In 1878, a mineral expert took a closer look at that pesky sand. Guess what he found? The sand was rich in both lead and silver!

The discovery of silver brought good times to Leadville. The city grew rapidly as miners flocked to the area. Then, in 1893, the silver boom ended. For a time, it looked as though Leadville would become an empty ghost town.

But Leadville was lucky. Other valuable minerals were found in this area. One is molybdenum. This metal is used to make high-strength steel. The town survived.

Today, Leadville is a tourist center. Some people come to learn about the history of this rich mining area. Others come to ski in winter or fish and hike in summer.

12.5 Sunny Southern California's Movie Industry

Watch your step! Look down at your feet and you will see stars set into the sidewalk. We are walking down Hollywood Boulevard. On this street, special movie, television, and music stars are honored with a star and their names placed in the sidewalk. This street in Los Angeles, California, is one of the most famous streets in the world.

Moviemaking is a giant industry in Southern California. America's first movies were made in the Northeast. But moviemakers needed sunny days to film outdoors. The Northeast is often cloudy and rainy. A few moviemakers found the sunshine they needed in Southern California. Others soon followed.

Today, thousands of people in Southern California work in the movie industry. Some work as writers, actors, set designers, and directors. Many more people work in jobs that help the movie industry. Some of these workers make costumes and equipment. Others provide important services such as transportation, food, and construction.

An artist creates a model of a dinosaur for a movie.

Each year, millions of tourists visit Southern California and enjoy its warm, sunny weather. Many of these tourists tour the movie studios, hoping to bump into a movie star at the same time!

12.6 California's Central Valley: America's Fruit and Salad Bowl

Do you snack on raisins? Spread strawberry jam on your toast? Look around you. Those foods probably came from California's Central Valley.

The Central Valley is shaped like a long bathtub. The sides are formed by mountain ranges. The bottom is covered with deep, rich soil. Summers here are long and warm.

Does this sound like a good place to farm? It is. But there is a problem. Almost no rain falls during the growing season.

California has solved this problem by building dams on rivers that flow down from the mountains. In winter, water collects behind the dams. In the summer, farmers use this water to irrigate crops.

Irrigation turned the Central Valley into what people call "America's fruit and salad bowl." Farmers here raise more than 300 crops, most of them fruits and vegetables. You probably eat some of them every day.

The Central Valley is also a center of farming technology. **Technology** is the use of tools and ideas to meet people's needs. Scientists here have invented many machines to help farmers pick their crops. One is a tomato-picking machine. It must be gentle so it won't crush the tomatoes. Scientists tested this machine with eggs. The machine can pick up an egg and pack it in a box—without breaking the egg!

technology the use of tools and ideas to meet people's needs

Farmers use a machine to harvest many California tomatoes at one time.

12.7 The Columbia River Gorge National Scenic Area

We have reached the Columbia River Gorge National Scenic Area. A **gorge** is a deep, narrow valley with steep walls. The Columbia River cut this beautiful gorge out of rock.

The Columbia River begins in the Rocky Mountains in Canada. It flows 1,200 miles south and west into the Pacific Ocean. For part of its journey, the river forms the boundary between the states of Washington and Oregon.

The Columbia looks lazy here. But don't let that fool you. This is one hardworking river. Dams on the river make a lot of electricity. Many businesses use this electric power. And farmers use water from the river to irrigate crops. Columbia River waters irrigate more than 8 million acres of land.

Farmers and businesspeople use the river for transportation. Many goods travel on the Columbia to shipping centers. It is one of the most traveled rivers in the country.

Putting the river to work has been good for people. Both Oregon and Washington are growing rapidly. But the use of the river has been bad for fish—especially salmon.

Since 1850, the number of salmon in the Columbia River has dropped sharply. Do you know why? You'll find out during our stop at the gorge.

Washington lies to the north of the Columbia River Gorge. Oregon lies to the south.

gorge a deep, narrow valley

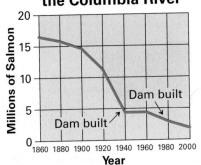

Salmon Returning to the Columbia River

Source: Pacific Salmon Coordination Office, U.S. Army Corps of Engineers

These stacks of lumber will eventually be shipped to customers around the world.

sawmill a factory where logs are turned into lumber

12.8 A Sawmill in Tacoma, Washington

Welcome to Tacoma, Washington. Tacoma was founded 150 years ago as a logging town. Today, Tacoma is still a center of the wood products industry. Wood products include lumber, plywood, cardboard, and paper.

Let's visit a **sawmill** in Tacoma. There are two things I like about touring a sawmill. The first is watching giant saws turn logs into lumber. The second is the smell of freshly sawed wood.

What I don't like is the noise. Every time a saw cuts into a log, it makes a screaming sound. When that happens, you may want to cover your ears.

Can you guess how much wood the average American uses each year? Over a ton! A lot of that wood is in the paper we use—681 pounds of paper per person. All that wood equals one 100-foot tall tree, 18 inches thick, for each American every year.

Much of that wood comes from the West. In the 1800s, forests attracted loggers and lumbermen to this region. The mountains of the West were covered with forests. Today, many westerners still work in the lumber industry.

We are heading now for Seattle-Tacoma International Airport. We'll take a plane to our next stop.

12.9 Anchorage, Alaska: Starting Point of the Iditarod

We are in Anchorage, Alaska. Alaska is by far the largest of the 50 states. Yet it has one of the lowest populations of any state. Can you guess why?

One reason is its chilly climate. Alaska is farther from the equator than any other state. This makes Alaska our coldest state. Its winters are so cold that car door handles can freeze and snap off in your hand.

People have been attracted to Alaska by its resources. In 1898, gold was discovered near the town of Nome. Within two years, Nome grew to more than 20,000 people. Another rush of people came in the 1960s. That was when oil was discovered in northern Alaska.

Today, many people come to Alaska to enjoy its open spaces and outdoor activities. A favorite sport here is dogsled racing. Alaskans used to depend on dogsleds to get around in winter. Now, they use airplanes and snowmobiles.

The most famous dogsled race is the Iditarod, held each year in March. The Iditarod begins right here in Anchorage. It ends 1,150 miles away in Nome. A few teams of dogs and their mushers, or drivers, cover that distance in an amazing 9 to 12 days. No wonder Alaskans call this event the "Last Great Race on Earth."

Iditarod teams usually have 12 to 16 dogs. The dogs pull the sled at an average speed of about 10 miles per hour.

12.10 Honolulu, Hawaii: A Tourist Paradise

Step out of the airplane into the warm sunshine. You have just flown from our country's coldest state to one of its warmest. Hawaii lies closer to the equator than any other U.S. state. Its climate is sunny and warm all year round.

Look at beautiful Waikiki Beach in Honolulu, Hawaii. I grew up near here. My father gave me my first surfing lesson at Waikiki. Maybe I'll have a chance to teach you how to surf here.

Today, tourists from all over the world enjoy this sunny beach. Tourism is Hawaii's most important industry. But it wasn't always such a big deal.

A hundred years ago, the main industry on the Hawaiian Islands was raising sugarcane. Hawaii's sugar planters needed lots of workers for their plantations. Those workers came from China, Japan, the Philippines, Portugal, and other places.

My great-great-grandparents came to Hawaii from Japan around 1890. They planned to work in the sugar fields for

a few years and then return home. But they liked Hawaii and decided to stay.

My grandfather remembers when jet airplanes began flying to Hawaii. That was in the late 1950s. Airplanes made it easier for tourists to come to Hawaii. Today, many jobs in Hawaii are related to tourism. So we are very happy that you are visiting our islands.

Thousands of tourists enjoy swimming, surfing, and sailing at Waikiki Beach each year.

Summary

What an awesome tour! We began high in the Rocky Mountains and ended up on Waikiki Beach. Along the way, we saw sights in eight states.

What was your favorite stop? The mine entrance in Leadville? Southern California? The Columbia River? Can you guess mine? It's Waikiki Beach, of course.

Remember the two questions I asked when we began our tour? What first attracted people to the West? And why are people still coming here today?

Here are my answers to the first question. People first came to the West in search of adventure, opportunity, and sunshine. The West had beautiful places to explore. It had valuable natural resources. These resources included furs, gold, silver, oil, and forests. And it had a climate that attracted farmers and moviemakers.

My answers to the second question are the same. People still come to the West for adventure, opportunity, and sunshine. The adventures have changed. We now hike and ski in the region where Lewis and Clark once almost starved.

The opportunities have changed too. Today, there are many jobs in the tourism and entertainment industries.

But the sunshine is the same—warm and bright. I hope you had fun in the sun on our trip.

Aloha!

The Golden Gate Bridge spans the San Francisco Bay. Thousands of tourists enjoy walking across this bridge each year.

Exploring the Pacific Crest Trail

At one end is the Mexican border. At the other end is Canada. In between stretches the Pacific Crest Trail. The trail rambles across deserts, over mountains, and along lakeshores. What can this trail teach us about the West?

In the 1930s, Clinton C. Clarke had a big idea: building a hiking trail from Mexico to Canada. Its path would follow the Pacific Crest. This ridge of mountains runs through California, Oregon, and Washington. Clarke wanted to preserve some of the beautiful wild areas of the West and help people enjoy the outdoors.

Making Clarke's idea happen was not easy. Some parts of the trail were already in place. But much of it was little more than a line on a map. The line showed the basic direction the trail would follow. But someone needed to walk and mark the trail Clarke had mapped out.

The person chosen for that job was a young man named Warren Rogers. As a child, Rogers had had a terrible disease called polio. It had harmed his legs, and he walked with a limp. Yet he still loved hiking and climbing.

In 1935, Rogers organized hikers into teams. For the next four summers, he led them in exploring different parts of the trail. The teams took notes on what they found. They mapped out a good route for the trail.

Rogers reached the end of the route in 1938. But it took decades of work before the trail itself was fully built. Not until 1993 did workers finally complete the Pacific Crest Trail.

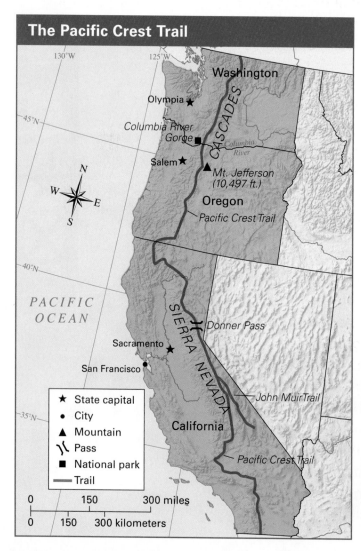

The Pacific Crest Trail

Washington
Olympia ★
Columbia River Gorge ■
CASCADES
Columbia River
Salem ★
▲ Mt. Jefferson (10,497 ft.)
Oregon
Pacific Crest Trail

PACIFIC OCEAN

SIERRA NEVADA
Donner Pass
Sacramento ★
San Francisco ●
John Muir Trail
California
Pacific Crest Trail

★ State capital
● City
▲ Mountain
)(Pass
■ National park
— Trail

0   150   300 miles
0   150   300 kilometers

130°W   125°W   45°N   40°N   35°N

Walking the Trail

Let's hike the Pacific Crest Trail. We will need to start in the spring and end in the fall. Climbing the trail's mountains in the winter is too dangerous. We'll also need to move quickly. To finish our hike we must cover about 17 miles each day.

The trail in Southern California is hot and dry. It winds through desertlike areas and over small mountains. Watch out for rattlesnakes!

The Sierra Nevada of central California are breathtaking. Now we're hiking between 8,000 and 13,000 feet above sea level. Brrrr! You usually find snow and ice here—even in midsummer. This stretch of trail is very wild. We might hike for 200 miles without crossing a road. Look out for coyotes, deer, and bears!

The Cascade Range will take us through Northern California, Oregon, and into Washington. These mountains were made by volcanoes. The forests here are thick and lush. The trail passes by many lakes and streams. We cross from Oregon to Washington over the beautiful Columbia River Gorge.

Get out your rain gear now. The Northern Cascades have very rainy weather. The wet climate helps rich forests grow. It also helps huckleberry bushes grow. If the time is right, we can feast on berries here—a tasty end to our trip.

Hikers face challenging terrain at many places along the trail.

Mount Jefferson offers hikers a dramatic view of the Cascade Range.

History Along the Trail

Hikers on the Pacific Crest Trail see beautiful scenery. But they also take a historical journey. The trail passes a number of key places in the history of the West.

Mount Jefferson, in the Cascade Mountains of Oregon, honors President Thomas Jefferson. In the early 1800s, it was Jefferson who picked Meriwether Lewis and William Clark to explore the nation's new territory in the West. Jefferson had purchased this land, called the Louisiana Territory, from France. Lewis and Clark mapped much of the territory, including areas along the Pacific Crest. On their trip, they named a mountain after the president.

High in the Sierra Nevada, the Pacific Crest Trail climbs through the Donner Pass. Here, in 1846, a group of settlers moving west tried to cross the mountains. Snowstorms forced them to spend a terrible winter in the mountains. Many of them died. The famous story of the Donner party reminds us of the challenges faced by early settlers of the West.

The trail also passes through gold country. In 1848, a man named James Marshall found gold in California. Thousands of gold-seekers flocked there to get rich. The gold rush changed the West forever. It brought new people and ideas to the region. New settlers built great cities such as San Francisco and Sacramento. These settlers helped create the modern states we know today.

Walking the John Muir Trail

A special path runs near the Pacific Crest Trail in the Sierra Nevada. It is known as the John Muir Trail.

John Muir lived in the late 1800s and early 1900s. He deeply loved the outdoors. He believed strongly in protecting the nation's great natural wonders. Muir was a leader of the effort to create our national parks. "Wildness," he said, "is a necessity."

Muir traveled widely. He explored parts of the United States—and beyond. But his favorite place on Earth was the Sierra Nevada. He called it the "range of light." Muir said that it was "the most divinely beautiful of all the mountain chains I have ever seen."

The John Muir Trail gives hikers a chance to experience the wilderness as John Muir did. The land around the trail looks very much as it did in the past. Hikers on this isolated trail catch a glimpse into the history of the West. They get to see the natural wonders that make this part of our country so special.

John Muir

Hikers on the John Muir Trail see the Sierra Nevada as Muir did.

Cities of the West

What attracts people to the cities of the West?

13.1 Introduction

"Go west, young man, and grow up with the country!" In the 1850s, these words were heard all over the United States. Americans have been following this advice ever since.

Americans have long viewed the West as a place to start new lives. In the 1800s, the West's wide-open spaces attracted farmers, miners, and ranchers. These pioneers loaded up their belongings in covered wagons and made the long trek west. A pioneer is someone who is among the first people to settle a region. Today, the West still has mines, ranches, and lots of land. It also has lively cities that draw people from around the world.

In this chapter, you will learn about seven of these cities. For each one, you'll visit an interesting place that tells something important about the city. As you read, ask yourself, "What is attracting people to the West today?"

Television Commercial Promoting the West

Cities of the WEST...

diverse people, jobs, and recreation that are the BEST!

POWER CHANNEL VOLUME

Denver is one of the nation's fastest-growing cities.

mint a factory where coins are made

13.2 Denver, Colorado

Denver, the capital city of Colorado, is home to the U.S. Mint. A **mint** is where coins—such as pennies, nickels, dimes, and quarters—are made. Back in the 1860s, miners brought their gold here. Their nuggets were melted and turned into valuable gold bars. The mint began producing gold and silver coins in 1906. Today, the mint makes about 50 million coins every day!

Geography

Denver sits where the Great Plains meet the Rocky Mountains. It is known as the "Mile-High City." If you stand on the 18th step of the state capitol building, you'll be exactly 5,280 feet, or one mile, above sea level. By the way, the dome of the capitol building is covered with real Colorado gold.

Denver has a dry, sunny climate. The city gets snow in the winter. To see how Denver's climate compares with those of other cities in the West, look at the chart on page 219.

History

Denver was founded in 1858 after people discovered gold in the area. Smaller mining communities grew up around the city.

During World War II, many U.S. government offices moved to Denver. When the war ended, many government workers decided to stay there.

Population

In 2006, more than half a million people lived in Denver. To see how Denver's population compares with those of other cities in the West, look at the chart on page 219.

Rodeo fans watch cowboys and cowgirls compete in events. These include bronco riding, calf roping, and steer wrestling.

The city's population is becoming more diverse. About one-half of Denver's residents are white. More than one-third are Latino. About one-tenth of the population is African American.

Economy

Many people in Denver work for the U.S. government. In fact, Denver has more government workers than Washington, D.C. Many large companies are also located in Denver.

Ways to Have Fun

Denver offers lots of opportunities to have fun. The city has more than 250 parks with trails for cycling, running, and walking. Denver even has a park where a herd of bison lives.

Denver is the center of professional sports in the Rocky Mountain region. The city's major league teams include the Denver Broncos (football), the Colorado Rockies (baseball), the Denver Nuggets (basketball), and the Colorado Avalanche (ice hockey). Every January, Denver hosts a national cattle show and rodeo.

Salt Lake City is the capital of Utah. It is named for the huge saltwater lake that lies west of the city.

Mormon a member of the Church of Jesus Christ of Latter-day Saints

13.3 Salt Lake City, Utah

If you stand in the center of downtown Salt Lake City, Utah, you will be in Temple Square. In front of you will be a huge white building, the Mormon Temple. Temple Square has always been the heart of Salt Lake City. The city was started by a group of people called **Mormons**. Mormons are members of the Church of Jesus Christ of Latter Day Saints. The Mormons built the city around their temple. The temple itself took 40 years to build.

Geography

Salt Lake City is in the north-central part of Utah. It is located in a high valley between the Wasatch Mountains and the Great Salt Lake Desert.

The climate in Salt Lake City is dry. The city has warm summers and some snow in the winter. (See the chart on page 219.)

History

Mormons founded Salt Lake City in 1847. They wanted a place where they could freely practice their religion. When they first arrived at the site of the city, it was a desertlike area. The Mormons used irrigation to bring water to the dry valley. They turned the desert into farmland.

In the 1880s, Salt Lake City's population more than doubled because of nearby mining. The city grew again during World War II. The government needed metal for ships and planes. So, more people came to work in the mines. After the war ended, many wartime workers stayed in the Salt Lake City area.

Population

In 2006, almost 180,000 people lived in Salt Lake City. (See the chart on page 219.) If you include the nearby towns, more than 1 million people live in the area.

Salt Lake City's population was once almost entirely white. But it has become more diverse. Whites make up almost seven-tenths of the city's population. Latinos are the second largest group, at more than two-tenths of the population. African Americans, American Indians, Asian Americans, and Pacific Islanders make up another one-tenth of the population.

People of all ages enjoy cross-country skiing in the Wasatch Mountains.

Economy

Mining is one of Salt Lake City's most important industries. Copper, silver, lead, zinc, coal, and iron ore are all mined nearby.

Ways to Have Fun

The Wasatch Mountains tower over Salt Lake City. They are a wonderful place for hiking and skiing. Because of this, Salt Lake City was chosen as the site of the 2002 Winter Olympics. The city also has many parks.

Salt Lake City has one major league sports team, the Utah Jazz (basketball).

13.4 Boise, Idaho

The summer is a fun time to visit Boise, Idaho. The weather is usually warm then. Some people start their day with an early-morning hot-air balloon ride. Then they might go fishing, hiking, or rafting down a nearby river.

People also walk or bike along the river that runs right through Boise. You can even float down the river in an inner tube or raft. And many families gather downtown once a week. There, people listen to live music, have picnics, and relax.

Geography

Boise is located on the Boise River in southwestern Idaho. It is near the Salmon River Mountains. Boise has a dry, sunny climate, with some snow in the winter. (See the chart on page 219.)

History

Boise was founded in 1863, following the discovery of gold in the region. The U.S. government built a fort near the Boise River. The city arose next to the fort.

Boise grew rapidly as miners rushed to the goldfields. Many of the miners were immigrants from China. In 1925, the Union Pacific Railroad ran its main line through Boise. This brought even more people to the city. Boise continued to grow in the 1980s, when new electronics factories created more jobs.

The state capitol building in Boise uses hot water pumped from the ground for heat. The water comes from natural hot springs that run below the area.

Population

Between 1990 and 2006, Boise's population grew from about 125,000 people to more than 204,000. (See the chart on page 219.) If you count nearby towns, more than 400,000 people live in the Boise area.

Almost nine-tenths of Boise's people are white. The next largest group is Latinos. They make up close to one-tenth of the population. The rest of Boise's population includes Asian Americans, African Americans, and American Indians.

Economy

Boise provides banking, shopping, and health services for many people. Companies that make computer chips and wood and paper products are also important in Boise.

Ways to Have Fun

Many people in Boise enjoy the outdoors. There are lots of paths for walking, bicycling, skating, and jogging. In a set of parks called the Greenbelt, people picnic, play sports, watch birds, and listen to concerts. Places for skiing and whitewater rafting are within an easy drive of the city.

Sports fans in Boise can root for the city's minor league baseball and ice hockey teams.

Fly-fishing is a popular sport in and around Boise.

Seattle is Washington's largest city. A fleet of ferryboats helps connect the city to other parts of the state and to Canada.

13.5 Seattle, Washington

The best place to see Seattle, Washington, is from the top of the city's most famous landmark, the Space Needle. An elevator lifts you 52 stories above the ground. From there, you can look out at Seattle's skyscrapers and the ferryboats crossing Elliott Bay.

The Space Needle was built for the 1962 World's Fair. It still looks like something out of the future. That makes it a perfect landmark for this modern city.

Geography

Seattle is in the northwestern corner of the United States, about 100 miles south of the border with Canada. The city lies next to a large bay of the Pacific Ocean. Mountains surround it.

Seattle has a mild, rainy climate. The city is often cloudy or foggy. (See the chart on page 219.)

History

Seattle was founded in 1851 by a small group of settlers. The city grew rapidly in the late 1800s with the growth of the timber industry and the discovery of gold. Miners poured into Seattle on their way to the goldfields. When the gold rush was over, many of them settled in the city.

Population

In 2006, over half a million people lived in Seattle. (See the chart on page 219.) More than 3 million people live in the surrounding area. This is one of the fastest-growing areas in the United States.

Whites make up just over two-thirds of Seattle's population. The next-largest groups are Asian Americans (more than one-tenth of the population), African Americans (about one-tenth), and Latinos (less than one-tenth).

Economy

Seattle is an important U.S. shipping port. There, many goods are traded with Japan and the rest of Asia. Fishing and the lumber industry are also important to the economy of Seattle.

For many years, most jobs in Seattle were at a company that made airplanes. Today, many people work in the computer industry.

Miles of paved trails make Seattle a great city for outdoor activities.

Ways to Have Fun

Seattle has more than 5,000 acres of public land. People enjoy miles of trails on which they can cycle, skate, jog, and walk. The nearby mountains offer excellent skiing, climbing, and hiking. Mount Rainier is a favorite hiking destination. And the area's many lakes make boating and fishing popular pastimes.

Seattle has three major league sports teams. They are the Mariners (baseball), the Seahawks (football), and the Supersonics (basketball).

The Willamette River winds through Portland.

13.6 Portland, Oregon

In spring, roses bloom in gardens all over the city of Portland, Oregon. In fact, one of Portland's biggest attractions is the International Rose Test Garden. Here you can see 10,000 rosebushes and more than 500 varieties of roses in all colors. Some people call Portland the "City of Roses."

Geography

Portland sits on the banks of the Willamette River, in northwestern Oregon. The city lies in a fertile valley between the Coast and Cascade mountain ranges.

Portland has a mild climate, with heavy rains in the late fall and winter. (See the chart on page 219.)

History

Portland got its start in 1845. Settlers arrived by the thousands over the Oregon Trail. During the California gold rush, Portland grew rapidly. Settlers sold lumber and grain to miners and their families in California.

Portland continued to grow at a steady pace. In 1905, a world's fair brought 3 million visitors to the city. Many of them decided to stay. In the 1930s, dams on the Columbia and Willamette rivers provided cheap electricity. This brought a number of industries to Portland. During World War II, thousands of workers arrived in the city to build ships for the United States Navy.

Population

In 2006, Portland's population was more than half a million people. (See the chart on page 219.) Close to 2 million people live in the city and its surrounding areas.

People of all ages enjoy walking and hiking in Portland's many parks.

About three-fourths of Portland's residents are white. Most of the rest of the population is divided equally among Latinos, African Americans, and Asian Americans.

Economy

People in Portland work for many different kinds of companies. Some companies make paper. Others make clothing and shoes. Portland also has new businesses, such as computer software companies.

Portland's harbor is one of the busiest in the country. Shipping companies have operated there for many years.

Ways to Have Fun

Portland has many parks and open spaces. Forest Park covers nearly 5,000 acres. It is one of the largest natural areas inside a U.S. city. Mount Hood, located less than 50 miles away from Portland, is a great place for skiing and other winter sports. Portland has one major league sports team, the Portland Trail Blazers (basketball).

San Jose is the largest city in Northern California. It has more than 2,000 miles of streets.

13.7 San Jose, California

People often call San Jose, California, the "Capital of Silicon Valley." Silicon Valley is a nickname for the area between the cities of San Jose and San Francisco. Silicon is a material used to make computers. The first computer companies began in Silicon Valley in the 1970s.

Geography

San Jose lies near the southern tip of San Francisco Bay. The city has a mild to warm climate. (See the chart on page 219.)

History

Spanish settlers founded San Jose in 1777. For many years, the area was home to vineyards and orchards. World War II brought new businesses and people to the city. By 1980, the city had grown to almost 10 times the size it was in 1950.

Population

San Jose's population reached more than 900,000 by the year 2006. (See the chart on page 219.)

The population is very diverse. About one-third of the people are white, one-third are Latinos, and one-third are Asian Americans. African Americans and American Indians also live in San Jose.

Economy

The San Jose region is famous for its technology companies. Silicon Valley is home to some of the most successful technology companies in the world. Thousands of computer and engineering students attend San Jose State University and other area schools. Many of them work in San Jose's technology companies after graduation.

Ways to Have Fun

San Jose has about 75 parks and playgrounds. The largest park is Alum Rock Park. It has miles of trails for hiking and horseback riding. Fans of thrill rides can go to amusement parks in nearby Santa Clara and Santa Cruz.

San Jose has two major league sports teams, the Sharks (ice hockey) and the Earthquakes (soccer).

Many people in San Jose work in the technology field.

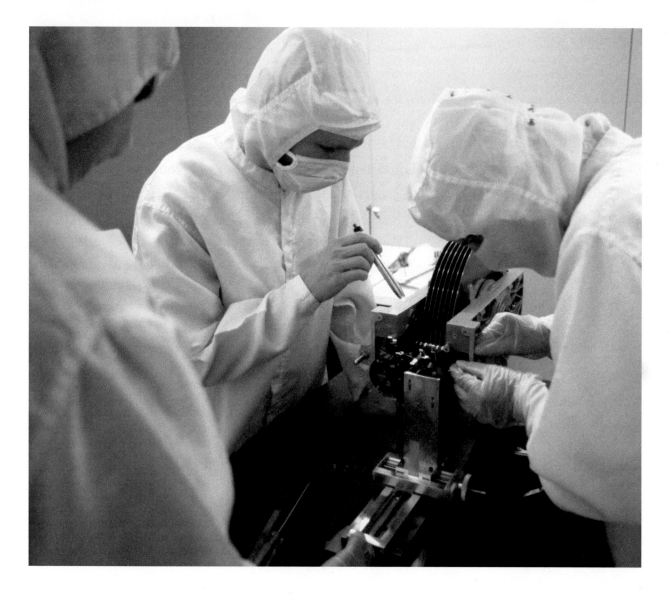

Las Vegas comes alive at night. It is the largest city in Nevada.

13.8 Las Vegas, Nevada

If you drive into Las Vegas, Nevada, you will see a sign that reads, "Welcome to Fabulous Las Vegas, Nevada." And fabulous is certainly the word for this city of bright lights and hotels. All around, colorful signs advertise music, comedy, and magic shows. It's no wonder many people call Las Vegas the "Entertainment Capital of the World."

Geography

Las Vegas is near the southern tip of Nevada. It sits in a desert valley surrounded by mountains.

Las Vegas has a dry climate. Winters are warm, and summers are hot. (See chart on page 219.)

History

oasis a place in the desert that has water and trees

Las Vegas lies in one of the few places in a desert that has water and trees. Such a place is called an **oasis**. American Indian tribes roamed the area thousands of years ago. In the late 1820s, Spanish explorers came upon the oasis. Settlers soon followed.

Las Vegas remained a small town until the 1930s. Then construction began on the Hoover Dam. The dam project created thousands of new jobs. Many of the workers stayed to settle in Las Vegas.

After World War II, Las Vegas grew rapidly as many hotels were built. Today, about 30 million visitors come to Las Vegas every year.

Population

In 2006, more than half a million people lived in Las Vegas. (See the chart on page 219.) Half of the city's people are white. The next largest group is Latinos, who make up one-third of the population. African Americans are more than one-tenth of the population, and Asian Americans are less than one-tenth.

Economy

Tourism is a big business in Las Vegas. The city's restaurants, hotels, and shops provide thousands of jobs. There is also great demand for home building and landscaping.

Ways to Have Fun

Las Vegas is famous for its shows. Many popular singers, dancers, and comics perform there. Championship boxing matches are often held in the city.

People in Las Vegas also enjoy outdoor activities. They can hike and camp. They can fish and boat on nearby lakes. And the Grand Canyon is only a five-hour drive from the city.

The building of new hotels and other structures in Las Vegas creates many construction jobs.

City Temperatures and Populations

City	Average January Temperature	Average July Temperature	Population
Denver	43.3°F	88.1°F	566,974
Salt Lake City	37.7°F	92.2°F	178,858
Boise	37.0°F	89.9°F	204,027
Seattle	45.8°F	75.2°F	562,106
Portland	46.0°F	80.1°F	539,950
San Jose	48.8°F	71.4°F	916,220
Las Vegas	57.0°F	104.1°F	569,753

Sources: Temperature data from the National Weather Service Forecast Office, based on monthly averages for the years 1971–2000. Population data from the U.S. Census Bureau, 2006 American Community Survey.

Summary

For more than 200 years, Americans have been moving west to start new lives. Today, the West still attracts people from all around the world. Of course, they don't arrive in covered wagons. And few will start a farm or a ranch. Instead, many are settling down in the West's thriving cities.

Have you discovered what attracts newcomers to the West today? Here are some attractions:

- scenery
- climate
- diverse populations
- new businesses and industries
- recreational opportunities

What do you think you might like in the cities of the West?

Portland, Oregon: Green and Clean

Portland, Oregon, has always been a beautiful place. That was true when the first white settlers chose the spot in the 1840s. As the city has grown, it has found ways to add more beauty—and to help keep Earth clean. What features help make Portland a city known for being green and clean?

It's not hard to imagine why people were first drawn to the area that is now Portland. In the distance rises magnificent Mount Hood. Covered with snow year round, the great peak stands like a guard over the surrounding land. It is truly an impressive sight.

Then there are the rivers. Portland sits where the Columbia and Willamette rivers come together. These rivers add to Portland's beauty. They provided resources such as water and fish. They helped make Portland an inviting place to settle.

And people did settle Portland. After its founding, lots of people moved in and set up lives in the new town. Many came to make their living by fishing. Others came to take trees from the rich forests. Some came to grow crops. Still others came as part of the many gold rushes in the West.

Portland's Washington Park offers breathtaking views of the city and Mount Hood.

The people of Portland live in a place full of natural beauty. Many of them work to keep it that way. The many roses there are a colorful example of this. These flowers earned Portland the nickname "City of Roses."

Roses have probably grown on the West Coast since before Portland was founded. Settlers brought bushes from the East. And the people of Portland really took to the plant. They found that their climate was perfect for growing roses.

Georgiana Pittock was a rose grower in Portland. In 1888, she started the Portland Rose Society. Its purpose was to get more people to grow and display roses. It was the first group of its kind in the country.

The Rose Society was a success. In 1905, Portland hosted a world's fair. The city lined its streets with flowers. Then, in 1907, Portland held a Rose Festival. It included a spectacular rose parade. Thousands of people celebrated the city's love for roses.

Portland still holds its Rose Festival every spring. Two million people come to the city to take part!

While in town, many visitors stop at the International Rose Test Garden. Since 1917, growers have been creating new types of roses there. The garden is a magnificent sight. It really helps the city live up to its nickname.

Visitors enjoy the thousands of rose plants tested and cared for at the International Rose Test Garden.

Georgiana Pittock

Laurelhurst Park offers hiking and biking paths, and play and picnic areas, as well as lots of shade for city residents.

The people of Portland do not stop at filling their city with flowers. They have a long tradition of keeping their city green.

From its earliest days, Portland has set aside land for parks. The settlers built a bustling city. But they wanted to make sure they had natural places, too.

Including natural places in a city can be a hard task. After all, a modern city needs highways for people and businesses to use. It needs buildings and parking lots. In Portland, people have put firm limits on this.

For example, in the 1970s, a wide highway ran along Portland's riverfront. The city decided to dig it up. In its place, they put a park. There, people can enjoy the outdoors and the beauty of the river.

Portland has many other parks, too. In fact, one out of every ten acres in the city is part of a park. There are also miles and miles of trails for people to wander. Portland is proud of the many outdoor recreation opportunities it offers.

One special Portland site is a huge wilderness area called Forest Park. A million people visit this park each year. They hike on nearly 70 miles of trails. They view interesting and unusual plants and birds. The park helps people escape from the busy city life for a time.

People in Portland want to keep their city clean as well as green. They are known for their work to protect the environment.

Look at the city's miles of bike paths, for example. These paths make it easy for people to get around by bike. Since cars cause air pollution, riding bikes instead of driving helps keep the air clean. In 2007, more than 14,000 riders cycled through the city each day.

Many other people use the city's public transportation system. You can ride it for free in the downtown area. This makes people want to use buses and trains. When they do, that too means fewer cars on the road.

Portland is also a leader in recycling. The city, along with the rest of Oregon, was the first place to require people to pay a small fee for each beverage bottle they buy. Buyers get the money back when they return the empty bottle for recycling. Many other states now use this program.

Portland was the first city to take action against greenhouse gases. Many scientists think these gases may harm the environment. In 1993, Portland made a plan to cut greenhouse gases. The plan worked. Portland now produces less greenhouse gas than it used to.

Portland is a city that believes in being green and clean. This is a big draw for people looking to visit—or live—there.

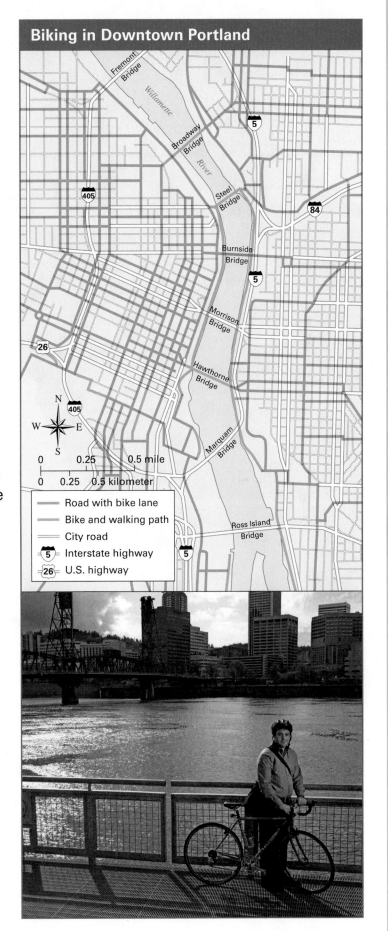

Biking in Downtown Portland

Road with bike lane
Bike and walking path
City road
Interstate highway
U.S. highway

Researching Your State's Geography

How has geography influenced life in your state?

14

14.1 Introduction

Suppose that you are flying in an airplane over your state. When you look down, do you see mountains or flat plains? A desert or a sandy coast? Are there lots of trees, lakes, and rivers? Is it cloudy? Or is the sun shining brightly on your state?

These features of land, water, and sky are all part of your state's **physical geography**. Studying the physical geography of a place is very important. It helps explain why and how people live in a place.

From your plane, you can also see cities and towns, roads and highways, bridges and dams. Geography includes the study of human features as well. **Human geography** explores how people have altered, or changed, their environment to make life more comfortable.

Now suppose that you are a geographer. What can you find out about the physical and human geography of your state? How do you think geography has influenced life in your state?

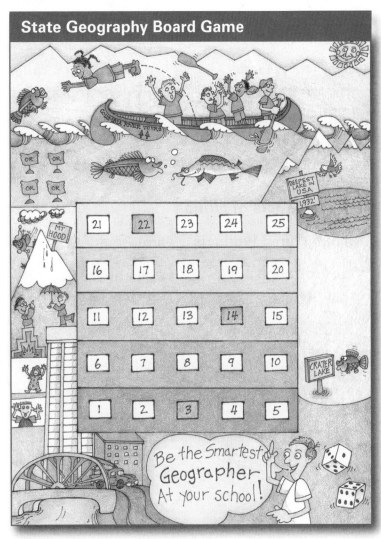

State Geography Board Game

14.2 Tools Geographers Use

Geographers use many tools to learn about places and the people who live there. Some of these tools are maps, charts, and graphs. They help organize facts and information.

In Chapter 2, you learned about three kinds of maps. They are physical, political, and special-purpose maps. You might use maps to help you discover facts about your state's geography. What could you learn about your state from a physical map or a political map? What could you discover from a special-purpose map that shows the growing seasons in your state?

You can also get interesting facts from charts and graphs. A chart might give information about industries in your state. These facts might give you clues about the natural resources in your area. Or you might find a graph showing the average monthly temperatures and rainfall in your state. What could these facts tell you about how people work and play in your state?

The facts you can study about a group of people are called **demographics**. Such facts might include the average age of people in a state. They might compare the number of men to the number of women living in a state. This information often appears on charts and graphs, too.

demographics the facts you can study about a certain group of people, such as their ages, genders, or jobs

Geographers use maps, charts, and graphs to organize information. What do these tools tell you about Florida?

Major Products of Florida

Manufactured Products	Farm Products
Transportation equipment	Cattle, hogs, and chickens
Electronic equipment	Citrus fruits
Chemicals	Vegetables
Machinery	Melons
	Potatoes
	Sugarcane
	Strawberries

People of Florida

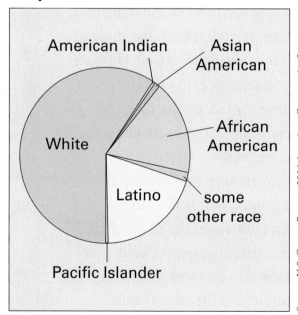

Source: U.S. Census Bureau, 2006 American Community Survey

14.3 Connecting Geography and History

When you study geography, you unlock lots of information. The history of a place is closely linked to its geography. The land and its features help tell the story of a place. They help shape how people live and how communities grow.

Think about Jamestown. This was the first permanent English settlement in America. In Chapter 6, you read how the site the Jamestown settlers chose caused problems. The land was swampy. Many people got sick and died. But the land and climate were good for growing tobacco. Growing this crop helped the colony survive.

In Chapter 7, you learned about the fall line on the edge of the Southeast's coastal plain. As English settlement spread, many settlers chose this point to live. They used falling water to power mills. They set up trading posts for farmers. Over time, cities were built along the fall line.

The land shaped the history of other parts of the country, too. St. Louis, Missouri, was founded near where two great rivers meet. This spot was a good departure point for western pioneers.

The history of the Southwest follows the path of the Colorado River. This waterway supported the region's first people. It helped attract modern-day settlers. People still depend on the river. What is the physical geography of your state? How might the land have helped shape your state's history?

This photograph was taken from space. It shows St. Louis, Missouri, and the rivers nearby.

14.4 Connecting Geography and Economics

Geography also helps us understand economics. Geography helps explain how certain industries have grown. It helps us understand how and why people work the way they do.

Think about the Midwest, for example. This region is perfect for farming. The land is very flat. The soil is fertile. Rivers help farmers ship crops to market. It is no surprise that agriculture is a major industry there.

Some parts of the country are rich in resources such as coal, oil, or silver. Others have pleasant climates or scenery. In the Northeast, harbors provide access to the sea. No wonder people use these resources to make a living. No wonder these industries help define these regions.

Geographers also study how people change the land. Recall from Chapter 8 that people in Michigan built the Soo Locks to connect two of the Great Lakes. The locks allow ships to carry goods from one lake to another. Elsewhere, people built canals. They constructed dams. These modifications have changed the way people live and work.

Think about the geography of your state. What natural features exist? How have people made changes to the land? What does the human geography tell you about the economy there?

Some industries develop in unlikely places. Here, sprinklers move in a circle to water fields in a dry part of Utah.

14.5 Finding Out About the Geography of Your State

There are many ways to research the geography of your state. Try these sources of information:

Atlases and encyclopedias. An atlas is a book of maps. An encyclopedia is a book of facts about all kinds of topics. Find a map of your state in an atlas. Look up your state in an encyclopedia.

The Internet. The Internet is a fast way to find information. First, connect to the Internet on a computer. Then, type in the name of your state plus a word such as *geography* or *climate*. Read the list of Web sites that appear on the screen. Click on any that sound interesting.

Libraries. Start your research in the reference section of the library. Look for books, newspaper and magazine articles, journals, and diaries about your state. Maps, drawings, and photographs might be interesting, too. Ask a librarian for help.

Chambers of commerce. Most cities and towns have an office called the chamber of commerce. You can visit yours. There you will find brochures, maps, postcards, and books about your state's geography and attractions.

State departments of tourism. Try writing to your state's department of tourism for information. Or visit its Web site on the Internet.

A U.S. atlas is a good place to look for geographic information about your state. It may include a few types of maps for each state.

geographic inquiry process a five-step process that helps answer geographic questions

14.6 Using the Geographic Inquiry Process

Knowing good sources of information can help you learn about your state. It also helps to have a process, or a set of steps, you can follow to achieve a goal. By following the **geographic inquiry process,** you can enjoy a more rewarding study of your state.

Step 1 is asking geographic questions. These are questions about what your state and its people are like. Say you live in Florida. You could ask these geographic questions about the state: Where do people live in my state? Why do people live there? How have people made changes to my state? What are some resources of my state? How do people use these resources?

Step 2 is acquiring geographic information. Once you have asked geographic questions, you need to look for information that will give you answers. You read about some of the tools and sources of information geographers use. These are ways of answering the questions. What kinds of tools would you use to answer the questions you asked in Step 1? What kinds of maps could you use? Where might you search for information?

Step 3 is organizing geographic information. You have collected data about your state. Now you need to put it into a useful form. This will help you find the data easily in later steps of the process.

What are some ways of organizing information? One is to make tables. Suppose you have found information about Florida's largest cities. You might make a table like the one at right. Maps are another useful tool. You could use your table to make a population map.

Step 4 is analyzing geographic information. The goal is to find patterns in what you have organized. Suppose you are making a map to show Florida's cities. Once you put the cities on the map, you would see that many of the large ones are along the coast.

Step 5 is answering geographic questions. Let's say you had asked, "Where do people live in my state?" By following Steps 1–4, you will find your answer. For Florida, you would find that many people live in coastal cities.

This is the end of the inquiry process. But it is also the beginning! Often, one answer will lead to new questions. Next you may wonder why so many cities were built along the coast. The process of learning never ends!

Cities in Florida	
City	Population
Jacksonville	794,555
Miami	404,048
Tampa	332,888

If you were researching cities in Florida, you would find out that Miami sits in the southeastern part of the state. It lies right along the coast.

Uncovering the Secrets of Ozette

Students are not the only ones who research the geography of their states. Archaeologists in the state of Washington spent years learning about an old American Indian village called Ozette. How did physical and human geography help them?

Long before Europeans came to North America, an American Indian tribe lived in the forests and along the coast of what is now the state of Washington. They were the Makahs (mah-KAWS).

The Makahs had five villages. One village was Ozette. Makahs lived at Ozette for thousands of years. But at some point, the village disappeared. Makah legend says that it was buried in an enormous mudslide several hundred years ago.

In the 1960s, an archaeologist named Richard Daugherty became interested in Ozette. He had a lot of questions. What happened to Ozette? Where had it been located? Could he find it?

Daugherty got permission to dig in the area from the Makah leader. Daugherty then found some evidence of Ozette. But he did not have enough time or money to continue digging.

The Makahs live at the tip of a stretch of land called the Olympic Peninsula. The area has both forests and coastal land.

Home of the Makahs

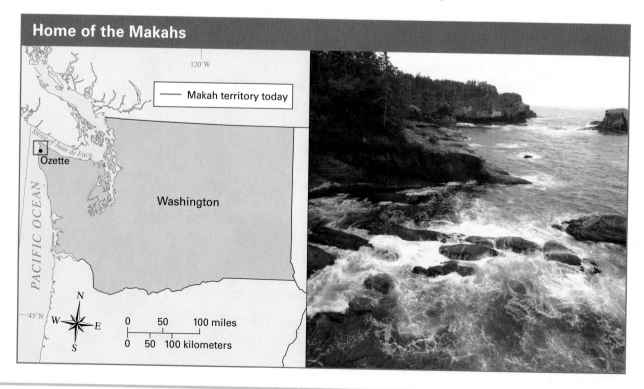

Makah territory today

Ozette

PACIFIC OCEAN

Strait of Juan de Fuca

Washington

125°W   120°W

45°N

N W E S

0   50   100 miles
0   50   100 kilometers

Geographic Research Solves a Mystery

In 1970, a huge storm hit Washington. Winds, rain, and waves from the Pacific Ocean pounded the coast. When the storm finally ended, people found old wooden items, such as canoe paddles, parts of homes, and fishing tools. Daugherty felt sure they were from Ozette.

Daugherty had always wanted to return to Ozette. Now, it seemed his chance had come. With a team of scientists and students, he spent the next 11 years investigating Ozette. Each new discovery they made answered some questions—and raised others.

When the team uncovered a village buried under 10 feet of mud, they knew the Makah legend was true. But where had the mud come from? And when exactly had the mudslide happened?

To learn about weather patterns hundreds of years ago, the team looked at books and other written records. They learned that in January of 1700, a powerful earthquake had occurred on the coast of Washington. It shook the nearby hills of Ozette and caused a huge mudslide. Mud swept down and buried the village.

Ten feet of mud covered Ozette for almost 300 years. Deep in that mud, the village was preserved just as it had once been. A wealth of information was waiting to be examined.

Daugherty's team pumped ocean water into hoses. They used the water to slowly remove the mud from houses and other remains.

This old photograph shows Makah hunters catching a whale. The Makahs used whales for food and whale oil to light lamps. Today, the U.S. government controls whale hunting.

Geography's Influence on Life in Ozette

Daugherty's team learned a lot about the Makahs of the past. They studied the physical geography of Ozette. They studied the constructed features found under the mud. Their discoveries gave us a detailed picture of Makah life long ago.

The sea and richly forested lands near Ozette offered the early Makahs a wealth of natural resources. They used these for food, shelter, and clothing. They knew where to hunt and gather the food and materials that helped them survive the cold and stormy coastal winters.

Many discoveries at the site showed how important the sea was to the people of Ozette. Various fish and sea animals—such as seals, otters, and whales—served as staple foods for the Makahs.

Huge cedar trees grow around the Ozette site. The people of Ozette relied heavily on cedars. They made their houses and boats from cedar wood. They pounded cedar bark into a soft material and made clothes from it. They also built a number of types of canoes from cedar wood. They used different canoes for war, hunting whales, hunting seals, fishing, and carrying large loads of goods for trade. They even made smaller canoes for children to use.

A Gift from the Past: Learning from Ozette

More than 55,000 artifacts have been uncovered at Ozette. It is one of the richest archaeological finds in the world.

Daugherty's team uncovered artifacts from all aspects of life. There were beautifully carved boards from houses and a riding saddle made of whalebone. There were baskets and boxes. There were toys, cradleboards for carrying babies, and ceremonial items. There were metal tools, fishing and whaling equipment, and many other items.

The team recognized much of what they found. But sometimes they could not identify an artifact. What was that piece of carved wood or shaped stone used for, they wondered?

They turned to the modern-day Makahs for answers. Perhaps some Makahs had seen something like it when they were young. Maybe they had heard about it from their grandparents.

The discoveries at Ozette have helped answer many questions about early coastal life. Now we know how close to the ocean people lived. We know what their houses looked like. We know how they cut down the giant trees and built their boats.

A Makah elder called the storm that uncovered Ozette "a gift from the past." For geographers, too, the site is a gift. It continues to provide details about how people have lived in the state of Washington for hundreds of years.

Today, you can see some of the treasures found at Ozette at the Makah Cultural and Research Center. These artifacts give us an understanding of what life was like long ago.

Researching Your State's History

15

How can you learn about your state's history?

15.1 Introduction

What is your state like? How did it get to be that way? Who settled your state? Who built its towns, cities, and farms? Why did these people choose your state as a place to live?

Questions like these are what history is all about. Studying history is like solving a mystery. When you study history, you use all kinds of clues to figure out what went on in the past.

These clues can be written records, like journals, newspapers, and letters. They can also be things you see around you, like old buildings. Each of these clues has a story to tell about the past.

Finding out about your state's history can help you appreciate the place where you live. It can help you understand why your state is the way it is today. It can even help you predict what your state might be like in the future.

Historical Building

15.2 How We Explore the Past

The clues historians use come in many forms. You must use many types of clues to build a clear understanding of the past.

You can find clues in letters and journals. You can find clues in newspapers and photographs. These are all **primary sources**. Primary sources are sources created by people who have seen or taken part in the events they describe. Suppose your state's first governor made a speech about his hopes for the state. That is a primary source. When you read it, you learn about the past from someone who was there.

You can also use **secondary sources**. Secondary sources are created by people who have not experienced the events described. This book is a secondary source. It has information about history. But its writers did not witness that history.

A secondary source may include primary sources. It may describe their importance. For example, a secondary source might explain why your state's first governor gave that speech. It might tell how people reacted to it.

Primary and secondary sources are both useful. They each give different types of information. A primary source may have rich detail. But it gives just one opinion. A good secondary source draws information from many sources. It can help explain how different views and opinions fit together. Use both types of sources when you study the past.

primary source

a source created by someone who has seen or taken part in the events described

secondary source

a source created by someone who has not seen or taken part in the events described

This primary source gives an account of the 1906 earthquake in San Francisco, California.

The Call=Chronicle=Examiner

SAN FRANCISCO, THURSDAY, APRIL 19, 1906.

EARTHQUAKE AND FIRE: SAN FRANCISCO IN RUINS

The Granger Collection, New York

15.3 Why We Study The Past

Why do we live where we do? Who were the people who came before us? What events did they live through? How did those events shape their actions? How did those events shape what they believed? By studying history, we can find the answers to questions like these. We can see that things did not come about by accident. There are reasons for the details of our lives. We can even find clues about how the future may unfold.

Personal records, such as this family album, help historians understand connections between people and the events they experienced.

History can teach us a great deal. If we understand our history, we can better understand who we are.

Think about yourself for a moment. What if you wanted to help someone understand who you are? You might describe your family members. You might say where they came from and how they came to live where they do. Or you might discuss your goals. You might tell about the things you want to do in your life.

Who you are is the result of things that happened long ago. And what happens in your future depends on what you do today. Historians think about those connections. Studying history helps them understand who we all are.

15.4 The Settlement of a State

Learning about your state's history can help you appreciate where you live. So, start at the beginning.

The first people to live in most of our states were American Indians. They probably came there looking for a good place to hunt or to grow food. Your state, community, or street may have an American Indian name. Names are often clues to a place's past.

In the early 1500s, Europeans began to settle in North America. Some of them hoped to find riches or natural resources. Others came here in search of religious or political freedom. You can find out when and why settlers came to your state.

In many areas, the new settlers drove the American Indians off of their land. The settlers brought their own ways of living. They introduced new languages, including English and Spanish. They built towns and farms. They formed governments. Many of us live in or near the towns the settlers built. We use a system of government these people created.

You can find many details about the settlement of your state. Then you'll know the story of your state.

The Cliff Palace in Colorado is the largest cliff dwelling in North America. Pueblo peoples lived in the area for 700 years.

15.5 The Expanding United States

Do you live in one of the original 13 states? If so, you may know about the rich history there. In many of these states, there are battle sites from the American Revolution. There are historic towns and buildings. There are monuments to many great events and people from our country's early history. You can learn a lot about these states by visiting or reading about such sites.

Other stories unfolded in states that joined the country later. After its founding, the United States expanded to the west. It began adding new states. Many of them were created as the result of a 1787 law. It was called the Northwest Ordinance. You can still read this law today. The document tells how states in the Great Lakes area were formed. If you live in one of those states, this primary source might interest you.

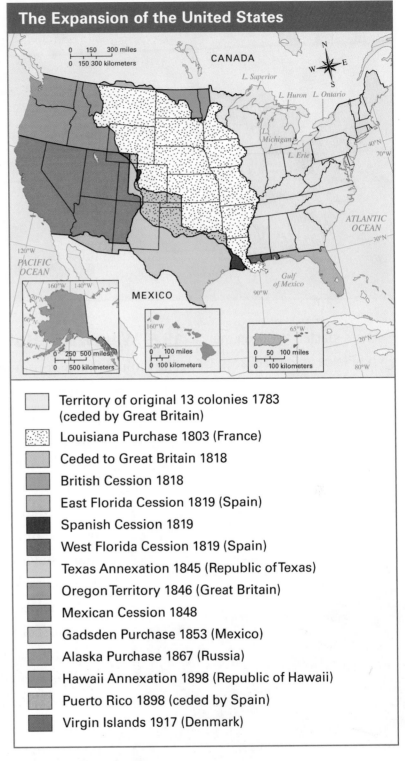

The Expansion of the United States

- Territory of original 13 colonies 1783 (ceded by Great Britain)
- Louisiana Purchase 1803 (France)
- Ceded to Great Britain 1818
- British Cession 1818
- East Florida Cession 1819 (Spain)
- Spanish Cession 1819
- West Florida Cession 1819 (Spain)
- Texas Annexation 1845 (Republic of Texas)
- Oregon Territory 1846 (Great Britain)
- Mexican Cession 1848
- Gadsden Purchase 1853 (Mexico)
- Alaska Purchase 1867 (Russia)
- Hawaii Annexation 1898 (Republic of Hawaii)
- Puerto Rico 1898 (ceded by Spain)
- Virgin Islands 1917 (Denmark)

The United States also got lands from other countries. Can you find these lands on the map? In 1803, it purchased a huge chunk of territory from France. This was the Louisiana Purchase. You can read primary and secondary sources about that purchase. These resources would help you learn how Louisiana and other states northwest of it were formed.

Settlers started farms on the Great Plains in the 1800s.

During the Gold Rush, miners helped California's population grow rapidly.

15.6 Westward, Ho!

The United States continued to expand west. New settlers arrived from other countries. As the population grew, new states were established.

What did these settlers come to find? In the 1800s, many people were looking for land and open space. They wanted to get as far away from other settlements as they could. Many people moved west because of the promise of inexpensive land. Farmers settled many states of the Great Plains, such as Kansas and Nebraska.

Some people who traveled west followed the Oregon Trail to the Pacific coast. They settled such states as Oregon and Washington. Some of them were drawn by dreams of finding riches. In 1848, a mill worker discovered gold in the West. Tens of thousands of people came looking to strike it rich. Many stayed. They formed a new state—California.

What drew people to your state? How did people build lives there? Every state has its own history. Asking questions like these and researching the answers can help you learn about the unique history of your state.

15.7 The Growth and Development of a State

The settling of your state is just part of its history. It continues to grow and develop today. People still come to the United States from all around the world. And many Americans move from state to the state. The new arrivals add to the history of your state.

The states in our country are alike in many ways. They are different in others. Each is special in its own way.

In some states, towns and cities crowd together. Other states have miles and miles of open space. Some states have lots of businesses and factories. Others are mostly farmland.

States developed in different ways because of their natural resources. Midwestern states like Iowa have rich soil for farming. In Colorado, miners found gold and silver. In Texas, ranchers found grasslands that were perfect for raising cattle.

States also differ because of the people who settled them. The colony of Pennsylvania welcomed people of all religions. Later, people from many countries settled in this state. Its population is still very diverse today. In California, settlers brought their grape-growing skills to their new home. They planted vineyards that today produce world-famous grapes.

Each state has its own story. What can you find out about how your state has grown and developed?

In the late 1890s, thousands of miners traveled through Washington on their way to seek gold in Alaska. The city of Seattle grew as people found work providing miners with clothing and transportation.

Lost and Found

Philadelphia is a city with a *lot* of history. Historian Ed Lawler is proud to know that history well. Yet one day he found a history mystery right in front of him. How did he uncover clues about the past?

Ed Lawler loves to show people around his hometown of Philadelphia, Pennsylvania. There are many historical sights to see, and Lawler knows a lot about them. One day, however, a cousin asked him a question he could not answer. Lawler had just explained that Philadelphia was once the capital of our nation. He showed his cousin the building where Congress had met. He showed him where the Supreme Court had gathered. "Where did the president live?" his cousin asked. Lawler didn't know.

Lawler set out to find the answer. He quickly discovered that no one was sure exactly where the first presidents had lived!

As a historian, Lawler knows how to do research. He's curious. And he's a good detective. So he got right to work to learn about the President's House. He wanted to know where it was, what it looked like, who lived there, and what happened there.

USHISTORY.org

USHISTORY.org

Philadelphia was the capital of the United States from 1790 to 1800. Congress met in Congress Hall (top). The Supreme Court met in Old City Hall (bottom). But where did the president live?

In 1800, the U.S. capital moved to Washington, D.C. From then on, presidents lived in the White House. Later, the President's House in Philadelphia was torn down. This drawing of the house was made in 1830.

Asking Questions

Lawler began by reading many books. Historians agreed that Presidents George Washington and John Adams had lived in the President's House. And they agreed that the house no longer stood.

The agreement stopped there. Historians said different things about where the house had been. They described how it looked in different ways, too. So Lawler started to ask some questions.

First, who owned the house? Lawler went to the **archives** of the city of Philadelphia. There he found the deed to the President's House. This told who owned it in the 1780s. After more searching, he found a newspaper advertisement that answered another question—where was the house? The ad gave the location. It stood on Market Street, one block north of Independence Hall.

But what did the house look like? At the Library of Congress, Lawler found another copy of the deed. It had a drawing of the house's layout. Lawler figured that people in Philadelphia in the 1700s would have bought insurance for their homes. So, he searched in a collection of old insurance records. Sure enough, there were papers describing the house. Lawler learned how large the rooms were and where the stairs were located. He found out how many fireplaces the house had and what the house looked like.

archives a collection of historical documents and records

At parties like this one, people could meet President and Mrs. Washington.

Words Tell a Story

What went on inside the house? Lawler wanted to know. He looked at other kinds of records. He read books, letters, and diaries. In them, he found many stories about life in the President's House.

Lawler read about fancy dinners that George and Martha Washington held on Thursdays. And every Tuesday, he learned, President Washington had an open house. That meant people could drop in and visit. One primary source explained, "Washington received his guests, standing between the windows in his back drawing room."

John Adams was the next president. He and his wife Abigail lived in the house until they moved to the new White House in Washington, D.C. Mrs. Adams is famous for the many letters she wrote. In one, she stated, "I feel more at home here [in the President's House] than I should any where else in the city."

The Adams' son, John Quincy Adams, also told stories about the house. In the room where Washington held his open houses, the Adams children once rolled up the rugs. Then they held a dance for their friends.

As Lawler read these old documents, he could feel the President's House come alive. He could picture the Washingtons living there. He could almost hear the Adams family talking to him.

Other Voices

Lawler found other voices from the past, too. He realized that there was an untold story about the building. During President Washington's time, it was the home of nine enslaved African Americans.

What were the stories of these nine men and women? Lawler uncovered them. From the writings of Washington's grandson, he learned about Hercules. This man was the chief cook for the house. Lawler read that "the whole household, treated the chief cook with such respect, as well for his valuable services as for his general good character and pleasing manners."

Hercules lived in Philadelphia for seven years. When the Washingtons moved from the city, he fled to freedom.

Lawler also found stories about a woman named Moll. She cared for the Washington children and grandchildren. He read about Oney Judge, who was Mrs. Washington's personal servant. Little by little, he learned about all the African Americans who lived and worked in the President's House.

For Lawler, it has been rewarding to learn about the lives of these African Americans. "In the past, they've been largely a list of names," he said. "I've tried to gather personal anecdotes and biographical information to help turn them back into real people."

Today, Lawler is still asking questions and finding answers. Because of his detective work with primary and secondary sources, historians can now tell the story of the President's House and the people who lived there.

Lawler's work helped architects design a memorial at the site of the President's House. The memorial will include some features to show what the house was like.

Researching Your State's Economy

What do you need to know to understand your state's economy?

16.1 Introduction

What kind of job would you like to have someday? Would you like to work with other people, perhaps as a teacher, a salesperson, or a lawyer? Would you like to design clothes or create computer programs? Would you like to work with your hands, as a carpenter or a mechanic does?

Thousands of jobs like these are a part of your state's economy. An economy is made up of all the ways in which people make, sell, and buy **goods** and **services**. Goods are physical objects, such as food, clothing, and cars. Services are things that we pay others to do for us. For example, restaurant workers save people the trouble of cooking. Travel agents help people plan their next vacation or business trip.

Studying your state's economy helps you understand how people live and work in your state. It can also help you learn what kinds of jobs you might have in the future.

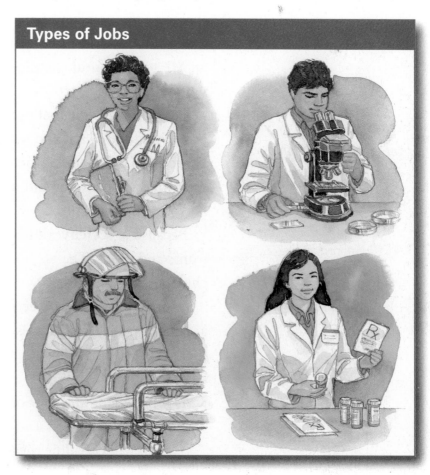

Types of Jobs

When people shop, they make choices about what goods and services to buy.

16.2 The Basics of Economics

In Chapter 1, you read about economics. Economists study the choices people make. Why are our choices so important? There are some things we all need. These are the items we must have to survive, including food and shelter. But there are also things we want. A new bike or an MP3 player would be nice to have, but we could survive without them.

Economists know that people cannot always get everything they want and need. Economists use the word **scarcity** to describe this fact of life. Scarcity means that the things people want and need, and the resources used to make them, are limited.

scarcity the idea that the things and the resources people want and need are limited

Because of scarcity, all people face choices about their wants and needs. The ways in which people make these choices shape an economy.

Your state has its own economy. It is made up of the actions of people, businesses, and governments. Together, these people and groups use their actions to answer three basic questions:

1. What goods and services should be produced?
2. How should goods and services be produced?
3. Who will consume these goods and services?

16.3 Understanding Markets

market a place where economic activity occurs

Economists have a word for a place where economic activity occurs. They call this place a **market**. You may have been shopping at a food market. But to an economist, the word *market* describes any place where buyers and sellers trade things.

A market can be an actual place, such as a store. But it does not have to be. In today's world, markets exist on computer networks and telephone systems. Some markets cover an entire state, the entire country, or even the entire world.

Markets are the center of our economy. In the marketplace, people work out answers to the three economic questions. There, buyers look to meet their wants and needs. Sellers seek to provide goods and services that buyers want.

Both buyers and sellers are interested in the prices of goods and services. When the price of a good or service is high, sellers tend to produce more of it. But high prices discourage buyers. Buyers are more likely to make a purchase as prices drop.

What happens when there is more than one seller in a marketplace? The result is competition. The sellers will compete for consumers. One seller may try to offer a better product. Another seller may offer a lower price. Competition is good for the buyer.

In the past, buyers and sellers traded one good or service for another. They had to agree on the terms of the exchange. Today, we can use money to make purchases. Because the value of money is set, exchanges are easier to make.

16.4 Workers in Your State

Before a seller sells a good, a worker must make it. These workers are also called producers. What is their role in the economy?

To make a product, businesses use what economists call the three **factors of production**. One factor is land. This includes raw materials—things that are found in nature and are used to make goods. Another factor is capital. Capital means tools, machines, and buildings that are used to make goods. The third factor is labor, or workers.

Businesses attract workers by paying them money. The higher the wage or salary offered, the more likely that people will be willing to work for that price.

Workers use their pay to meet their needs and wants. When workers spend their money on products, they also help sellers. You can see, then, why jobs are important to an economy. More and better jobs help everyone. Jobs enable workers to buy what they need or want, which helps sellers earn money, too.

Workers also pay **taxes** on their earnings. Taxes support the government. They pay for services that the government provides to people. For example, salaried firefighters work for the government. Taxpayer money pays their wages.

factors of production the resources, including land, capital, and workers, used to create a good or service

tax the money that people and businesses pay to the government to support its functions

Here, you see two of the factors of production: capital (the machine) and labor (the worker).

My Budget for the Month

Money I Will Earn

Washing our car: $5
Sweeping outside our house: $5
Mowing lawns: $15
Carrying groceries for neighbors: $15
Walking dogs for neighbors: $15

Total: $5 + $5 + $15 + $15 + $15 = $55

Money I Will Spend

Going to a movie: $7
Buying music: $10
Buying a birthday gift: $10
Riding the bus: $8

Total: $7 + $10 + $10 + $8 = $35

Money I Will Save

$55 − $35 = $20

16.5 The Role of the Consumer

When a worker spends money to buy something, that producer becomes a consumer. Consumers also play a key role in the economy. They buy the goods and services that producers make.

You are a consumer. And you can learn to be a smart consumer. Being a smart consumer will help keep your state's economy strong. And it will help you plan how much money you need. As you know, money is what we trade for goods and services to meet our needs and wants.

You can be a smart consumer by spending wisely. To do so, you can make a **budget**. A budget details how much money you expect to have in a given time period. And it details how you will spend that money. Following a budget helps you avoid spending more than you have.

You can also be a smart consumer by saving some of your money. Many people save money by putting it in the bank. Saving your money helps ensure that you will always have a way of meeting your needs. Savings also helps the economy because banks then have a supply of money to loan out. This helps businesses grow.

You can write a budget for any length of time. First, list what you will earn. Next, list what you will spend. Then, subtract your spending from your earnings. Make sure you don't spend more than you have.

budget a plan for how you will spend the money you expect to have

Cranberries grow well in the state of Washington, an example of how climate can affect a state's economy.

16.6 A State's Economy Grows and Develops

Each state's economy grows and develops in different ways. A state's natural resources and climate can affect what producers in the state choose to make and sell.

To see how resources shape economic decisions, look at the state of Florida. Florida's first big industry was agriculture because of the state's rich soil. Florida also has a warm, wet climate. These features allow farmers to grow sugarcane and citrus fruits, such as oranges. These valuable crops cannot be grown easily in most other states.

People saw another way to develop Florida's economy, again by using the warm weather and the natural features— tourism. To attract tourists, people built hotels, restaurants, shops, and amusement parks. Today, tourism is Florida's most important industry. Florida's pleasant climate also attracted millions of retired people. New businesses arose to meet their needs. With plenty of buyers, these businesses grew.

Like Florida's economy, Montana's economy grew from its natural resources. The state developed agriculture. Lumbering, mining, and ranching industries also formed. Later, as the state's population grew and changed, so did its economy. Today, more people in Montana work in service jobs than in any other type of business.

16.7 Types of Jobs in Our States

Each state has many types of industries and jobs. Here are some that you may find in your state as you research its economy. Can you think of others?

Agriculture. The agriculture industry is made up of businesses that grow food. Farm workers and ranchers work in agriculture. Scientists and businesspeople do, too.

Manufacturing. Any business that makes goods is part of the manufacturing industry. Factory workers, scientists, and engineers are just a few of the people who work in manufacturing.

Retail. Stores that sell goods to consumers make up the retail industry. Supermarkets, video stores, and car dealerships are all retail businesses. Two of the main jobs in retail are salesclerk and store manager.

Government. Millions of people work for federal, state, and local governments. Governments need many kinds of workers. Many teachers, firefighters, and police officers work for governments.

Service. Many people work in service businesses. Hair stylists, dry cleaners, mechanics, waiters, and security guards all provide services in a state.

As you research your state's economy, look for the ways in which it is linked to other economies. Many people in your state may do business throughout the country or throughout the world. They may also compete with businesses around the globe.

The service industry is made up of many types of jobs. This airport ground crewman is part of the service industry.

Doing Real Work in the Real World

What is it like to do jobs that adults usually do? Students across the country answer that question as they participate in real-world work projects. What do they learn about work?

In 2004, the Robert E. Byrd Academy School was a crumbling building in a run-down part of Chicago. The building had no heat. In winter, it was so cold that students had to wear coats in class. The bathrooms had wet floors from leaking pipes. There were no soap dispensers.

Teacher Brian Shultz asked his fifth graders what community project they wanted to work on. They answered "our school." They knew they couldn't make the repairs themselves. But they also knew they could build public support for solving their school's problems. In the adult world, community organizers work to educate the public and elected officials about a specific issue. In effect, the students became junior community organizers to win supporters and get official solutions.

Students in Chicago became community organizers to help fix their school.

For five months, the students worked to bring attention to the problems in the school building. They made lists of projects that needed to be done. They researched the costs for the projects. They looked at the school department's budget to find where the money might come from. They wrote letters and e-mails to school and city officials about their school's problems.

Students saw their hard work pay off. Officials listened to their arguments. Workers fixed many problems. And they put soap dispensers in the bathrooms. "The students were so excited," said Mr. Shultz. "They were coming out of the bathrooms with their hands full of bubbles, yelling, 'We've got soap!'"

4-H members learn real-world skills by working at home and in their community. Here, a girl cares for a goat.

Learning By Doing

"Learn by doing" is the official saying of 4-H. 4-H is an organization of clubs for children and teenagers. (The four "H"s stand for Head, Heart, Hands, and Health.) Learning by doing has been the focus of 4-H since its beginning. Kids learn practical skills by doing real work projects.

4-H had an interesting beginning. It was created in the early 1900s so that kids could teach adults about new farming discoveries. Teachers working at agricultural colleges discovered that many adults in the farming community did not easily accept new technologies. But kids were happy to experiment with these new ideas and then share their experiences and successes with adults.

For many years, 4-H clubs were mostly agricultural clubs for boys and girls. With help from adult experts, kids learned new ways to raise animals, grow crops, and preserve food.

Today, the goal of 4-H is to help kids develop citizenship, leadership, and life skills. The clubs still focus on hands-on learning. Club member do projects that teach them skills and help their community. They raise and train seeing-eye dogs. They care for endangered animals. They learn first aid and work as camp counselors.

Running Businesses, Being Smart Consumers

In many schools, students learn about business by running their own. At Benjamin Cosor Elementary School in Fallsburg, NY, sixth grade students run a school supply store. The store is built into nooks in the front hallway of the school. It is stocked with items such as pens, pencils, notebooks, and folders. The students who run the store order supplies, stock shelves, wait on customers, and run the cash register.

At Canyon Creek Elementary School in Richardson, Texas, groups of students take turns running Enterprise City for a day. Enterprise City has 16 businesses, including a city hall and a bank. Students become shop owners, managers, accountants, and salespeople. They run the radio station and the newspaper. They act as police officers, judges, and the mayor.

At Enterprise City, students are "paid" for their work and learn how to be smart consumers. Using checkbooks, students buy what they need and want in the Enterprise City stores. They have to pay attention, though, to make sure that they do not spend more than they have earned.

"I learned how to check how much money I had, and not to spend it all!" one student explained.

BUSINESSES

1. Distribution and Mail Center 2. Print Shop 3. Television Studio 4. City Hall 5. Radio Station
6. Gift Shop 7. Souvenir Shop 8. Professional Services 9. Jewelry Shop 10. T-Shirt Shop 11. Photo Shop
12. Web Design Shop 13. Sports Shop 14. Snack Shop 15. Newspaper 16. Bank

This illustration shows the businesses and activities that students run in Enterprise City.

Working for Your Community

Look around your own community. Can you find kids who are doing real-world work? Some kids run farmers markets or work in stores. Some work with children or older people in schools, hospitals, and senior centers. Others work in parks or in playgrounds.

What real world work projects could you and your friends do? Look around your school, your neighborhood, your community. Do you see any problems? Are there things your community needs?

What skills and interests do you have to share? Do you love books? Can you read to people who cannot read? Do you love animals? Are there animals that need to be cared for in your community? Do you love being outside? Are there parks, rivers, or lakes that need cleaning and tending?

Here are some steps to take to do a real-world work project of your own:

1. Identify a problem and decide on a project.

2. Find other kids who want to help.

3. Get help from adult experts.

4. Make a plan.

5. Do it!

In many places, kids plan, plant, and tend community gardens. Some kids even help distribute the food they grow to food pantries.

Researching Your State's Government

How does your state's government work?

17.1 Introduction

Do you see things that you would like to change in your state? Perhaps you'd like to see schools get more money to fix their buildings. Maybe you'd like to see somebody take better care of your state parks. Or maybe you'd like to see stronger laws against dangerous driving.

There are always new problems to worry about. Governments try to solve problems that are bigger than people can solve on their own. Our national government is called the **federal government**. It is concerned with problems that affect the whole country. The federal government makes laws for the entire United States. **State governments** deal with problems that affect their state. Your state government makes laws for your state. It also makes sure people obey these laws.

And remember, as a **citizen**— or a person who by law has a right to live in a community—you can have a big effect on what your state government does. But first, you need to know how your state government works.

State Capitol Building

Local governments provide services, such as fire protection, to their communities.

17.2 The Federal System

Citizens of individual states are also citizens of the United States. That is because we have a federal system of government. In this system, the power of government is shared. The federal government holds some powers. The states hold the rest.

The founders of our country created a federal system in the United States. They had a deep fear of government that was too powerful. The country had just won independence from the too-powerful British king. They favored government with limited power. So, they chose a federal system. This way, power would rest with different levels of governments, not just one.

The federal system is set up to protect our rights. It ensures that no government—state or federal—gains too much power over the people.

The United States has one other level of government. This is **local government**. Your city, town, or county government is your local government. State governments create local governments to meet local needs. For example, local governments run schools. They pick up trash or run garbage dumps. They offer fire protection. They provide police services to help protect people and property. They do many things for the people in their community.

local government
city, town, and county governments

17.3 The Separation of Powers

State governments work the same way as the federal government. They are divided into three parts, or branches. The legislative branch writes the laws. Just as Congress makes laws for the United States, your state legislature makes laws for your state. Most state legislatures have two houses. What are the houses called in your state?

The executive branch carries out the laws. In the federal government, the president is in charge of the executive branch. In each state, the governor is in charge of the executive branch. Who is the governor of your state?

The judicial branch makes sure that justice is done, or that people are treated fairly. In the federal government, this branch includes the Supreme Court and other federal courts. In the states, the judicial branch is made up of state courts and judges.

Having three branches creates a separation of powers. The **system of checks and balances** makes sure no branch will have too much power. Each branch's power is limited by the other two branches. For example, the governor of a state may veto, or stop, a law passed by the legislature. But in most states, two-thirds of the members of the legislature can agree to overrule the veto and pass the law.

system of checks and balances a system set up in the U.S. Constitution to allow each branch of government ways to limit the power of the other two branches

The Three Branches of State Government

Executive

- The executive branch enforces state laws.
- The leader of the executive branch is the governor.

Legislative

- The state legislature makes the laws.
- Most state legislatures have two houses.

Judicial

- The judicial branch makes sure people are treated fairly.
- The judicial branch includes the state courts and judges.

17.4 The Importance of Leadership

As you learned in the early chapters of this book, the United States has a democratic form of government. The word *democracy* means "rule by the people." In our country, and in our states, the people rule. They have the power. The government serves the people.

Even though the people rule, we still need leaders. A good leader sets examples for others to follow. A good leader inspires people. He or she helps people put aside differences to solve problems together. They help people make decisions.

republic a type of government in which people choose leaders to act for them

We need leaders for another reason. Our nation is also a republic. In a **republic,** people choose leaders to act for them. Usually, citizens do not vote on laws. They do not directly decide what the government will do. Instead, they choose leaders to act for them. These men and women do the day-to-day work of government.

We have leaders in the federal government who act on our behalf. The president is one. Members of Congress and federal judges also represent us.

The state government works the same way. Have you heard your governor speak? Do you know who represents you in the state legislature? These are some of your state's leaders.

The president leads the executive branch. In each state, a governor leads the executive branch.

17.5 Choosing Our Leaders

We use elections to choose many of our leaders. In an election, citizens choose by voting.

Candidates campaigning for office meet voters at rallies like this one.

In elections in the United States, voters choose candidates based on many factors. Voters want someone whose views they agree with. They want a fair and honest leader. They often vote for candidates who have shown wisdom or courage. To learn about candidates, people can listen to what the candidates say—in person, on the radio, or on television. People can also read about candidates' views. They can listen to what others say about candidates, too. What would you look for in a leader?

Voters in your state elect your governor. They also elect your representatives to Congress and the state legislature. In some states, citizens vote on judges for some courts. When is the next election in your state?

Voting is a key part of being a citizen. Elections let the people have their say. They allow us to choose leaders to settle conflicts and make decisions. Are people happy with their leaders? Do they want new ones? On election day, we find out.

legislator a member of the branch of government that makes laws

bill a proposal for a new law

state constitution a written statement of a plan for a state government

17.6 How Ideas Become Laws

Most laws begin in the legislature. Laws are made to protect people's rights and the common good. Suppose you have an idea for a new state law. How could you make your law a reality?

The first step is to get other people's support. When many citizens get behind an idea, state governments will listen to them. That's because citizens elect their governors and state **legislators**.

There are many ways to get people's support. For example, you could hang posters around town. You could write letters to the newspaper. You could speak at town meetings. You could call up television or radio talk shows. You could organize rallies.

For an idea to become law, a state legislator must write it up as a **bill**. The entire legislature then debates the bill and often makes changes to it. Finally, the legislature votes on the bill.

If the legislature approves the bill, the governor must agree to sign it. Otherwise, the bill does not become a law.

Sometimes people believe that a state law is unfair. When that happens, they might ask state courts to take a look at the law. Courts can overrule a law if it disagrees with the U.S. Constitution or with the **state constitution**.

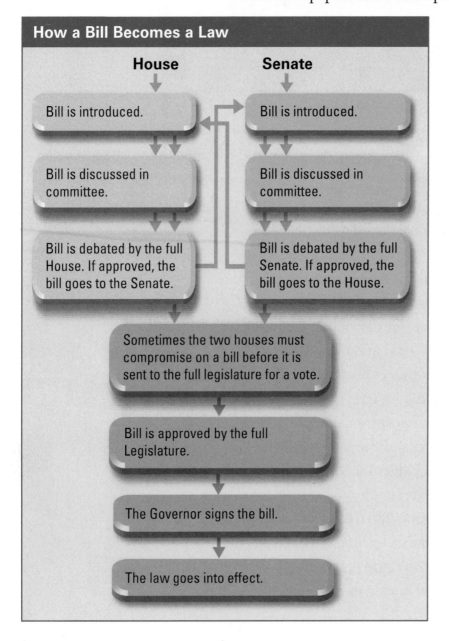

How a Bill Becomes a Law

House   **Senate**

Bill is introduced.   Bill is introduced.

Bill is discussed in committee.   Bill is discussed in committee.

Bill is debated by the full House. If approved, the bill goes to the Senate.   Bill is debated by the full Senate. If approved, the bill goes to the House.

Sometimes the two houses must compromise on a bill before it is sent to the full legislature for a vote.

Bill is approved by the full Legislature.

The Governor signs the bill.

The law goes into effect.

17.7 The Rights and Responsibilities of Citizenship

Citizens have many rights and responsibilities. Voting is one important right as well as a responsibility. Citizens can vote for leaders to represent them. The Constitution grants citizens over 18 years old this right.

Another right is freedom of speech. All citizens are entitled to these and other rights. The government cannot take away a citizen's rights without a very good reason.

Citizens have responsibilities, too. These are things you must do to help support the government. One responsibility is paying taxes. Another is being on a jury. Most adult citizens share these responsibiliities.

There are also many ways to be a good citizen before you become an adult. You can obey the laws of the country and your state. You can show respect for the rights of others. You can develop leadership traits, such as courage, honesty, fairness, and wisdom. And you can learn to recognize these traits in others.

Helping to get a law passed or changed is one way you can practice good citizenship. Although citizens usually cannot make laws directly, they can suggest an idea and help it become a law. Citizens can work with elected leaders to write and encourage support for new laws. Next, you'll meet a group of student citizens from Massachusetts who did just that.

Voting in elections is a right and a responsibility of citizenship.

Student Citizens Help Make a Law

In Franklin, Massachusetts, Ms. Johnson's students were discussing state symbols, like the state flag. They thought of a new symbol for their state. They used their idea to help make a law. What did the students learn about their state's government in the process?

Many states choose state symbols from plants and animals found in the state.

In 1974, Palma Johnson's class at the Kennedy School was studying Massachusetts state symbols. They looked at the Massachusetts flag and the state seal. They looked at pictures of the state bird (the chickadee) and the state tree (the American Elm). Massachusetts even had a state fish (the Atlantic cod).

"I think Massachusetts should have a state bug," said one student. The rest agreed. Several students suggested the ladybug. Ladybugs are found in yards and parks all over Massachusetts.

"Every citizen of Massachusetts has the right to suggest new laws for our state," Ms. Johnson told her class. "Maybe our class can make the ladybug the state bug. Maybe we can make it a law."

Atlantic Cod

Chickadee

American Elm

Petitioning the Massachusetts Legislature

Ms. Johnson's class agreed to try to turn their idea into law. The first thing to do was find out how.

As citizens of Massachusetts, they had the right to give their legislators ideas for new laws. This right is called the **right of free petition**. The first step was to write to the State House in Boston, the state capital. This is where the state's legislators work. In the letter, the class asked for a petition form.

When the form arrived, the class filled it out carefully. They explained why they proposed the ladybug as the state bug.

Next, they had to find a legislator to sign the petition. Any petition for a new law needs the support of a legislator. The class decided to ask Representative Robert Ficco to help them. Mr. Ficco represented the town of Franklin in the Massachusetts state legislature. The class wrote to ask him to sign their petition. He wrote back to say he would be glad to help.

Mr. Ficco sent the petition to the Massachusetts House of Representatives. The ladybug idea was on its way.

The Massachusetts legislature works in the state capitol building in Boston.

right of free petition the right of the people to give legislators ideas for new laws

From a Petition to a Bill

When Representative Ficco sent the ladybug petition to Boston, it started the long journey to becoming a state law.

First, the petition needed to become a bill. The House Clerk for the House of Representatives gave it a number—H.5155. The petition was now a bill.

Next, the House Clerk assigned it to a committee. Different committees are responsible for different issues. The Clerk sent copies of the bill to all the legislators on this committee. They started to study and talk about the bill.

The students hoped to go to Boston when anything important happened with their bill. One event they did not want to miss was the public hearing the committee would hold on their bill. The students knew that just proposing a bill was not enough. They needed to show that there was support for the bill.

On the day of the hearing, Ms. Johnson's class dressed in ladybug costumes that they had made. Then they rode to Boston on a school bus. At the hearing, the students were allowed to speak. They explained why the bill was important to them.

The committee listened carefully. Afterward, they told the House of Representatives what they thought. They said the ladybug bill should be passed into law. This was a good start. But there was a long way to go.

How the Ladybug Petition Became a State Law

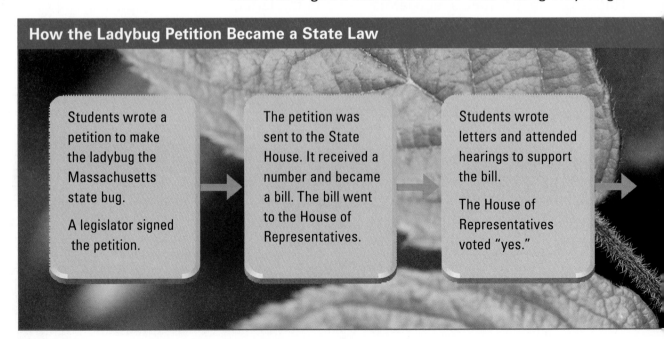

Students wrote a petition to make the ladybug the Massachusetts state bug.

A legislator signed the petition.

→

The petition was sent to the State House. It received a number and became a bill. The bill went to the House of Representatives.

→

Students wrote letters and attended hearings to support the bill.

The House of Representatives voted "yes."

→

From a Bill into Law

Over the next few weeks, the class went back to hearings at the state capitol several times. The representatives in the House discussed their bill on three different occasions. Between hearings, the students wrote letters to representatives to convince them to vote for their bill. They also talked to some representatives. In the end, the House of Representatives voted "yes" on the bill.

Next, the bill went to the other house of the legislature, the Senate. It was the Senate's turn to read, discuss, and vote on the bill. When the Senate voted "yes" on the bill, the students cheered.

The bill was almost a law, but not quite. First it was printed on special paper. Then, all the legislators voted together to enact the bill. That meant that the bill could become law.

The governor of Massachusetts was the final person who had to say "yes." When he signed the bill, it became a state law. Ms. Johnson's students attended the signing cremony. Now it was official. The ladybug was the state bug of Massachusetts.

The students knew that all their hard work had paid off. Ms. Johnson was happy, too. "I wanted my students to know how important it is to be active in our public life," she said. "After all, no voice is too small to be heard."

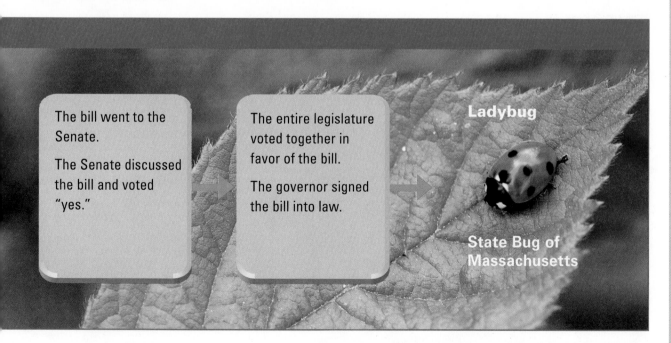

The bill went to the Senate.

The Senate discussed the bill and voted "yes."

The entire legislature voted together in favor of the bill.

The governor signed the bill into law.

Ladybug

State Bug of Massachusetts

Ideas That Unite Us as Americans

What connects Americans are shared ideals. Ideals are ideas that seem very good and worth trying to achieve. Our country is based on ideas about freedom and equality for everyone.

The Declaration of Independence: Creating a New Country

People have lived in our land for thousands of years. But the United States is less than 250 years old. It was founded in 1776.

At that time, our country was a group of 13 colonies. The colonies belonged to country called Great Britain. They were ruled by the British king.

Many colonists grew unhappy with British rule. They felt the British did not treat them fairly. They had little say in their own government.

In 1775, colonial leaders met in Philadelphia, Pennsylvania. This group was called the Second Continental Congress. For over a year, they discussed what to do about the conflict with Great Britain. In July 1776, they decided the colonies should form their own country. They declared independence from Great Britain.

This was a huge step. It was a crime to be disloyal to the British king. But the colonists believed in something more powerful than British law. They believed they had basic rights. No government or king could take these rights away.

A man named Thomas Jefferson explained this thinking. He did so in the Declaration of Independence.

From the Declaration of Independence

We hold these truths to be self-evident, that all men are created equal, that they are endowed by their Creator with certain unalienable Rights, that among these are Life, Liberty, and the pursuit of Happiness.

American Ideals

The Declaration of Independence describes the ideals of the new country.

Thomas Jefferson wrote, "All men are created equal." This was a new idea in 1776. In most countries, people were not born equal. But the United States was founded on the ideal of equality.

It has taken time to live up to this promise. Until 1865, most African Americans lived in slavery. Women could not vote until 1920.

Jefferson also wrote that all people have basic rights. These rights are "unalienable." This means they cannot be taken away.

Our basic rights include the right to life, liberty, and the pursuit of happiness. *Liberty* is another word for freedom. We believe in the freedom to make choices. We decide what we will do for a living. We choose how we will worship. We make other basic choices. We are free to pursue happiness.

Thomas Jefferson

Jefferson believed that government should get its power "from the consent of the governed." In other words, power belongs to the people. They can choose to let the government use it. The United States is a democracy. We choose our leaders. We give them the power to make laws. Over time, our democracy has grown. More and more people have been invited to take part. Today, nearly all citizens aged 18 or older can vote.

The Constitution of the United States: Creating a Government

The Declaration of Independence listed the ideals that would guide the nation. But it did not create a government.

In 1787, a group of leaders again met in Philadelphia. They met to create a plan for the new government. The plan they wrote is the Constitution of the United States of America.

The Constitution begins with a special paragraph. We call this the Preamble. The words make clear that "we the people" are forming the government. It exists to serve us. The words also tell the purposes of our government. These are to:

- create a more perfect union
- establish justice
- insure domestic tranquility— peace among the people
- provide for the common defense
- secure the blessings of liberty.

In 1789, the states adopted the plan.

Preamble to the United States Constitution

We the people of the United States, in order to form a more perfect union, establish justice, insure domestic tranquility, provide for the common defense, promote the general welfare, and secure the blessings of liberty to ourselves and our posterity, do ordain and establish this Constitution of the United States of America.

How Government Achieves Its Purposes

The Preamble tells us the purposes of the government. But how does the Constitution achieve them?

One way is by giving government power. The Constitution gives government power to create an army. The army helps defend us. It keeps us safe.

The Constitution allows government to coin money. With this power, government helps people do business. It helps them build better lives.

The Constitution gives government the power to tax. Taxes are how government raises money. Money allows government to offer important services. For example, government helps give people medicine. It helps the needy. Government helps keep our air and water clean. Such services promote our welfare.

The Constitution meets the purposes of the Preamble by putting limits on government power, too. One way it does this is with elections. The people can change leaders if they do not like the ones they have. This gives the people great power.

The Constitution also gives power to the states. For example, states make their own laws. They run schools. They build roads. The states have power. And the federal government has power. But nobody has too much.

The Bill of Rights: Protecting the Rights of Individuals

The Constitution achieves the purposes of the Preamble in another way. It promises to protect people's rights. It does so in the first ten amendments to the Constitution. Together, these amendments are called the Bill of Rights.

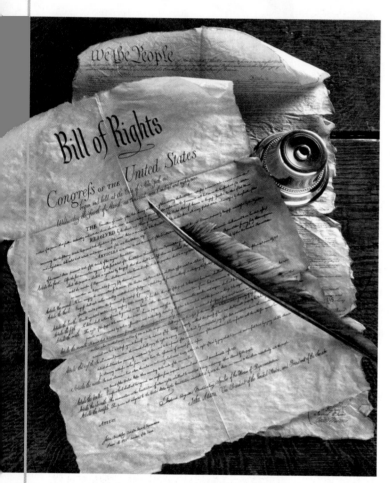

What rights does the Bill of Rights guarantee? They include:

- *The freedom of speech and freedom of the press* Government cannot stop us from sharing our ideas and views. We can even criticize the government.

- *The freedom of religion* This means we can worship in any way we want.

- *The right to bear arms* People are allowed to own guns.

- *The right not to be searched or arrested without good reason* Government must follow certain rules.

- *The right to a speedy public trial in front of a jury* Everyone who is arrested has the right to a trial.

Our rights have limits. For example, we do not have the freedom to say things that might create danger. We cannot shout out "Fire!" in a crowded place and cause a panic. We cannot put hurtful lies about a person in a newspaper.

With our rights come responsibilities. We hear the ideas of different candidates in an election. We must choose wisely when we vote.

We are free to practice any religion we like. We are responsible for respecting other people's choices.

Four Freedoms

Americans believe in freedom. We also believe in helping others enjoy freedom and equality. Sometimes, this is not easy. Sometimes, we must fight for freedom. We must resist those who would take freedom away.

The United States faced this kind of challenge in 1940. The country was about to go to war—World War II. Our enemies were dictators. In a dictatorship, people have no freedom.

Our president was Franklin Roosevelt. He gave a speech to help prepare the country for the challenge ahead. This speech is called the Four Freedoms speech.

Roosevelt reminded Americans of their own freedom. He challenged them to spread American ideals. "In the future days, which we seek to make secure, we look forward to a world founded upon four essential human freedoms."

These four freedoms included the freedoms of speech and religion. Roosevelt also named two other freedoms. One he called the "freedom from want." People should be free to work and earn a good living.

The fourth freedom was "freedom from fear." This was the fear of one country taking away the freedom of another.

Roosevelt's ideas still ring true today. Americans want their freedom. They want freedom for the people of the world.

Franklin D. Roosevelt

Respect for the Flag

The flag should never be displayed with the union (the blue portion) down, except as a signal of dire distress.

The flag should never touch anything beneath it, such as the ground.

The flag should never be carried flat or horizontally, but aloft and free.

The flag should not be used as wearing apparel, bedding, or drapery.

The flag should never be fastened, used, displayed, or stored in a way that would allow for easy tearing, soiling, or damage.

The flag should never be used to cover the ceiling.

The flag should never have placed upon it any mark, letter, word, figure, design, picture, or drawing of any nature.

The flag should never be used as a container for receiving, holding, or carrying anything.

The flag should never be used for advertising or printed on anything designed to be thrown away.

No part of the flag should ever be used as a costume or athletic uniform.

When a flag is in such condition that it is no longer fit for display, it should be destroyed in a dignified way, such as by burning.

The Pledge of Allegiance

I pledge allegiance to the flag
of the United States of America,
and to the Republic
for which it stands,
one nation under God, indivisible,
with liberty and justice for all.

Symbols of the United States of America

France gave the Statue of Liberty to the United States in the 1800s as a sign of friendship. The world has come to see the statue as a symbol of freedom and democracy. It has welcomed millions of people to the United States.

The bald eagle became a national symbol in 1782. The powerful bird was chosen because it was found only in North America. To our early leaders, the bird stood for strength, courage, and freedom.

The Great Seal of the United States shows the main ideas of the nation's founding. The colors come from the American flag. The eagle represents strength, freedom, and courage. The 13 arrows and the olive branch show the power of war and peace. The cluster of stars in the sky stand for a new nation taking its place among the other nations. The motto *E Pluribus Unum* means "from many, one." It means that we are one people made up of many different types.

The pyramid stands for strength. The eye over the pyramid stands for a greater power watching over people. Latin words celebrate the start of a new time in history. The letters on the pyramid's base are Roman numerals for 1776, the year of the nation's founding.

National Holidays in the United States

Fourth of July—Independence Day
This holiday celebrates the day that the Continental Congress approved the Declaration of Independence. It is celebrated across the United States with picnics, parades—and, of course—fireworks.

Thanksgiving
In 1621, the Pilgrims of the Plymouth colony and local American Indians celebrated the harvest. Presidents Washington and Lincoln later called for national days of thanksgiving. Today we hold this celebration on the fourth Thursday in November.

President's Day
In February, the country notes the birthdays of two of our greatest presidents: George Washington and Abraham Lincoln. Americans today honor both of these great leaders with the celebration of President's Day. It takes place on the third Monday in February.

Memorial Day
Americans remember the men and women who died in the service of our country on Memorial Day. The holiday began in the years following the Civil War. It was called Decoration Day, after the practice of placing flowers on the graves of the war dead. Today, it is celebrated on the last Monday in May.

Labor Day
On the first Monday in September, Americans celebrate the contributions of the American worker.

Flag Day
The first Flag Day was in 1877. It honored the adoption of the American flag by the Continental Congress. That took place 100 years earlier, on June 14. Now, each year on that date, we honor the great symbol of our nation.

Constitution Day
Constitution Day falls on September 17. It celebrates the signing of the United States Constitution on that day in 1787.

I Have a Dream

Reverend Martin Luther King Jr. fought hard for equality for all Americans. On August 28, 1963, he spoke before a huge crowd in Washington, D.C., about his dream for our country. This speech is remembered today as the "I Have a Dream" speech. Here are some parts of that speech.

I say to you today, my friends, so even though we face the difficulties of today and tomorrow, I still have a dream. It is a dream deeply rooted in the American dream.

I have a dream that one day this nation will rise up and live out the true meaning of its creed: "We hold these truths to be self-evident: that all men are created equal."

I have a dream that my four little children will one day live in a nation where they will not be judged by the color of their skin but by the content of their character.

I have a dream today.

I have a dream that one day... little black boys and black girls will be able to join hands with little white boys and white girls as sisters and brothers.

I have a dream today.

And if America is to be a great nation, this must become true... Let freedom ring... from every mountainside, let freedom ring.

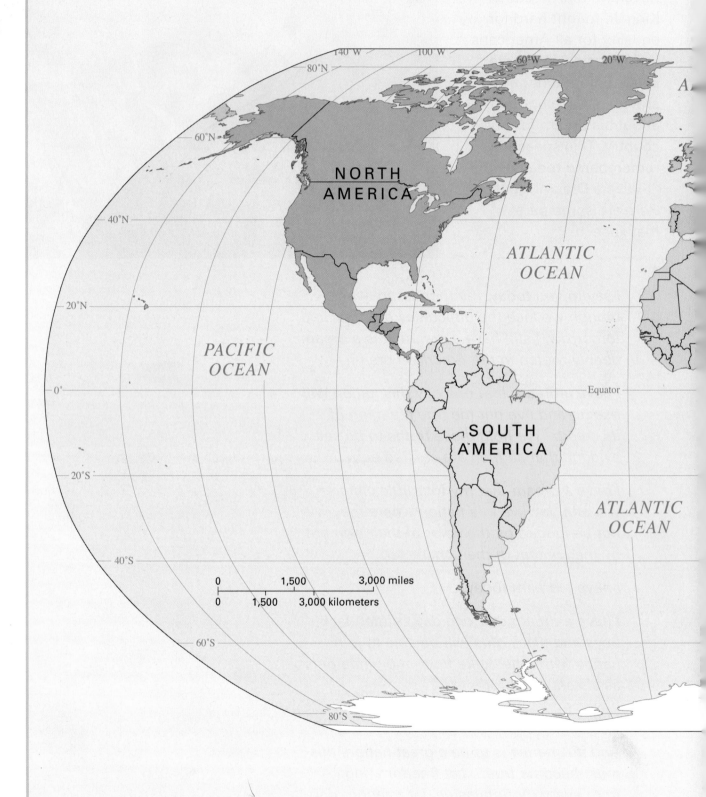

NORTH
AMERICA

ATLANTIC
OCEAN

PACIFIC
OCEAN

Equator

SOUTH
AMERICA

ATLANTIC
OCEAN

0   1,500   3,000 miles
0   1,500   3,000 kilometers

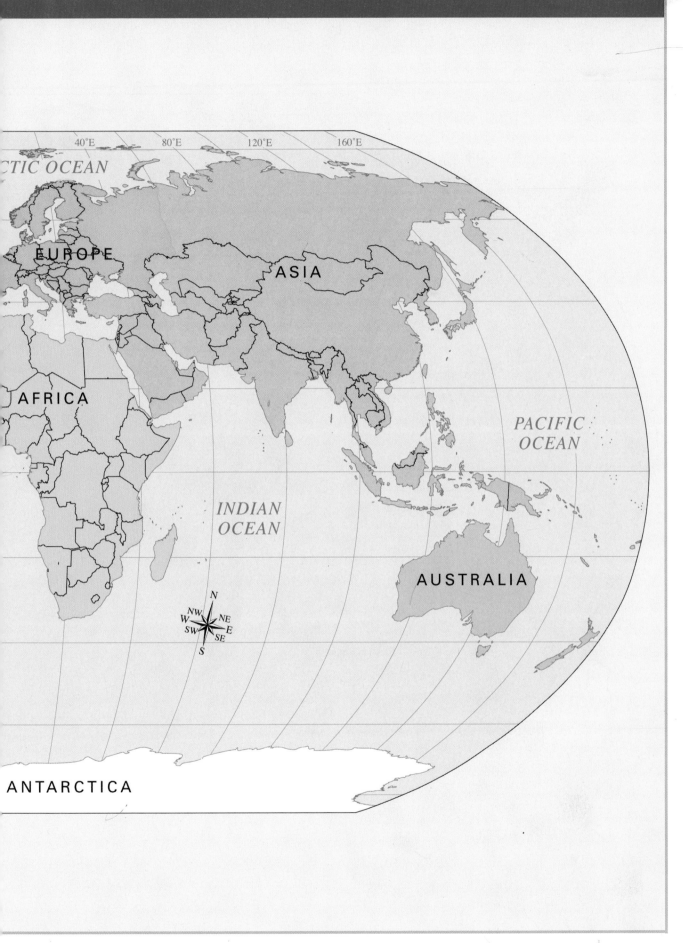

CTIC OCEAN

40°E   80°E   120°E   160°E

EUROPE

AFRICA

ASIA

PACIFIC
OCEAN

INDIAN
OCEAN

AUSTRALIA

N
NW   NE
W   E
SW   SE
S

ANTARCTICA

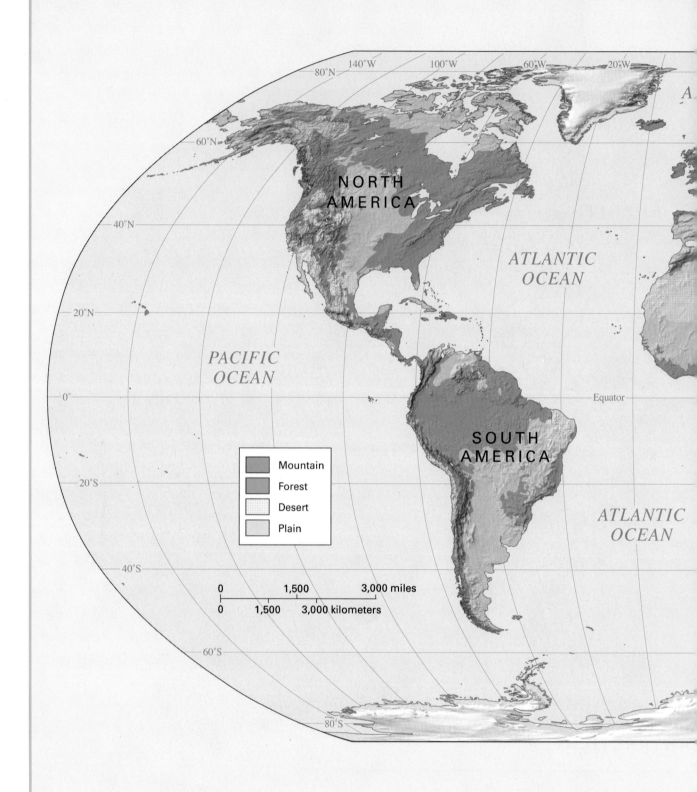

80°N 140°W 100°W 60°W 20°W

A

60°N

NORTH
AMERICA

40°N

ATLANTIC
OCEAN

20°N

PACIFIC
OCEAN

0°

Equator

SOUTH
AMERICA

20°S

	Mountain
	Forest
	Desert
	Plain

ATLANTIC
OCEAN

40°S

| 0 | | 1,500 | | 3,000 miles |
| 0 | 1,500 | 3,000 kilometers | | |

60°S

80°S

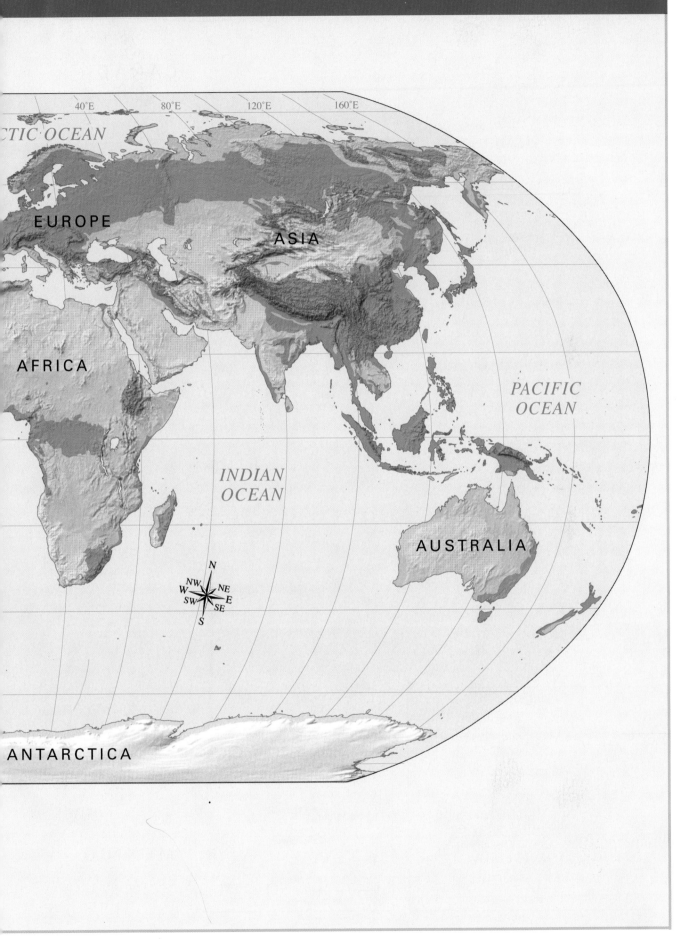

CTIC OCEAN

40°E   80°E   120°E   160°E

EUROPE

ASIA

AFRICA

PACIFIC
OCEAN

INDIAN
OCEAN

AUSTRALIA

N
NW   NE
W   E
SW   SE
S

ANTARCTICA

CANADA

Washington
★
Olympia

★ Salem

Oregon

★ Boise

Idaho

★ Helena
Montana

North
Dakota

Bismarck ★

South
Dakota

Pierre ★

Wyoming

Cheyenne
★

Nebraska

★ Salt Lake
City

Nevada

★ Carson City

Sacramento
★

Utah

★ Denver

Colorado

Kansas

California

35°N

Arizona

★ Phoenix

★ Santa Fe

New Mexico

Oklahoma
City

PACIFIC
OCEAN

120°W

Texas

Austin ★

45°N

40°N
125°W

ARCTIC OCEAN

70°N

Alaska

60°N
170°W

PACIFIC
OCEAN

160°W

150°W

140°W

Juneau ★

0   400 miles

0   400 kilometers

160°W   Hawaii

Kauai

Niihau

Oahu

Honolulu ★ Molokai

Lanai   Maui

Kahoolawe

PACIFIC
OCEAN

20°N

Hawaii

0   150 miles

0   150 kilometers

MEXICO

500 miles
500 kilometers

N
NW NE
W E
SW SE
S

Minnesota
★ St. Paul
Wisconsin
★ Madison
Michigan
★ Lansing

Maine
★ Augusta
New Hampshire
Vermont
★ Montpelier
★ Concord
Boston
Massachusetts
Albany ★
★ Providence
New York
Hartford ★
Rhode Island
Connecticut

Iowa
★ Des Moines
Illinois
★ Springfield
Indiana
★ Indianapolis
Ohio
★ Columbus

Pennsylvania
Harrisburg ★
Trenton ★
New Jersey
Annapolis ★ Dover
Delaware
Washington D.C.
Maryland
70°W

★ Lincoln
★ Topeka
Jefferson City ★
Missouri
Kentucky
★ Frankfort
West Virginia
★ Charleston
Virginia
Richmond ★
70

Oklahoma
Arkansas
★ Little Rock
Tennessee
★ Nashville
North Carolina
★ Raleigh
South Carolina
★ Columbia
★ Atlanta
Georgia
Alabama
★ Montgomery
Mississippi
★ Jackson
Louisiana
Baton Rouge ★
★ Tallahassee
Florida

ATLANTIC OCEAN

75°W

Gulf of Mexico

95°W   90°W   85°W   80°W

U.S. capital
State capital

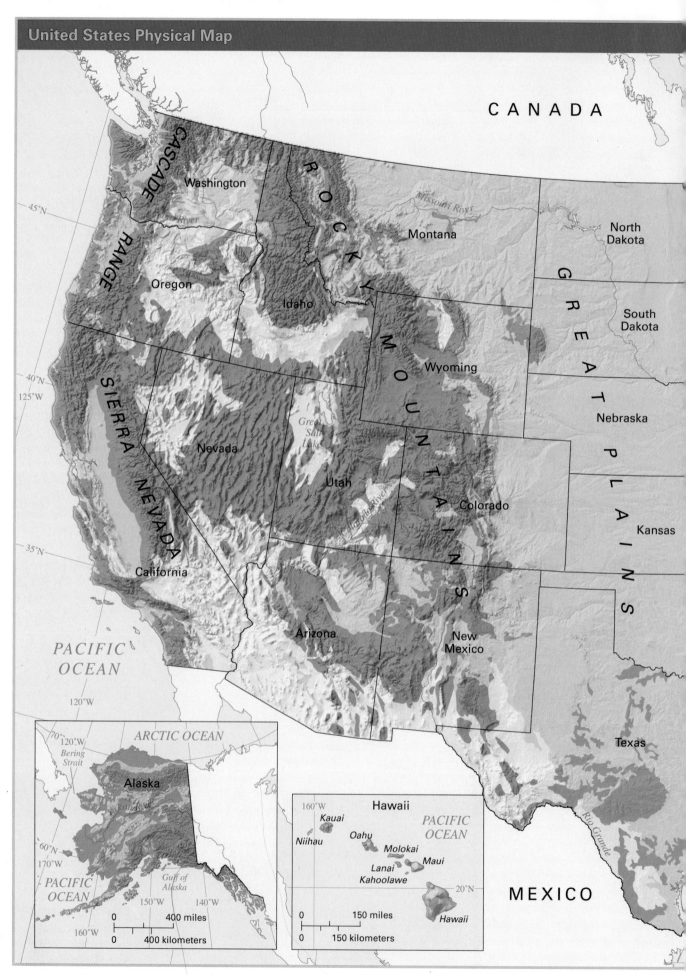

CANADA

CASCADE RANGE

Washington

River

R O C K Y

Missouri River

Montana

North Dakota

45°N

Oregon

Idaho

G R E A T

South Dakota

SIERRA NEVADA

40°N
125°W

Nevada

Great Salt Lake

M O U N T A I N S

Wyoming

P L A I N S

Nebraska

Utah

Colorado River

Colorado

35°N

California

Kansas

PACIFIC OCEAN

120°W

Arizona

New Mexico

Texas

Rio Grande

70°
120°W
Bering Strait

ARCTIC OCEAN

Alaska

60°N
170°W

PACIFIC OCEAN

Gulf of Alaska

150°W   140°W

160°W

0   400 miles

0   400 kilometers

160°W   Hawaii

Kauai

PACIFIC OCEAN

Niihau   *Oahu*

Molokai

Lanai   *Maui*

Kahoolawe

20°N

0   150 miles

0   150 kilometers

Hawaii

MEXICO

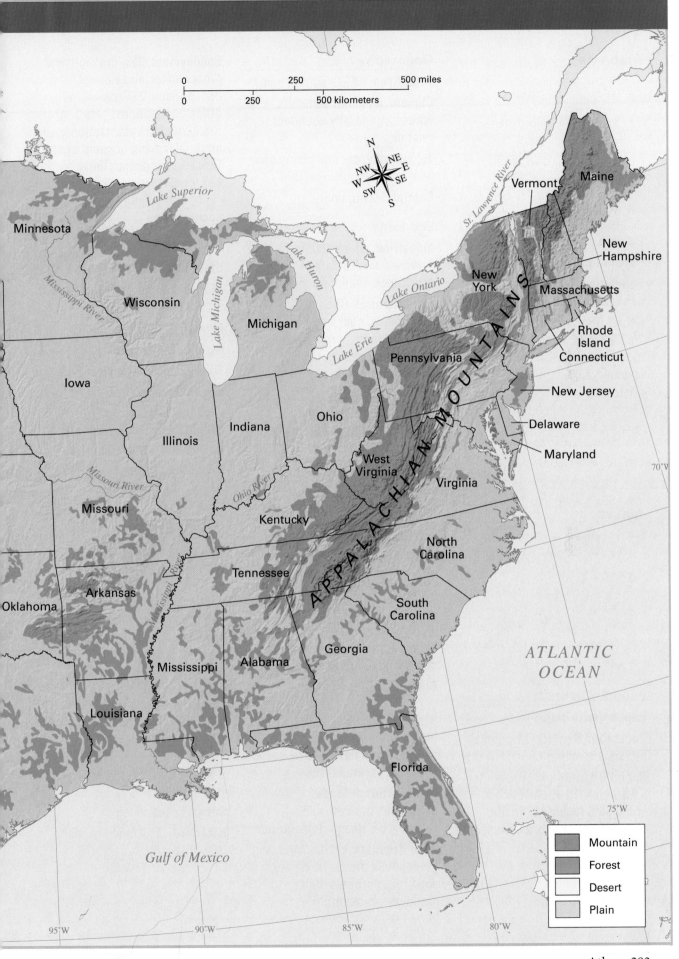

0   250   500 miles

0   250   500 kilometers

N
NW   NE
W   E
SW   SE
S

Lake Superior

Minnesota

Lake Michigan

Lake Huron

Wisconsin

Michigan

Mississippi River

Lake Ontario

St. Lawrence River

Vermont

Maine

New
Hampshire

New
York

Massachusetts

Rhode
Island
Connecticut

Lake Erie

Iowa

Illinois

Indiana

Ohio

Pennsylvania

New Jersey

Delaware

Maryland

Missouri River

Missouri

Ohio River

West
Virginia

Virginia

APPALACHIAN MOUNTAINS

70°V

Kentucky

Tennessee

North
Carolina

Arkansas

Mississippi River

Oklahoma

South
Carolina

Mississippi

Alabama

Georgia

ATLANTIC
OCEAN

Louisiana

Florida

75°W

Gulf of Mexico

	Mountain
	Forest
	Desert
	Plain

95°W   90°W   85°W   80°W

Alabama

★Montgomery

People (2006)

Population: 4,599,030

Population Density: 87.6 people per square mile

Racial Distribution: 69% white; 26.3% black; 0.5% American Indian; 1% Asian; 0.5% Pacific Islander; 2.5% Latino; 1% some other race

Geography

Total Area: 52,218 square miles

Climate: long, hot summers; mild winters; generally abundant rainfall

Topography: coastal plains give way to hills, broken terrain

Capital: Montgomery

Economy

Industries: educational services, health care, and social assistance; manufacturing

Manufactured Goods: electronics, cast iron, fabricated steel products, paper products, poultry processing, tires, lumber, and paints

Farm Products: cattle, hogs, chickens; cotton, peanuts, sweet potatoes, potatoes, other vegetables

Employment: 31% management, professional, and related occupations; 25% sales and office occupations; 17% production, transportation, and material moving occupations; 15% service occupations; 12% construction, extraction, maintenance and repair occupations.

Fun Facts

State Date: December 14, 1819

Motto: We dare maintain our rights.

Flower: Camellia

Bird: Yellowhammer

Tree: Southern Longleaf Pine

Song: Alabama

Nicknames: Heart of Dixie, Cotton State, Yellowhammer State (unofficial)

Web Site: alabama.gov

Alaska

Juneau

People (2006)

Population: 670,053

Population Density: 1.1 people per square mile

Racial Distribution: 66% white; 3.7% black; 15.4% American Indian; 5% Asian; 1% Pacific Islander; 6% Latino, 2% some other race

Geography

Total Area: 616,240 square miles

Climate: moist and mild; far N, extremely dry; extended summer days/winter nights; high winds and snow storms in W

Topography: mountains with central plateau and Arctic slope

Capital: Juneau

Economy

Industries: educational services, and health care, social assistance; retail trade

Manufactured Goods: petroleum, tourism, mining, forestry, canned and frozen fish

Farm Products: cattle, chickens; greenhouse products, barley, oats, hay, potatoes, dairy products, aquaculture

Employment: 35% management, professional, and related occupations; 24% sales and office occupations; 17% service occupations; 12% construction, extraction, maintenance and repair occupations; 11% production, transportation, and material moving occupations.

Fun Facts

State Date: January 3, 1959

Motto: North to the future

Flower: Forget-Me-Not

Bird: Willow Ptarmigan

Tree: Sitka Spruce

Song: Alaska's Flag

Nickname: The Last Frontier

Web Site: state.ak.us

Arizona

★ Phoenix

People (2006)

Population: 6,166,318

Population Density: 55.2 people per square mile

Racial Distribution: 59.7% white; 3.8% black; 5% American Indian; 2% Asian; 0.5% Pacific Islander; 29% Latino, 11% some other race

Geography

Total Area: 113,998 square miles

Climate: clear and dry in southern regions and northern plateau; heavy winter snows in high central areas

Topography: plateau in the N, Grand Canyon; desert in the SW

Capital: Phoenix

Economy

Industries: educational services, and health care, social assistance; retail trade

Manufactured Goods: electronics, metals, aircraft and missiles, food processing

Farm Products: cattle, sheep, hogs; cotton, lettuce, cauliflower, broccoli, sorghum, barley, corn, wheat, citrus fruits

Employment: 33% management, professional, and related occupations; 27% sales and office occupations; 17% service occupations; 12% construction, extraction, maintenance and repair occupations; 10% production, transportation, and material moving occupations.

Fun Facts

State Date: February 14, 1912

Motto: God enriches.

Flower: Blossom of the Saguaro Cactus

Bird: Cactus Wren

Tree: Palo Verde

Song: Arizona

Nickname: Grand Canyon State

Web Site: az.gov

Arkansas

Little Rock ★

People (2006)

Population: 2,810,872

Population Density: 51.3 people per square mile

Racial Distribution: 76% white; 16% black; 1% American Indian; 1% Asian; 0.1% Pacific Islander; 5% Latino; 2% some other race

Geography

Total Area: 53,178 square miles

Climate: long, hot summers, mild winters; generally abundant rainfall

Topography: eastern delta and prairie, southern lowland forests, northwestern highlands

Capital: Little Rock

Economy

Industries: educational services, health care, and social assistance; manufacturing

Manufactured Goods: food, chemicals, shoes, lumber, paper, electrical machinery, furniture, transportation equipment, clothing, machinery, steel

Farm Products: cattle, hogs, chickens; rice, soybeans, cotton, tomatoes, grapes, apples, vegetables, peaches, wheat

Employment: 29% management, professional, and related occupations; 25% sales and office occupations; 18% production, transportation, and material moving occupations; 16% service occupations; and 10% construction, extraction, maintenance and repair occupations.

Fun Facts

State Date: June 15, 1836

Motto: The people rule.

Flower: Apple Blossom

Bird: Mockingbird

Tree: Pine

Song: Arkansas

Nicknames: The Natural State, The Razorback State

Web Site: state.ar.us

California

★ Sacramento

People (2006)

Population: 36,457,549

Population Density: 217.2 people per square mile

Racial Distribution: 43% white; 6.7% black; 1% American Indian; 12.4% Asian; 0.4% Pacific Islander; 36% Latino; 16.7% some other race

Geography

Total Area: 158,854 square miles

Climate: moderate temperatures and rainfall along the coast; extremes in the mountainous areas

Topography: mountainous coastline, central valley, mountains to E and N, desert basins in southern interior

Capital: Sacramento

Economy

Industries: educational services, health care, and social assistance; professional, scientific, and management; administrative and waste management services

Manufactured Goods: electronic equipment, computers

Farm Products: cattle, sheep, hogs, chickens; grapes, cotton, flowers, oranges, rice, nursery products, hay, tomatoes, lettuce, strawberries, almonds, asparagus; dairy products

Employment: 35% management, professional, and related occupations; 26% sales and office occupations; 17% service occupations; 12% production, transportation, and material moving occupations; 10% construction, extraction, maintenance and repair occupations.

Fun Facts

State Date: September 9, 1850

Motto: Eureka (I have found it.)

Flower: Golden Poppy

Bird: California Valley Quail

Tree: California Redwood

Song: I Love You, California

Nickname: Golden State

Web Site: state.ca.us

Colorado

Denver ★

People (2006)

Population: 4,753,377

Population Density: 41.5 people per square mile

Racial Distribution: 72% white; 4% black; 1% American Indian; 3% Asian; 0.1% Pacific Islander; 20% Latino; 6.2% some other race

Geography

Total Area: 104,093 square miles

Climate: low humidity; wide daily/seasonal temperature ranges; alpine conditions

Topography: high plains, hilly/mountainous central plateau; western mountains; wide valleys, deep canyons

Capital: Denver

Economy

Industries: educational services, health care, and social assistance; professional, scientific, and management; administrative and waste management services

Manufactured Goods: industrial machinery, aerospace products

Farm Products: cattle, sheep, hogs, chickens; corn, wheat, hay, sugar beets, barley, potatoes, apples, peaches, dry beans, sorghum, oats, sunflowers, vegetables, melons, and lettuce

Employment: 37% management, professional, and related occupations; 26% sales and office occupations; 16% service occupations; 11% construction, extraction, maintenance and repair occupations; and 10% production, transportation, and material moving occupations.

Fun Facts

State Date: August 1, 1876

Motto: Nothing without Providence

Flower: Rocky Mountain Columbine

Bird: Lark Bunting

Tree: Colorado Blue Spruce

Song: Where the Columbines Grow

Nickname: Centennial State

Web Site: colorado.gov

Connecticut

★ Hartford

People (2006)

Population: 3,504,809

Population Density: 702.9 people per square mile

Racial Distribution: 74.8% white; 10% black; 0.5% American Indian; 3% Asian; 0.1% Pacific Islander; 11% Latino; 5% some other race

Geography

Total Area: 5,543 square miles

Climate: moderate; winters slightly below freezing; long, warm summers

Topography: western uplands; narrow central lowland; hilly eastern upland drained by rivers

Capital: Hartford

Economy

Industries: educational services, health care, and social assistance; manufacturing

Manufactured Goods: aircraft engines and parts, submarines, helicopters, computers, electronic equipment, plastics and metalwork

Farm Products: cattle, dairy products, chickens; nursery plants, vegetables, tobacco, apples

Employment: 39% management, professional, and related occupations; 26% sales and office occupations; 16% service occupations; 10% production, transportation, and material moving occupations; 8% construction, extraction, maintenance and repair occupations.

Fun Facts

State Date: January 9, 1788

Motto: He who transplanted still sustains.

Flower: Mountain Laurel

Bird: American Robin

Tree: White Oak

Song: Yankee Doodle

Nicknames: Constitution State, Nutmeg State

Web Site: ct.gov

Delaware

★ Dover

People (2006)

Population: 853,476

Population Density: 401.0 people per square mile

Racial Distribution: 69% white; 21% black; 0.5% American Indian; 3% Asian; 0.1% Pacific Islander; 6% Latino; 2.2% some other race

Geography

Total Area: 2,396 square miles

Climate: hot and humid summers, moderate winters

Topography: piedmont plateau sloping to near sea-level plain

Capital: Dover

Economy

Industries: educational services, health care, and social assistance; retail trade

Manufactured Goods: paints, rubber and plastic goods, processed meats and vegetables, transportation equipment

Farm Products: cattle, hogs, chickens; soybeans, potatoes, vegetables, barley, wheat, corn, peaches

Employment: 35% management, professional, and related occupations; 27% sales and office occupations; 17% service occupations; 11% production, transportation, and material moving occupations; 10% construction, extraction, maintenance and repair occupations.

Fun Facts

State Date: December 7, 1787

Motto: Liberty and independence

Flower: Peach Blossom

Bird: Blue Hen Chicken

Tree: American Holly

Song: Our Delaware

Nicknames: First State, Diamond State

Web Site: de.gov

Florida

Tallahassee

People (2006)

Population: 18,089,888

Population Density: 296.4 people per square mile

Racial Distribution: 61% white; 16% black; 0.5% American Indian; 2% Asian; 0.1% Pacific Islander; 20% Latino; 4% some other race

Geography

Total Area: 59,909 square miles

Climate: subtropical N, tropical S

Topography: flat or rolling land

Capital: Tallahassee

Economy

Industries: educational services, health care, and social assistance; retail trade

Manufactured Goods: electronic equipment, transportation equipment, chemicals, industrial machinery

Farm Products: cattle, bee colonies, chickens; citrus fruits, vegetables, melons, potatoes, sugarcane, strawberries

Employment: 31% management, professional, and related occupations; 29% sales and office occupations; 18% service occupations; 12% construction, extraction, maintenance and repair occupations; 9% production, transportation, and material moving occupations.

Fun Facts

State Date: March 3, 1845

Motto: In God we trust.

Flower: Orange Blossom

Bird: Mockingbird

Tree: Sabal Palmetto Palm

Song: Old Folks at Home

Nickname: Sunshine State

Web Site: myflorida.com

Georgia

Atlanta

People (2006)

Population: 9,363,941

Population Density: 141.4 people per square mile

Racial Distribution: 59% white; 30% black; 0.5% American Indian; 3% Asian; 0.1% Pacific Islander; 7.5% Latino; 4% some other race

Geography

Total Area: 58,970 square miles

Climate: hot and humid in summer; cold in the N and mild in the SE in winter

Topography: mountains; central piedmont to fall line of rivers; coastal plain

Capital: Atlanta

Economy

Industries: educational services, health care, and social assistance; manufacturing

Manufactured Goods: textiles, processed food, pulp and paper products

Farm Products: cattle, hogs, chickens; peanuts, cotton, corn, tobacco, hay, soybeans, cucumbers, squash

Employment: 33% management, professional, and related occupations; 26% sales and office occupations; 15% service occupations; 14% production, transportation, and material moving occupations; 11% construction, extraction, maintenance and repair occupations.

Fun Facts

State Date: January 2, 1788

Motto: Wisdom, justice, and moderation

Flower: Cherokee Rose

Bird: Brown Thrasher

Tree: Live Oak

Song: Georgia on My Mind

Nicknames: Empire State of the South, Peach State

Web Site: georgia.gov

Hawaii

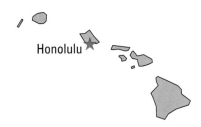

Honolulu

People (2006)

Population: 1,285,498

Population Density: 188.6 people per square mile

Racial Distribution: 25% white; 3% black; 0.5% American Indian; 40% Asian; 9.1% Pacific Islander; 8% Latino; 1% some other race

Geography

Total Area: 6,461 square miles

Climate: tropical with wide variations in rainfall

Topography: islands that are tops of partially submerged volcanic mountains; two main active volcanoes

Capital: Honolulu

Economy

Industries: educational services, health care, and social assistance; arts, entertainment, and recreation; accommodation and food services

Manufactured Goods: processed sugar, canned pineapple, clothing

Farm Products: cattle, hogs, chickens; sugar, pineapples, macadamia nuts, tropical fruits, coffee, vegetables, flowers

Employment: 33% management, professional, and related occupations; 27% sales and office occupations; 21% service occupations; 10% construction, extraction, maintenance and repair occupations; 8% production, transportation, and material moving occupations.

Fun Facts

State Date: August 21, 1959

Motto: The life of the land is perpetuated in righteousness.

Flower: Yellow Hibiscus (pua ma'o hau hele)

Bird: Hawaiian Goose (nene)

Tree: Candlenut (kukui)

Song: Hawaii's Own (Hawai'i Pono'i)

Nickname: Aloha State

Web Site: hawaii.gov

Idaho

Boise

People (2006)

Population: 1,466,465

Population Density: 15.6 people per square mile

Racial Distribution: 86% white; 0.7% black; 1% American Indian; 1% Asian; 0.1% Pacific Islander; 9.5% Latino; 2.2% some other race

Geography

Total Area: 83,570 square miles

Climate: moderate with westerly winds; drier, colder in SE

Topography: plains in the S; central region of mountains, canyons, gorges

Capital: Boise

Economy

Industries: educational services, health care, and social assistance; retail trade

Manufactured Goods: computers, flour, meat processing, lumber, paper, chemicals

Farm Products: cattle, hogs, chickens; sheep, mink, bee colonies, hay, wheat, barley, potatoes, sugar beets

Employment: 31% management, professional, and related occupations; 25% sales and office occupations; 16% service occupations; 13% construction, extraction, maintenance and repair occupations; 12% production, transportation, and material moving occupations.

Fun Facts

State Date: July 3, 1890

Motto: Let it be perpetual.

Flower: Syringa

Bird: Mountain Bluebird

Tree: White Pine

Song: Here We Have Idaho

Nickname: Gem State

Web Site: state.id.us

Illinois

★ Springfield

People (2006)

Population: 12,831,970

Population Density: 223.4 people per square mile

Racial Distribution: 65% white; 15% black; 0.5% American Indian; 4% Asian; 0.1% Pacific Islander; 15% Latino; 9% some other race

Geography

Total Area: 57,914 square miles

Climate: cold, snowy winters and warm summers

Topography: prairie and fertile plains throughout; open hills in the southern region

Capital: Springfield

Economy

Industries: educational services, health care, and social assistance; manufacturing

Manufactured Goods: machinery, electronic equipment, metals, chemicals

Farm Products: cattle, hogs, chickens; corn, soybeans, wheat, sorghum, hay, dairy products

Employment: 34% management, professional, and related occupations; 26% sales and office occupations; 16% service occupations; 15% production, transportation, and material moving occupations; 8% construction, extraction, maintenance and repair occupations.

Fun Facts

State Date: December 3, 1818

Motto: State sovereignty, national union

Flower: Native Violet

Bird: Cardinal

Tree: White Oak

Song: Illinois

Nickname: Prairie State

Web Site: illinois.gov

Indiana

★ Indianapolis

People (2006)

Population: 6,313,520

Population Density: 169.5 people per square mile

Racial Distribution: 84% white; 9% black; 0.5% American Indian; 1% Asian; 0.1% Pacific Islander; 5% Latino; 2% some other race

Geography

Total Area: 36,418 square miles

Climate: long humid summers and cool winters

Topography: hilly southern region; fertile rolling plains in central region; dunes along Lake Michigan shore

Capital: Indianapolis

Economy

Industries: educational services, health care, and social assistance; manufacturing

Manufactured Goods: metals, automobiles, industrial machinery, electronics

Farm Products: cattle, turkey, hogs, chickens; corn, soybeans, wheat, nursery and greenhouse products, vegetables, hay, tobacco, mint

Employment: 30% management, professional, and related occupations; 24% sales and office occupations; 20% production, transportation, and material moving occupations; 15% service occupations; 10% construction, extraction, maintenance and repair occupations.

Fun Facts

State Date: December 11, 1816

Motto: The Crossroads of America

Flower: Peony

Bird: Cardinal

Tree: Tulip Poplar

Song: On the Banks of the Wabash

Nickname: Hoosier State

Web Site: in.gov

Iowa

Des Moines ★

People (2006)

Population: 2,982,085

Population Density: 53.4 people per square mile

Racial Distribution: 91% white; 2% black; 0.5% American Indian; 2% Asian; 0.1% Pacific Islander; 4% Latino; 2% some other race

Geography

Total Area: 56,271 square miles

Climate: humid summers and cold winters with blizzard-like conditions

Topography: watershed runs down the western side of the state; flat land in north-central area

Capital: Des Moines

Economy

Industries: educational services, health care, and social assistance; manufacturing

Manufactured Goods: processed foods, farm machinery, electronic products, appliances, auto accessories, ball point pens, wood products and motor homes

Farm Products: cattle, sheep, hogs, chickens; corn, soybeans, oats, hay

Employment: 33% management, professional, and related occupations; 25% sales and office occupations; 17% production, transportation, and material moving occupations; 16% service occupations; 9% construction, extraction, maintenance and repair occupations.

Fun Facts

State Date: December 28, 1846

Motto: Our liberties we prize and our rights we will maintain.

Flower: Wild Prairie Rose

Bird: Eastern Goldfinch

Tree: Oak

Song: The Song of Iowa

Nickname: Hawkeye State

Web Site: iowa.gov

Kansas

Topeka ★

People (2006)

Population: 2,765,074

Population Density: 32.9 people per square mile

Racial Distribution: 81% white; 6% black; 1% American Indian; 2% Asian; 0.1% Pacific Islander; 9% Latino; 3% some other race

Geography

Total Area: 82,276 square miles

Climate: great extremes between summer and winter

Topography: hilly plains in the E; prairie in the NE; hills in central area; high plains in the W

Capital: Topeka

Economy

Industries: educational services, health care, and social assistance; manufacturing

Manufactured Goods: transportation equipment, machinery, electrical equipment, processed foods

Farm Products: cattle, turkey, hogs, chickens; wheat, sorghum, corn, hay, soybeans, sunflowers

Employment: 34% management, professional, and related occupations; 25% sales and office occupations; 16% service occupations; 14% production, transportation, and material moving occupations; 10% construction, extraction, maintenance and repair occupations.

Fun Facts

State Date: January 29, 1861

Motto: To the stars through difficulties

Flower: Native Sunflower

Bird: Western Meadowlark

Tree: Cottonwood

Song: Home on the Range

Nickname: Sunflower State

Web Site: kansas.gov

Kentucky

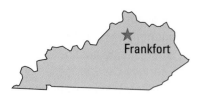
Frankfort

People (2006)

Population: 4,206,074

Population Density: 101.7 people per square mile

Racial Distribution: 88% white; 7.5% black; 0.5% American Indian; 1% Asian; 0.2% Pacific Islander; 2% Latino; 1% some other race

Geography

Total Area: 40,409 square miles

Climate: moderate, with plentiful rainfall

Topography: mountainous in the E; rounded hills in the N; bluegrass plains; wooded rocky hillsides

Capital: Frankfort

Economy

Industries: educational services, health care, and social assistance; manufacturing

Manufactured Goods: transportation and industrial machinery, electronic equipment, chemicals, steel, bricks

Farm Products: cattle, hogs, chickens; tobacco, corn, soybeans

Employment: 31% management, professional, and related occupations; 25% sales and office occupations; 17% production, transportation, and material moving occupations; 15% service occupations; 11% construction, extraction, maintenance and repair occupations.

Fun Facts

State Date: June 1, 1792

Motto: United we stand, divided we fall.

Flower: Goldenrod

Bird: Cardinal

Tree: Tulip Poplar

Song: My Old Kentucky Home

Nickname: Bluegrass State

Web Site: kentucky.gov

Louisiana

Baton Rouge

People (2006)

Population: 4,287,768

Population Density: 102.6 people per square mile

Racial Distribution: 63% white; 32% black; 1% American Indian; 1% Asian; 0.5% Pacific Islander; 3% Latino; 1% some other race

Geography

Total Area: 49,650 square miles

Climate: subtropical

Topography: mashes and river flood plain; valley lowlands; upland hills

Capital: Baton Rouge

Economy

Industries: educational services, health care, and social assistance; retail trade

Manufactured Goods: chemicals, transportation equipment, electronics, petroleum products, lumber, paper

Farm Products: cattle, chickens, dairy products; soybeans, sugarcane, rice, corn, cotton, sweet potatoes, pecans

Employment: 30% management, professional, and related occupations; 26% sales and office occupations; 18% service occupations; 13% production, transportation, and material moving occupations; 13% construction, extraction, maintenance and repair occupations.

Fun Facts

State Date: April 30, 1812

Motto: Union, justice, and confidence

Flower: Magnolia

Bird: Eastern Brown Pelican

Tree: Bald Cypress

Song: Give Me Louisiana

Nickname: Pelican State

Web Site: state.la.us

Maine

People (2006)

Population: 1,321,574

Population Density: 41.3 people per square mile

Racial Distribution: 95.6% white; 1% black; 1% American Indian; 1% Asian; 0.1% Pacific Islander; 1% Latino; 0.1% some other race

Geography

Total Area: 37,738 square miles

Climate: mild summers; cold, harsh winters averaging between 60 and 90 inches of snow

Topography: mountains and rugged terrain in the W; sandy/rocky coast with peninsulas and fjords

Capital: Augusta

Economy

Industries: educational services, health care, and social assistance; retail trade

Manufactured Goods: paper and wood products, transportation equipment

Farm Products: cattle, chickens, sheep; potatoes, blueberries, apples, fish and shellfish

Employment: 33% management, professional, and related occupations; 25% sales and office occupations; 17% service occupations; 12% production, transportation, and material moving occupations; 11% construction, extraction, maintenance and repair occupations.

Fun Facts

State Date: March 15, 1820

Motto: I direct.

Flower: White Pine Cone and Tassel

Bird: Chickadee

Tree: Eastern White Pine

Song: State of Maine Song

Nickname: Pine Tree State

Web Site: state.me.us

Maryland

People (2006)

Population: 5,615,727

Population Density: 541.9 people per square mile

Racial Distribution: 58% white; 29.5% black; 0.5% American Indian; 5% Asian; 0.1% Pacific Islander; 6% Latino; 3% some other race

Geography

Total Area: 12,297 square miles

Climate: moderate in the W; humid subtropical in the E

Topography: coastal plain and piedmont plateau

Capital: Annapolis

Economy

Industries: educational services, health care, and social assistance; professional, scientific, and management; administrative and waste management services.

Manufactured Goods: electronic equipment, processed foods, chemicals, printed materials

Farm Products: cattle, hogs, chickens; greenhouse and nursery products, soybeans, corn

Employment: 43% management, professional, and related occupations; 25% sales and office occupations; 15% service occupations; 9% construction, extraction, maintenance and repair occupations; 8% production, transportation, and material moving occupations.

Fun Facts

State Date: April 28, 1788

Motto: Manly deeds, womanly words

Flower: Black-eyed Susan

Bird: Baltimore Oriole

Tree: White Oak

Song: Maryland, My Maryland

Nickname: Old Line State

Web Site: maryland.gov

Massachusetts

Boston

People (2006)

Population: 6,437,193

Population Density: 821.1 people per square mile

Racial Distribution: 79% white; 6% black; 0.5% American Indian; 5% Asian; 0.5% Pacific Islander; 8% Latino; 4% some other race

Geography

Total Area: 9,240 square miles

Climate: moderate; warm, humid summers and cold winters

Topography: jagged, indented coast; flat land yields to stony upland near central region and gentle hills in W

Capital: Boston

Economy

Industries: educational services, health care, and social assistance; professional, scientific, and management; administrative and waste management services.

Manufactured Goods: electronic equipment, industrial machinery, fabricated metal products

Farm Products: cattle, chickens, turkey; cranberries, vegetables

Employment: 41% management, professional, and related occupations; 25% sales and office occupations; 16% service occupations; 10% production, transportation, and material moving occupations; 8% construction, extraction, maintenance and repair occupations.

Fun Facts

State Date: May 16, 1788

Motto: By the sword we seek peace, but peace only under liberty.

Flower: Mayflower

Bird: Black-capped Chickadee

Tree: American Elm

Song: Hail Massachusetts

Nickname: Bay State

Web Site: mass.gov

Michigan

Lansing

People (2006)

Population: 10,095,643

Population Density: 175.0 people per square mile

Racial Distribution: 78% white; 14% black; 1% American Indian; 2% Asian; 0.1% Pacific Islander; 4% Latino; 2% some other race

Geography

Total Area: 96,716 square miles

Climate: four seasons

Topography: low rolling hills in S to northern tableland of hills; level in NE with swampy areas; higher, rugged terrain in W

Capital: Lansing

Economy

Industries: educational services, health care, and social assistance; manufacturing.

Manufactured Goods: automobiles, machinery, metals, plastics, office furniture

Farm Products: cattle, sheep, hogs, chickens; corn, wheat, soybeans, dry beans, hay, potatoes, sweet corn, apples, cherries, sugar beets, blueberries, cucumbers, grapes

Employment: 33% management, professional, and related occupations; 25% sales and office occupations; 17% service occupations; 16% production, transportation, and material moving occupations; 9% construction, extraction, maintenance and repair occupations.

Fun Facts

State Date: January 26, 1837

Motto: If you seek a pleasant peninsula, look about you.

Flower: Apple Blossom

Bird: Robin

Tree: White Pine

Song: Michigan, My Michigan

Nicknames: Great Lakes State, Wolverine State

Web Site: michigan.gov

Minnesota

St. Paul

People (2006)

Population: 5,167,101

Population Density: 61.8 people per square mile

Racial Distribution: 86% white; 4.5% black; 1% American Indian; 4% Asian; 0.1% Pacific Islander; 4% Latino; 1.4% some other race

Geography

Total Area: 86,938 square miles

Climate: moist Great Lakes storm belt; semiarid plains to the W

Topography: over 15,000 lakes cover the state; rocky ridges in NE; flat plain in NW; rolling plains and deep river valleys in S

Capital: St. Paul

Economy

Industries: educational services, health care, and social assistance; manufacturing.

Manufactured Goods: chemicals, paper, machinery, electronic equipment, computers, medical instruments, metals

Farm Products: cattle, sheep, hogs, chickens, milk and dairy products; corn, soybeans, wheat, sugar beets, hay, barley, potatoes, sunflowers

Employment: 36% management, professional, and related occupations; 25% sales and office occupations; 15% service occupations; 13% production, transportation, and material moving occupations; 8% construction, extraction, maintenance and repair occupations.

Fun Facts

State Date: May 11, 1858

Motto: The star of the north

Flower: Pink and White Lady's-Slipper

Bird: Common Loon

Tree: Red Pine

Song: Hail! Minnesota

Nicknames: North Star State, Gopher State

Web Site: state.mn.us

Mississippi

Jackson

People (2006)

Population: 2,910,540

Population Density: 60.6 people per square mile

Racial Distribution: 59% white; 37.1% black; 0.5% American Indian; 1% Asian; 0.1% Pacific Islander; 2% Latino; 1% some other race

Geography

Total Area: 48,282 square miles

Climate: semitropical, with abundant rainfall

Topography: low, fertile delta; sandy gulf coastal terraces followed by piney woods and prairie

Capital: Jackson

Economy

Industries: educational services, health care, and social assistance; manufacturing.

Manufactured Goods: chemicals, plastics, processed foods, furniture, lumber and wood products, electrical machinery, transportation equipment

Farm Products: cattle, hogs, chickens, milk, dairy products; cotton, rice, soybeans

Employment: 28% management, professional, and related occupations; 24% sales and office occupations; 18% production, transportation, and material moving occupations; 16% service occupations; 12% construction, extraction, maintenance and repair occupations.

Fun Facts

State Date: December 10, 1817

Motto: By valor and arms

Flower: Magnolia

Bird: Mockingbird

Tree: Magnolia

Song: Go, Mississippi

Nickname: Magnolia State

Web Site: www.ms.gov

Missouri

Jefferson City

People (2006)

Population: 5,842,713

Population Density: 81.2 people per square mile

Racial Distribution: 83% white; 12% black; 0.5% American Indian; 1% Asian; 0.1% Pacific Islander; 3% Latino; 1% some other race

Geography

Total Area: 69,704 square miles

Climate: humid, hot summers; winter temperatures can vary from cool to cold

Topography: rolling hills; open, fertile plains; prairies

Capital: Jefferson City

Economy

Industries: educational services, health care, and social assistance; manufacturing.

Manufactured Goods: transportation equipment, processed foods, electronic equipment, chemicals

Farm Products: cattle, sheep, hogs, chickens; soybeans, corn, wheat, hay, cotton

Employment: 32% management, professional, and related occupations; 27% sales and office occupations; 17% service occupations; 14% production, transportation, and material moving occupations; 10% construction, extraction, maintenance and repair occupations.

Fun Facts

State Date: August 10, 1821

Motto: The welfare of the people shall be the supreme law.

Flower: Hawthorn

Bird: Bluebird

Tree: American Dogwood

Song: Missouri Waltz

Nickname: Show Me State

Web Site: mo.gov

Montana

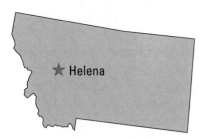

Helena

People (2006)

Population: 944,632

Population Density: 6.5 people per square mile

Racial Distribution: 89% white; 0.5% black; 6% American Indian; 1% Asian; 0.1% Pacific Islander; 2% Latino; 1% some other race

Geography

Total Area: 147,042 square miles

Climate: mild in the west; colder winters, warmer summers and more rainfall in the east

Topography: mountains in western third of the state; gently rolling plains in rest of state

Capital: Helena

Economy

Industries: educational services, health care, and social assistance; retail trade

Manufactured Goods: wood and paper products, metals, petroleum and coal products

Farm Products: cattle, sheep, hogs, chickens; wheat, barley, sugar beets, hay, oats

Employment: 33% management, professional, and related occupations; 23% sales and office occupations; 18% service occupations; 13% construction, extraction, maintenance and repair occupations; 10% production, transportation, and material moving occupations.

Fun Facts

State Date: November 8, 1889

Motto: Gold and silver

Flower: Bitterroot

Bird: Western Meadowlark

Tree: Ponderosa Pine

Song: Montana

Nickname: Treasure State

Web Site: mt.gov

Nebraska

Lincoln ★

People (2006)

Population: 1,768,331

Population Density: 23.0 people per square mile

Racial Distribution: 89% white; 4% black; 1% American Indian; 2% Asian; 0.1% Pacific Islander; 7% Latino; 3% some other race

Geography

Total Area: 77,354 square miles

Climate: semi-arid

Topography: plains and hills

Capital: Lincoln

Economy

Industries: educational services, health care, and social assistance; manufacturing

Manufactured Goods: processed foods, industrial machinery, printed materials, electronic equipment, metal products

Farm Products: cattle, sheep, hogs, chickens; corn, sorghum, soybeans, hay, wheat, dry beans, oats, potatoes, sugar beets

Employment: 34% management, professional, and related occupations; 25% sales and office occupations; 16% service occupations; 14% production, transportation, and material moving occupations; 9% construction, extraction, maintenance and repair occupations.

Fun Facts

State Date: March 31, 1867

Motto: Equality before the law

Flower: Goldenrod

Bird: Western Meadowlark

Tree: Cottonwood

Song: Beautiful Nebraska

Nickname: Cornhusker State

Web Site: state.ne.us

Nevada

Carson City ★

People (2006)

Population: 2,495,529

Population Density: 22.7 people per square mile

Racial Distribution: 74% white; 7% black; 1% American Indian; 6% Asian; 0.1% Pacific Islander; 24% Latino; 9% some other race

Geography

Total Area: 110,561 square miles

Climate: semiarid and arid

Topography: rugged mountain ranges; desert

Capital: Carson City

Economy

Industries: arts, entertainment, and recreation; accommodation and food services; educational services, health care, and social assistance

Manufactured Goods: food products, plastics, chemicals, furniture, printed materials

Farm Products: cattle, sheep, hogs; hay, alfalfa seed, potatoes, onions, garlic, barley, wheat

Employment: 27% management, professional, and related occupations; 25% sales and office occupations; 24% service occupations; 14% construction, extraction, maintenance and repair occupations; 10% production, transportation, and material moving occupations.

Fun Facts

State Date: October 31, 1864

Motto: All for our country

Flower: Sagebrush

Bird: Mountain Bluebird

Trees: Single-Leaf Piñon, Bristle-Cone Pine

Song: Home Means Nevada

Nickname: Silver State

Web Site: nv.gov

New Hampshire

Concord ★

People (2006)

Population: 1,314,895

Population Density: 147 people per square mile

Racial Distribution: 95% white; 1% black; 0.5% American Indian; 2% Asian; 0.1% Pacific Islander; 2% Latino; 1% some other race

Geography

Total Area: 9,350 square miles

Climate: highly varied, due to nearby high mountains and ocean

Topography: low, rolling coast followed by hills and mountains rising out of a central plateau

Capital: Concord

Economy

Industries: educational services, health care, and social assistance; manufacturing

Manufactured Goods: machinery, electronic products, plastics, fabricated metal products

Farm Products: cattle, hogs, chickens; dairy products, nursery and greenhouse products, hay, vegetables, apples, maple syrup/sugar products

Employment: 36% management, professional, and related occupations; 27% sales and office occupations; 15% service occupations; 12% production, transportation, and material moving occupations; 10% construction, extraction, maintenance and repair occupations.

Fun Facts

State Date: June 21, 1788

Motto: Live free or die.

Flower: Purple Lilac

Bird: Purple Finch

Tree: White Birch

Song: Old New Hampshire

Nickname: Granite State

Web Site: state.nh.us

New Jersey

★ Trenton

People (2006)

Population: 8,724,560

Population Density: 1,176 people per square mile

Racial Distribution: 70% white; 14% black; 0.5% American Indian; 8% Asian; 0.1% Pacific Islander; 16% Latino; 8% some other race

Geography

Total Area: 8,721 square miles

Climate: moderate, with marked difference between NW and SE

Topography: mountain peaks and valleys; flat-topped NE-SW mountain ranges; low plains broken by high ridges; coastal plain

Capital: Trenton

Economy

Industries: educational services, health care, and social assistance; professional, scientific, and management; administrative and waste management services

Manufactured Goods: chemicals, electronic equipment, processed food

Farm Products: cattle, chickens; nursery and greenhouse products, corn, blueberries, peaches, peppers, cranberries, soybeans

Employment: 38% management, professional, and related occupations; 28% sales and office occupations; 16% service occupations; 11% production, transportation, and material moving occupations; 8% construction, extraction, maintenance and repair occupations.

Fun Facts

State Date: December 18, 1787

Motto: Liberty and prosperity

Flower: Common Meadow Violet

Bird: Eastern Goldfinch

Tree: Red Oak

Song: I'm from New Jersey

Nickname: Garden State

Web Site: state.nj.us

New Mexico

People (2006)

Population: 1,954,599

Population Density: 16.1 people per square mile

Racial Distribution: 68% white; 2% black; 10% American Indian; 1% Asian; 0.1% Pacific Islander; 44% Latino; 16% some other race

Geography

Total Area: 121,590 square miles

Climate: sunny and mild, with a cooler, wetter climate in the higher elevations

Topography: plains, mountains, high plateau

Capital: Santa Fe

Economy

Industries: educational services, health care, and social assistance; retail trade

Manufactured Goods: processed food, machinery, clothing, lumber, printing, electronics, semiconductors

Farm Products: cattle, sheep, hogs; hay, onions, chilis, greenhouse and nursery products, pecans, cotton

Employment: 34% management, professional, and related occupations; 25% sales and office occupations; 18% service occupations; 12% construction, extraction, maintenance and repair occupations; 10% production, transportation, and material moving occupations.

Fun Facts

State Date: January 6, 1912

Motto: It grows as it goes.

Flower: Yucca

Bird: Roadrunner

Tree: Piñon

Song: O, Fair New Mexico

Nickname: Land of Enchantment

Web Site: state.nm.us

New York

People (2006)

Population: 19,306,183

Population Density: 409 people per square mile

Racial Distribution: 66% white; 16% black; 0.5% American Indian; 7% Asian; 0.5% Pacific Islander; 16% Latino; 9% some other race

Geography

Total Area: 54,556 square miles

Climate: variable due to nearby ocean and variations in elevation and terrain

Topography: some of the highest and most rugged mountains in the NE region; lowland river basin, coastal plain

Capital: Albany

Economy

Industries: educational services, health care, and social assistance; retail trade

Manufactured Goods: books, magazines, clothing, chemicals, machinery, electronic equipment

Farm Products: cattle, sheep, hogs, chickens; fruits, onions, corn, hay, wheat, oats, maple syrup, grapes; milk, cheese

Employment: 37% management, professional, and related occupations; 26% sales and office occupations; 19% service occupations; 10% production, transportation, and material moving occupations; 8% construction, extraction, maintenance and repair occupations.

Fun Facts

State Date: July 26, 1788

Motto: Higher

Flower: Rose

Bird: Bluebird

Tree: Sugar Maple

Song: I Love New York

Nickname: Empire State

Web Site: state.ny.us

North Carolina

People (2006)

Population: 8,856,505

Population Density: 182 people per square mile

Racial Distribution: 70% white; 21% black; 1% American Indian; 2% Asian; 0.1% Pacific Islander; 7% Latino; 4% some other race

Geography

Total Area: 53,819 square miles

Climate: subtropical in SE; moderate in mountainous area

Topography: coastal plain and tidewater; piedmont plateau; gentle to rugged hills; mountains

Capital: Raleigh

Economy

Industries: educational services, health care, and social assistance; manufacturing

Manufactured Goods: processed foods, textiles, industrial machinery, electronic equipment, furniture, tobacco products

Farm Products: cattle, hogs, chickens; tobacco, cotton, soybeans, corn, wheat, peanuts, sweet potatoes

Employment: 33% management, professional, and related occupations; 24% sales and office occupations; 16% service occupations; 15% production, transportation, and material moving occupations; 12% construction, extraction, maintenance and repair occupations.

Fun Facts

State Date: November 21, 1789

Motto: To be rather than to seem

Flower: Dogwood

Bird: Cardinal

Tree: Pine

Song: The Old North State

Nickname: Tar Heel State

Web Site: nc.gov

North Dakota

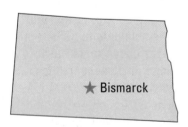

People (2006)

Population: 635,867

Population Density: 9.2 people per square mile

Racial Distribution: 91% white; 1% black; 5% American Indian; 1% Asian; 0.1% Pacific Islander; 1% Latino; 1% some other race

Geography

Total Area: 70,700 square miles

Climate: wide range of temperature and moderate rainfall

Topography: prairie and plains

Capital: Bismarck

Economy

Industries: educational services, health care, and social assistance; retail trade

Manufactured Goods: farm equipment, processed foods, fabricated metals, electronics

Farm Products: cattle, sheep, hogs; durum wheat, barley, flaxseed, oats, corn, dry beans, honey, soybeans, sugar beets, sunflowers, hay

Employment: 34% management, professional, and related occupations; 25% sales and office occupations; 17% service occupations; 12% production, transportation, and material moving occupations; 10% construction, extraction, maintenance and repair occupations.

Fun Facts

State Date: November 2, 1889

Motto: Liberty and union, now and forever, one and inseparable

Flower: Wild Prairie Rose

Bird: Western Meadowlark

Tree: American Elm

Song: North Dakota Hymn

Nickname: Peace Garden State

Web Site: nd.gov

Ohio

★ Columbus

People (2006)

Population: 11,478,006

Population Density: 280.3 people per square mile

Racial Distribution: 84% white; 12% black; 0.5% American Indian; 2% Asian; 0.1% Pacific Islander; 2% Latino; 1% some other race

Geography

Total Area: 44,825 square miles

Climate: variable; much precipitation

Topography: varies from rolling plains to hills

Capital: Columbus

Economy

Industries: educational services, health care, and social assistance; manufacturing

Manufactured Goods: transportation equipment, machinery, metal products

Farm Products: cattle, sheep, hogs, chickens; corn, hay, wheat, oats, soybeans

Employment: 32% management, professional, and related occupations; 26% sales and office occupations; 17% production, transportation, and material moving occupations; 16% service occupations; 8% construction, extraction, maintenance and repair occupations.

Fun Facts

State Date: March 1, 1803

Motto: With God, all things are possible.

Flower: Scarlet Carnation

Bird: Cardinal

Tree: Buckeye

Song: Beautiful Ohio

Nickname: Buckeye State

Web Site: state.oh.us

Oklahoma

★ Oklahoma City

People (2006)

Population: 3,579,212

Population Density: 52 people per square mile

Racial Distribution: 75% white; 7% black; 7% American Indian; 2% Asian; 0.1% Pacific Islander; 7% Latino; 3% some other race

Geography

Total Area: 69,898 square miles

Climate: humid eastern and dry western zones

Topography: high plains in the W; hills and small mountains in the N and E; river basin and plains

Capital: Oklahoma City

Economy

Industries: educational services, health care, and social assistance; retail trade

Manufactured Goods: machinery, transportation equipment, processed foods, metal products

Farm Products: cattle, sheep, hogs, chickens; wheat, cotton, hay, peanuts, sorghum, soybeans, corn, pecans

Employment: 31% management, professional, and related occupations; 26% sales and office occupations; 17% service occupations; 14% production, transportation, and material moving occupations; 12% construction, extraction, maintenance and repair occupations.

Fun Facts

State Date: November 16, 1907

Motto: Labor conquers all things.

Flower: Mistletoe

Bird: Scissor-tailed Flycatcher

Tree: Redbud

Song: Oklahoma!

Nickname: Sooner State

Web Site: state.ok.us

Oregon

People (2006)

Population: 3,700,758

Population Density: 39 people per square mile

Racial Distribution: 86% white; 2% black; 2% American Indian; 4% Asian; 0.1% Pacific Islander; 10% Latino; 4% some other race

Geography

Total Area: 98,381 square miles

Climate: coastal mild and humid climate; dryness and extreme temperatures in central area

Topography: coastal range of rugged mountains; fertile river valley; volcanic peaks; plateau

Capital: Salem

Economy

Industries: educational services, health care, and social assistance; manufacturing

Manufactured Goods: electronics and semiconductors, lumber and wood products, metals, transportation equipment, processed foods, paper

Farm Products: cattle, chickens; hay, wheat, grass seed, potatoes, onions, pears, mint

Employment: 33% management, professional, and related occupations; 26% sales and office occupations; 16% service occupations; 13% production, transportation, and material moving occupations; 10% construction, extraction, maintenance and repair occupations.

Fun Facts

State Date: February 14, 1859

Motto: She flies with her own wings.

Flower: Oregon Grape

Bird: Western Meadowlark

Tree: Douglas Fir

Song: Oregon, My Oregon

Nickname: Beaver State

Web Site: oregon.gov

Pennsylvania

People (2006)

Population: 12,440,621

Population Density: 278 people per square mile

Racial Distribution: 84% white; 10% black; 0.5% American Indian; 2% Asian; 0.1% Pacific Islander; 4% Latino; 2% some other race

Geography

Total Area: 46,055 square miles

Climate: wide range of seasonal temperatures

Topography: mountains with piedmont and coastal plain; rugged plateau falls to lowland in N

Capital: Harrisburg

Economy

Industries: educational services, health care, and social assistance; manufacturing

Manufactured Goods: metal products, processed food, rubber and plastics, electronics, chemicals

Farm Products: cattle, sheep, hogs, chickens; corn, hay, mushrooms, apples, potatoes, wheat, oats

Employment: 34% management, professional, and related occupations; 26% sales and office occupations; 16% service occupations; 14% production, transportation, and material moving occupations; 9% construction, extraction, maintenance and repair occupations.

Fun Facts

State Date: December 12, 1787

Motto: Virtue, liberty, and independence

Flower: Mountain Laurel

Bird: Ruffed Grouse

Tree: Hemlock

Song: Pennsylvania

Nickname: Keystone State

Web Site: state.pa.us

Rhode Island

Providence ★

People (2006)

Population: 1,067,610

Population Density: 1,022 people per square mile

Racial Distribution: 83% white; 5% black; 0.5% American Indian; 3% Asian; 0.0% Pacific Islander; 11% Latino; 7% some other race

Geography

Total Area: 1,545 square miles

Climate: variable

Topography: eastern lowlands; western uplands of flat and rolling hills

Capital: Providence

Economy

Industries: educational services, health care, and social assistance; manufacturing

Manufactured Goods: costume jewelry, textiles, electrical equipment

Farm Products: cattle, hogs, chickens; nursery products, hay, vegetables, honey

Employment: 35% management, professional, and related occupations; 26% sales and office occupations; 18% service occupations; 13% production, transportation, and material moving occupations; 8% construction, extraction, maintenance and repair occupations.

Fun Facts

State Date: May 29, 1790

Motto: Hope

Flower: Violet

Bird: Rhode Island Red

Tree: Red Maple

Song: Rhode Island It's For Me

Nickname: Ocean State

Web Site: state.ri.us

South Carolina

★ Columbia

People (2006)

Population: 4,321,249

Population Density: 144 people per square mile

Racial Distribution: 67% white; 29% black; 0.5% American Indian; 1% Asian; 0.1% Pacific Islander; 3% Latino; 1% some other race

Geography

Total Area: 32,020 square miles

Climate: humid subtropical

Topography: mountains; piedmont and coastal plain

Capital: Columbia

Economy

Industries: educational services, health care, and social assistance; manufacturing

Manufactured Goods: textiles, chemicals, metal and paper products

Farm Products: cattle, hogs, chickens; tobacco, cotton, soybeans, corn, wheat, peaches, tomatoes

Employment: 30% management, professional, and related occupations; 26% sales and office occupations; 17% production, transportation, and material moving occupations; 16% service occupations; 11% construction, extraction, maintenance and repair occupations.

Fun Facts

State Date: May 23, 1788

Motto: While I breathe, I hope.

Flower: Carolina Yellow Jessamine

Bird: Great Carolina Wren

Tree: Palmetto

Song: Carolina

Nickname: Palmetto State

Web Site: sc.gov

South Dakota

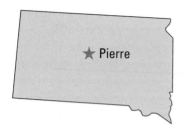

★ Pierre

People (2006)

Population: 781,919

Population Density: 10.3 people per square mile

Racial Distribution: 87% white; 1% black; 9% American Indian; 1% Asian; 0.0% Pacific Islander; 2% Latino; 1% some other race

Geography

Total Area: 77,117 square miles

Climate: variable temperatures, persistent winds, low precipitation and humidity

Topography: prairie plains and rolling hills

Capital: Pierre

Economy

Industries: educational services, health care, and social assistance; retail trade

Manufactured Goods: processed foods, machinery, electronic equipment

Farm Products: cattle, sheep, hogs, chickens; corn, soybeans, oats, wheat, sunflowers, hay

Employment: 35% management, professional, and related occupations; 25% sales and office occupations; 16% service occupations; 14% production, transportation, and material moving occupations; 9% construction, extraction, maintenance and repair occupations.

Fun Facts

State Date: November 2, 1889

Motto: Under God, the people rule.

Flower: American Pasqueflower

Bird: Ring-necked Pheasant

Tree: Black Hills Spruce

Song: Hail, South Dakota

Nickname: Mount Rushmore State

Web Site: state.sd.us

Tennessee

★ Nashville

People (2006)

Population: 6,038,803

Population Density: 147 people per square mile

Racial Distribution: 79% white; 17% black; 0.5% American Indian; 1% Asian; 0.0% Pacific Islander; 3% Latino; 1% some other race

Geography

Total Area: 42,143 square miles

Climate: humid subtropical

Topography: mountains and valleys; plateaus; coastal plain with streams; a narrow strip of swamp and flood plain in the extreme W

Capital: Nashville

Economy

Industries: educational services, health care, and social assistance; manufacturing

Manufactured Goods: chemicals, machinery, transportation equipment, metal products, rubber/plastic products

Farm Products: cattle, hogs, chickens; tobacco, cotton, soybeans, grain, corn

Employment: 31% management, professional, and related occupations; 26% sales and office occupations; 17% production, transportation, and material moving occupations; 15% service occupations; 10% construction, extraction, maintenance and repair occupations.

Fun Facts

State Date: June 1, 1796

Motto: Agriculture and commerce

Flower: Iris

Bird: Mockingbird

Tree: Tulip Poplar

Song: Tennessee Waltz

Nickname: Volunteer State

Web Site: state.tn.us

Texas

Austin ★

People (2006)

Population: 23,507,783

Population Density: 90 people per square mile

Racial Distribution: 70% white; 12% black; 0.5% American Indian; 3% Asian; 0.1% Pacific Islander; 36% Latino; 13% some other race

Geography

Total Area: 268,581 square miles

Climate: extremely varied from dry to wet

Topography: coastal plain; inland plains broken by low mountains

Capital: Austin

Economy

Industries: educational services, health care, and social assistance; retail trade

Manufactured Goods: industrial machinery, electronic products, chemicals, food products

Farm Products: cattle, sheep, hogs, chickens; cotton, wheat, sorghum, vegetables, citrus and other fruits, greenhouse/nursery products, pecans, peanuts; milk, eggs

Employment: 32% management, professional, and related occupations; 26% sales and office occupations; 16% service occupations; 13% production, transportation, and material moving occupations; 12% construction, extraction, maintenance and repair occupations.

Fun Facts

State Date: December 29, 1845

Motto: Friendship

Flower: Bluebonnet

Bird: Mockingbird

Tree: Pecan

Song: Texas, Our Texas

Nickname: Lone Star State

Web Site: state.tx.us

Utah

★ Salt Lake City

People (2006)

Population: 2,550,063

Population Density: 31.0 people per square mile

Racial Distribution: 89% white; 1% black; 1% American Indian; 2% Asian; 1% Pacific Islander; 11% Latino; 5% some other race

Geography

Total Area: 84,899 square miles

Climate: arid; ranging from warm desert to alpine

Topography: brilliantly colored canyons; broad, flat, desert-like basin; mountains, valleys, and plateaus

Capital: Salt Lake City

Economy

Industries: educational services, health care, and social assistance; retail trade

Manufactured Goods: transportation equipment, electronic components, processed foods, steel and copper

Farm Products: cattle, sheep, hogs, chickens; hay, corn, wheat, barley, apples, potatoes, cherries, onions, peaches, pears

Employment: 32% management, professional, and related occupations; 28% sales and office occupations; 15% service occupations; 13% production, transportation, and material moving occupations; 11% construction, extraction, maintenance and repair occupations.

Fun Facts

State Date: January 4, 1896

Motto: Industry

Flower: Sego Lily

Bird: American Seagull

Tree: Blue Spruce

Song: Utah, We Love Thee

Nickname: Beehive State

Web Site: utah.gov

Vermont

★Montpelier

People (2006)

Population: 623,908

Population Density: 67.5 people per square mile

Racial Distribution: 96% white; 1% black; 0.5% American Indian; 1% Asian; 0.5% Pacific Islander; 1% Latino; 0.5% some other race

Geography

Total Area: 9,614 square miles

Climate: long, cold winters and brief, warm summers; heavy snowfall in winter

Topography: mountainous

Capital: Montpelier

Economy

Industries: educational services, health care, and social assistance; manufacturing

Manufactured Goods: tools, paper products, computer components, specialty foods

Farm Products: cattle, hogs, chickens; dairy products, apples, maple syrup, greenhouse/nursery products, corn, hay, potatoes

Employment: 37% management, professional, and related occupations; 23% sales and office occupations; 18% service occupations; 11% production, transportation, and material moving occupations; 10% construction, extraction, maintenance and repair occupations.

Fun Facts

State Date: March 4, 1791

Motto: Freedom and unity

Flower: Red Clover

Bird: Hermit Thrush

Tree: Sugar Maple

Song: Hail Vermont

Nickname: Green Mountain State

Web Site: vermont.gov

Virginia

Richmond ★

People (2006)

Population: 7,642,884

Population Density: 193.0 people per square mile

Racial Distribution: 71% white; 20% black; 0.5% American Indian; 5% Asian; 0.1% Pacific Islander; 6% Latino; 3% some other race

Geography

Total Area: 42,774 square miles

Climate: hot, humid summers and mild winters

Topography: mountains and valleys; rolling piedmont plateau; tidewater, or coastal plain

Capital: Richmond

Economy

Industries: educational services, health care, and social assistance; professional, scientific, and management; administrative and waste management services

Manufactured Goods: textiles, transportation equipment, chemicals, paper products, beverages

Farm Products: cattle, sheep, hogs, chickens; tobacco, grain, corn, soybeans, wheat, peanuts, cotton

Employment: 40% management, professional, and related occupations; 24% sales and office occupations; 15% service occupations; 11% production, transportation, and material moving occupations; 10% construction, extraction, maintenance and repair occupations.

Fun Facts

State Date: June 25, 1788

Motto: Thus always to tyrants

Flower: Dogwood

Bird: Cardinal

Tree: Dogwood

Song: Carry Me Back to Old Virginia

Nickname: Old Dominion

Web Site: virginia.gov

Washington

★ Olympia

People (2006)

Population: 6,395,798

Population Density: 96.1 people per square mile

Racial Distribution: 81% white; 3% black; 2% American Indian; 7% Asian; 0.1% Pacific Islander; 9% Latino; 4% some other race

Geography

Total Area: 71,300 square miles

Climate: mild and wet in the west, drier with more temperature variation in the east

Topography: mountains; open land along coast

Capital: Olympia

Economy

Industries: educational services, health care, and social assistance; manufacturing

Manufactured Goods: software, aircraft, paper, wood, wine, processed fruits and vegetables, electronics

Farm Products: cattle, chickens; apples, potatoes, hay, cherries, grapes

Employment: 37% management, professional, and related occupations; 25% sales and office occupations; 16% service occupations; 12% production, transportation, and material moving occupations, 9% construction, extraction, maintenance and repair occupations.

Fun Facts

State Date: November 11, 1889

Motto: By and by

Flower: Coast Rhododendron

Bird: Willow Goldfinch

Tree: Western Hemlock

Song: Washington, My Home

Nickname: Evergreen State

Web Site: access.wa.gov

West Virginia

★ Charleston

People (2006)

Population: 1,818,470

Population Density: 76 people per square mile

Racial Distribution: 94% white; 3% black; 0.5% American Indian; 1% Asian; 0.1% Pacific Islander; 1% Latino; 0.5% some other race

Geography

Total Area: 24,230 square miles

Climate: humid and warmer in lowlands; cooler in the mountains

Topography: ranging from hilly to mountainous

Capital: Charleston

Economy

Industries: educational services, health care, and social assistance; retail trade

Manufactured Goods: plastic and hardwood products, metals, chemicals, automotive parts

Farm Products: cattle, sheep, hogs, chickens; apples, peaches, hay, tobacco, corn, wheat, soybeans

Employment: 28% management, professional, and related occupations; 25% sales and office occupations; 17% service occupations; 15% production, transportation, and material moving occupations; 13% construction, extraction, maintenance and repair occupations.

Fun Facts

State Date: June 20, 1863

Motto: Mountaineers are always free.

Flower: Big Rhododendron

Bird: Cardinal

Tree: Sugar Maple

Songs: The West Virginia Hills; This Is My West Virginia; West Virginia, My Home

Nickname: Mountain State

Web Site: wv.gov

Wisconsin

Madison ★

People (2006)

Population: 5,556,506

Population Density: 102.3 people per square mile

Racial Distribution: 88% white; 6% black; 1% American Indian; 2% Asian; 0.0% Pacific Islander; 5% Latino; 3% some other race

Geography

Total Area: 65,498 square miles

Climate: long, cold winters and short, warm summers

Topography: plains, hills, lowlands

Capital: Madison

Economy

Industries: educational services, health care, and social assistance; manufacturing

Manufactured Goods: motor vehicles, paper products, plastics, machinery, cheese, beverages

Farm Products: cattle, sheep, hogs, chickens; corn, hay, soybeans, potatoes, cranberries, sweet corn, peas, oats, snap beans; milk, butter, cheese

Employment: 32% management, professional, and related occupations; 25% sales and office occupations; 18% production, transportation, and material moving occupations; 16% service occupations; 9% construction, extraction, maintenance and repair occupations.

Fun Facts

State Date: May 29, 1848

Motto: Forward

Flower: Wood Violet

Bird: Robin

Tree: Sugar Maple

Song: On, Wisconsin!

Nickname: America's Dairyland

Web Site: wisconsin.gov

Wyoming

Cheyenne ★

People (2006)

Population: 515,004

Population Density: 5.3 people per square mile

Racial Distribution: 92% white; 1% black; 2% American Indian; 1% Asian; 0.1% Pacific Islander; 7% Latino; 2% some other race

Geography

Total Area: 97,814 square miles

Climate: semi-desert conditions throughout; true desert in the Bighorn and Great Divide Basins

Topography: plains rising to foothills of Rocky Mountains

Capital: Cheyenne

Economy

Industries: educational services, health care, and social assistance; retail trade

Manufactured Goods: refined petroleum, electronic devices, refined sugar, beverages, metal containers

Farm Products: cattle, sheep, hogs, chickens; wheat, beans, barley, oats, sugar beets, hay

Employment: 30% management, professional, and related occupations; 22% sales and office occupations; 17% service occupations; 15% construction, extraction, maintenance and repair occupations; 14% production, transportation, and material moving occupations.

Fun Facts

State Date: July 10, 1890

Motto: Equal rights

Flower: Indian Paintbrush

Bird: Western Meadowlark

Tree: Cottonwood

Song: Wyoming

Nicknames: Equality State, Cowboy State

Web Site: state.wy.us

Source: U.S. Census Bureau, 2006 American Community Survey. Note: Entries under "Racial Distribution" may not add up to 100% due to rounding and nonlisting of other categories.

A

adapt to change in order to survive

African American someone who is an African immigrant or a descendant of an African immigrant or slave

agribusiness a large-scale farming enterprise

agriculture the business of growing crops and raising animals

American Indian someone who is a descendant of the first people to live in North and South America

American Revolution the war in which the American colonies won independence from Great Britain

the Americas the landmasses and islands of North America, Central America, and South America

aqueduct a pipe or canal for carrying a large quantity of water from one place to another

archaeologist a social scientist who studies the past by looking at artifacts people have left behind

archives a collection of historical documents and records

Asian American someone who is an Asian immigrant or a descendant of an Asian immigrant

assembly line a process in which each worker assembles one part of a product before passing it on to the next worker down the line

B

basin a bowl-shaped landform that is lower than the surrounding land

bayou a stream that flows through a swamp

bill a proposal for a new law

border a boundary line that separates two places

budget a plan for how you will spend the money you expect to have

C

canal a ditch dug across land that often connects two waterways

canning preserving food by cooking and sealing it in cans or jars

canyon a deep, narrow valley with steep sides

capital a city where the government of a country or state is located

cave a natural underground hole

cavern a large cave

citizen a person who by law has a right to live in a community

coastal plain low, flat land that runs along a coast

colony a settlement that is ruled by another country

combine a machine, pulled by horses, for cutting and threshing grain

conservation the careful use of a resource

Constitution the plan of government for the United States

culture a way of life shared by a group of people

D

dairy a farm that produces milk and milk products

dam a wall built across a river to stop the flow of water

Declaration of Independence document declaring the United States free from Great Britain

delta a triangle-shaped area of land at the end of a river

democracy a form of government in which people vote for their leaders

demographics the facts you can study about a certain group of people, such as their ages, genders, or jobs

desert an area of land that receives very little rain

diverse made up of different groups of people

drought a time when little or no rain falls

E

economist a social scientist who studies the economy of a community

economy the way people in a community use resources to meet their needs and wants

European American someone who is an immigrant from Europe or a descendant of a European immigrant

expedition a journey with a purpose

F

factors of production the resources, including land, capital, and workers, used to create a good or service

fall line an imaginary line, marked by rapids and waterfalls, where rivers start to drop from higher land to lower land

federal government our national government that deals with problems that affect the entire country

feedlot an area or a building where livestock are kept while fattened for slaughter

fertile soil able to produce good crops

fertilizer a substance added to the soil to improve plant growth

floodplain the low, flat land along a river that may be underwater during a flood

foothills a hilly region at the base of a mountain range

frontier the beginning of unexplored land

G

geographer a social scientist who studies the natural and human features of Earth's surface, and its climate and life-forms

geographic inquiry process a five-step process that helps answer geographic questions

geyser a spring that throws jets of heated water and steam into the air

global grid the grid formed by crisscrossing lines of latitude and longitude on a map

goods objects such as food, clothing, and cars

gorge a deep narrow valley

H

habitat the place where a type of animal typically lives in nature

historian a social scientist who studies the past

human geography human-made features of a place

hurricane a storm with heavy rains and high winds

I

immigrant someone who comes from another place to live in a country

industry an organized economic activity connected with the production, manufacture, or construction of a particular product or range of products

inland not bordering an ocean

irrigation a way to bring water to dry land, using water from another location

L

Latino someone who was born in Latin America or is a descendant of someone born in Latin America

legislator a member of the branch of government that makes laws

levee a wall typically made of dirt, built along a river to keep it from flooding

line of latitude an imaginary line that runs east and west around the globe; also called a parallel

line of longitude an imaginary line that runs around the globe between the North and South Poles; also called a meridian

livestock animals raised on farms, such as cattle, hogs, and chickens

local government city, town, and county governments created to meet local needs

lock a water elevator used to raise and lower boats

M

maize a tall plant that produces large cobs of sweet corn

map key an explanation of what the symbols on a map stand for

market any place where economic activity occurs

mass production a way of making large quantities of products

meatpacking the preparing of meat for sale

megalopolis a "great city" consisting of a string of towns and cities where many people live

mesa a flat-topped hill

mill a factory in which people make products out of raw materials

mineral a natural material found in rock

mint a factory where coins are made

mission a Spanish settlement built to teach Christianity in North America

Mormon a member of the Church of Jesus Christ of Latter-day Saints

N

natural resource a resource supplied by nature

navigable deep enough and wide enough for ships to use

O

oasis a place in the desert that has water and trees

P

pass a route across mountains

peak the top of a mountain

pesticide a substance used on crops to kill insects and other pests

petroleum a thick, black, oily liquid found underground

physical geography features of land, water, and sky

plantation a large farm, usually worked by many laborers

plateau a high, flat landform that rises steeply from the land around it

political scientist a social scientist who studies governments

pollution any substance that makes air, water, or soil dirty or unsafe to use

population density a measure of the average number of people living in one unit of area

population distribution map a map showing where, and how many, people live in a region or an area

prairie a flat or gently rolling land that is covered with tall grasses and wildflowers

primary source a source created by someone who has seen or taken part in the events described

R

reaper a machine for cutting grain

rebellion an armed fight against a government

renewable resource something that renews itself, or re-grows, even as people use up the original supply of it

republic a type of government in which people choose leaders to act for them

reservation public land set aside by the government for use by American Indians

reservoir an area where water is stored for people's use

right of free petition the right of the people to give legislators ideas for new laws

river basin the area around a river and its tributaries

S

sawmill a factory where logs are turned into lumber

scale a diagram that explains distances on a map

scarcity the idea that the things and resources people want and need are limited

secondary source a source created someone who has not seen or taken part in the events described

segregation the separation of people because of race, religion, or gender

self-sufficient doing everything necessary to take care of yourself on your own

services things we pay others to do for us

skyscraper a very tall building

social science the study of how people live in groups

social scientist a person who studies how people live in groups

sod a mixture of dirt and roots of grass

source the beginning of a river

special-purpose map a map that shows just one kind of information, such as rainfall or elevation

state constitution a written statement of a plan for a state government

state government the government of an individual state that deals with problems that affect that state

strip mine a place where minerals are scraped from the ground

swamp a low area of land that is covered by water at least part of the year

system of checks and balances a system set up in the U.S. Constitution to allow each branch of government ways to limit the power of the other two branches

T

tax the money that people and businesses pay to the government to support its functions

technology the use of tools and ideas to meet people's needs

tenement a four- to six-story building with many small apartments

tornado a violent windstorm whose center is a cloud in the shape of a funnel

transportation hub a city that serves as a center for moving goods and people

tributary a river that joins another, larger river

W

wage a payment of money for work

wastewater water that has been used

W

Y

Photography

Cover
David Olsen/Getty Images

Title Page
David Olsen/Getty Images

Table of Contents
ii background: RF **ii TL:** RF **ii TR:** RF **ii ML:** RF **ii MR:** RF **ii B:** RF **iv:** RF **v:** NASA **vi:** RF **vii L:** Richard Hamilton Smith/Corbis **viii:** RF **x:** © Robert Glusic/Corbis **xi:** Lowell Georgia/Corbis **xii:** RF/Corbis **xiii:** RF/Corbis **xiv:** RF **xv:** Kevin Fleming/Corbis **xvi:** Jim West/Alamy **xvii:** Paul Conklin/PhotoEdit

Chapter 1
4: RF/Corbis **6:** RF/Corbis **7:** courtesy of Steely Studios **8:** RF/Corbis **10:** Jim Wark/Peter Arnold Inc. **11:** The Daily Times, Marc F. Henning/AP Photo **12:** Cahokia Mounds Museum Society and Art Grossman. **13 TR, BM:** Cahokia Mounds State Historic Site **ix:** Minnesota Historical Society/Corbis

Chapter 2
14 background: RF **14 TL:** RF **14 TR:** RF **14 ML:** RF **14 MR:** RF **14 B:** RF **18:** Howard Kingsnorthzefa/Corbis **19:** Howard Kingsnorth-zefa/Corbis **25:** GO-Image Bank/Getty Images **26 TR:** Penguin Classics **26 BL:** Bettmann/Corbis **27:** Erich Lessing/Art Resource, NY **28:** North Wind Picture Archives **29:** Thinkstock Images/Jupiter Images

Chapter 3
30: Ed Honowitz/Getty Images **33:** Bettmann/Corbis **35:** Lindsay Hebberd/Corbis **36:** Bettmann/Corbis **39:** Bettmann/Corbis **40:** Corbis **41:** © 2002 Jim Cummins/Getty Images/FPG **42 TM:** Southern Pacific News Bureau/AP Photo **42 TR:** Bruce Dale/NGS Image Collection **42 BL:** Tom Bean/Corbis **42 BM:** Bruce Dale/National Geographic Image **42 BR:** Visions of America, LLC/Alamy **43:** © 2002 Arthur Tilley/Getty Images/FPG **45:** The Granger Collection

46: New York Public Library **47 TR:** Bob Krist/Corbis **47 BL:** Andrew Prokos

Chapter 4
48 background: RF **48 TL:** RF **48 TM:** RF **48 TR:** RF **48 M:** RF **48 BL:** RF **48 BR:** RF **52:** RF/Digital Vision **53:** Phil Schermeister/Corbis **54:** RF **55:** Rudi Von Briel/RF/Corbis **56:** Joe Viesti **57:** Alan Schein Photography/Corbis **58 TL, TR:** Richard T. Nowitz/Corbis **59:** RF **60:** RF **61 T:** Adam Woolfitt/Corbis **61 B:** Stephanie Kuykendal-Bloomberg News/Landov **62:** Alexis C. Glenn-UPI/Landov **63:** RF **64:** Library of Congress **66:** Lowell National Historical Park **67:** Center for Lowell History University of Massachusetts Lowell **68:** North Wind Picture Archives **69:** Lowell National Historical Park

Chapter 5
70: NASA **72 L:** Richard Laird/Getty Images **72 R:** VisionsofAmerica/Joe Sohm-Digital Vision/RF/Getty **74 T:** GO- Bank-Michael Pasdzior/RF/Getty Images **74 B:** Mick Roessler/RF/Corbis **75 L:** Jeff Greenberg/Alamy **75 R:** Steve Dunwell/The Image Bank **76 L:** Hiroyuki Matsumoto-Stone/Getty Images **76 R:** Superstock **77 T:** Roger Wood/Corbis **77 B:** James T. Blair-PhotoDisk/RF/Getty Images **78 T:** Patrick Ward/Corbis **78 B:** Mike Brinson/Getty Images **79 T:** Barry Howe/RF/Corbis **79 B:** Visions of America-Joe Sohm/RF/Getty Images **80:** Popperfoto/Getty Images **81 T:** Library of Congress **81 B:** Bettmann/Corbis **82 T:** AP Wideworld Photo **82 B:** Corbis **83:** Minnesota Historical Society/Corbis

Chapter 6
84 Background: RF **84 CL:** RF **84 TR:** RF **84 ML:** RF **84 MR:** RF **84 BL:** RF **84 BR:** RF **88:** RF **89:** RF **90:** Nik Wheeler/Corbis **91:** Charles E. Rotkin/Corbis **92:** RF **93:** RF **94:** Nicolas Russell-Riser/Getty Images **95:** Philip Gould/Corbis **96:** Raymond Gehman/Corbis **97:** Alex Brandon/AP Photo **98:** United States Postal Service **99:** Library of Congress **100:** Jamie Martin/AP Photo **101:** Chitose Suzuki/AP Photo

Chapter 7

102: Tony Arruza/Corbis **104:** Neil Rabinowitz/Corbis **104 T:** RF/Corbis **104 B:** Corbis **106:** Cathlyn Melloan/Getty Images **107:** Cameron Davidson/Workbook Stock **108:** Corbis **109 L:** Richard Hamilton Smith/Corbis **109 R:** David R. Frazier Photolibrary, Inc./Alamy **110:** Kent F. Berg/The Miami Herald/Getty Images **111:** Skip Nall/RF/Getty Images **112:** NASA/NOAA **113:** Franz-Marc Frei/Corbis **114:** Warren Faidley/Corbis **115 T:** Reuters/Corbis **115 B:** Steve Starr/Corbis

Chapter 8

116 background: RF **116 TL:** RF **116 TC:** RF **116 TR:** RF **116 ML:** RF **116 MR:** RF **116 BL:** RF **116 BR:** RF **120:** RF **121:** David Frazier/RF/Corbis **122 L:** Bettmann/Corbis **122 R:** Andre Jenny/The Image Works **123 T:** RF **123 B:** Newscom **124:** Phil Schermeister/Corbis **125:** Bettmann/Corbis **126:** iStockphoto **127:** Joseph Sohm-Visions of America/Corbis **128:** Bill Ross/Corbis **129:** Alvis Upitis-The Image Bank/Getty Images **130:** Library of Congress **131:** Bettmann/Corbis **132:** Library of Congress **133:** The Art Archive/Culver Pictures

Chapter 9

134 T: Culver Pictures **134 M:** Minnesota Historical Society/Corbis **134 B:** Paul A. Souders/Corbis **136:** RF/Getty Images **137:** Culver Pictures **138:** Culver Pictures **139:** Brown Brothers **140:** Corbis **141:** Bettmann/Corbis **142:** George D. Lepp/Corbis **143:** Tony Hertz/Alamy **144:** Paul A. Souders/Corbis **145:** Rob Crandall/The Image Works **146:** John Elk III/Alamy **147 T:** G.Frysinger/Travel-Images.com **147 B:** Marilyn Angel Wynn/Nativestock Pictures **149:** Roger Ressmeyer/Corbis

Chapter 10

150 background: RF **150 TL:** RF **150 TR:** RF **150 ML:** RF **150 MR:** RF **150 BL:** RF **150 BM:** RF **150 BR:** RF **154:** © Robert Glusic/Corbis **155:** RF/Corbis **156:** RF/Corbis **157:** RF/Corbis **158:** © William A. Bake/Corbis **159:** RF **160:** SuperStock

161: © Kelly-Mooney Photography/Corbis **162:** Bettmann/Corbis **163:** David Mendelsohn/Masterfile **164:** Courtesy of Texas State Library and Archives Commission. **165:** Bettmann/Corbis **166:** Bob Daemmrich **167:** Randy Faris/Corbis

Chapter 11

168: © Tom Bean/Corbis **170:** Salt River Project Heritage **171:** Bettmann/Corbis **172:** Adam Woolfitt/Corbis **173:** Herbert Hoover Presidential Library **174:** Phil Degginger/Animals Animals-Earth Scenes **175:** RF/Getty Images **176:** Lowell Georgia/Corbis **177:** RF/Getty Images **178:** Jeff Greenberg/PhotoEdit **179:** Tony Roberts/Corbis **180:** National Geographic/SuperStock **181:** Fred Hirschmann-Science Faction/Getty Images **182:** Library of Congress **183:** Fred Hirschmann/Science Faction/Getty Images

Chapter 12

184 background: RF **184 TL:** RF/Getty Images **184 TM:** RF/Getty Images **184 TR:** RF **184 ML:** RF/Getty Images **184 MR:** RF/Getty **184 BL:** RF/Getty Images **184 BR:** RF/Getty Images **188:** Macduff Everton/Corbis **189:** RF/Getty Images **190:** Joseph Sohm/Visions of America/Corbis **191:** Louie Psihoyos/Corbis **192:** Ed Young/Corbis **193:** RF/Corbis **194:** Gary Braasch/Corbis **195:** Paul A. Souders/Corbis **196:** © 2002 Peter Timmermans-Stone/Getty Images **197:** RF/Corbis **199:** Andre Jenny/Alamy **200:** Danita Delimont/Alamy **201 T:** Library of Congress **201 B:** Wyatt Shudlick/Alamy

Chapter 13

202 TL: © James L. Amos/Corbis **202 TR:** RF/Getty **202 TM:** RF/Corbis **202 ML:** RF/Corbis **202 ML:** RF/Corbis **202 BL:** RF/Corbis **202 BR:** RF/Getty Images **203 TL:** Tony Anderson/Getty Images **203 TC:** © 2002 Richard Price/Getty Images **203 TR:** RF/Corbis **203 B:** © 2002 Scott Markewitz/Getty Images **204:** © 2002 James Balog/Getty Images **205:** RF/Corbis **206:** © 2002 R. Derek Smith/Getty Images **207:** © 2002 Richard Price/Getty Images **208:** RF/Getty Images **209:** RF/Corbis **210:** © 2002 Nick Gunderson/Getty Images **211:** © 2002 Scott Markewitz/Getty Images

212: © Jim Richardson/Corbis 213: Tony Anderson/Getty Images 214: © 2002 Michael Melford, Inc.-The Image Bank/Getty Images 215: Jerry McElroy/Pro-Vision 216: RF/Corbis 217: © 2002 Jay S Simon-Stone/Getty Images 218: © 2002 American Images, Inc./Getty Images 220: Photodisc/Alamy 221 T: Craig Lovell/Eagle Visions Photography/Alamy 221 B: Michael Henley of Contemporary Images 222: Bruce Forster 223: Digital Vision/Alamy

Chapter 14

227: NASA 228: Aufwind-Luftbilder/Visum/The Image Works 229: RF 230: Lawrence Migdale 231: David Frazier/Corbis 232: Randy Green 233: Paul Gleeson/Makah Cultural and Research Center 234: Library of Congress 235: Makah Cultural And Research Center

Chapter 15

336: Richard Cummins/Corbis 238: The Granger Collection, New York 239: SGM/ Stock Connection 240: Kevin Fleming/Corbis 242 T: The Granger Collection, New York 242 B: RF/ Getty Images 243: RF 244 T: USHistory.org 244 B: USHistory.org 245: Library Company of Philadelphia 246: Richard Cummins/Corbis 247 T: Museo Thyssen-Bornemisza, Spain 247 B: Kelly/Maiello Inc.

Chapter 16

248: Bettmann/Corbis 250: Jeff Greenberg/ PhotoEdit 251: EuroStyle Graphics/Alamy 252: RF 254: Jim West/Alamy 255: © 2002 Willie Maldonado-Stone/Getty Images 256: Alan Klehr/Churchill & Klehr Photography 257: AP Photo/Hatttiesburg American, Barry Beard 258: Enterprise City 259: Frances Roberts/Alamy

Chapter 17

260: Paul Conklin/PhotoEdit 262: Superstock/ Alamy 264: CJ Gunther-epa/Corbis 265: Digital Vision/RF/Getty Image 267: Jim West/Alamy 268 T: Florian Graner/Minden Pictures 268 BL: Thomas & Pat Leeson/Photo Researchers, Inc.

268 BR: William Harlow/Photo Researchers, Inc 269: Robert E.Klein/AP Wide World 270: Ball Miwako/Alamy 271: Ball Miwako/Alamy

Ideas that Unite Us as Americans

272 background: Corbis 272: L: Lawrence Migdale 272 R: Jon Feingersh/Corbis 273 L: Ariel Skelley/ Corbis 273 M: Corbis 273 R: RF/Masterfile 274: Atwater Kent Museum of Philadelphia/Bridgeman Art Collection 275: The Granger Collection, New York 276: Superstock 277 T: Alex Wong/Getty Images 277 M: J.Pat Carter/AP Photo 277 B: Frank Siteman 278: RF/Fotosearch 279: The Granger Collection, New York 281: Michael Ventura/ PhotoEdit 282 L: Bill Ross/Corbis 282 R: Daniel J. Cox/Corbis 283 T: United States Diplomacy Center 283 B: United States Diplomacy Center 285: Bob Adelman/Corbis

Art

3: Rosiland Solomon 15: Len Ebert 31 C: Susan Jaekel 31 TR: Doug Roy 31 BR: Renate Lohmann 31 TL: Siri Weber Feeney 31 BL: Len Ebert 49 T: DJ Simison 49 B: Len Ebert 65: Len Ebert 71: Doug Roy 85 T: DJ Simison 85 B: Len Ebert 103: Doug Roy 117 T: DJ Simison 117 B: Len Ebert 124: Len Ebert 135: Susan Jaekel 148: Jon Goodell 151 T: DJ Simison 151 B: Len Ebert 185 T: DJ Simison 185 B: Len Ebert 225: Doug Roy 231: Doug Roy 237: Doug Roy 249: Gary Undercuffler 253: Doug Roy 261: Renate Lohmann 263: Gary Undercuffler

Artists represented by Ann Remen-Willis, Artist Representative and Art Manager:
Len Ebert
Jon Goodell
Susan Jaekel
Renate Lohmann
Doug Roy
DJ Simison
Rosiland Solomon
Gary Undercuffler
Siri Weber Feeney